Writing in Science
in Action

Writing in Science

in Action

Strategies, Tools, and Classroom Video

Betsy Rupp Fulwiler

HEINEMANN • Portsmouth, NH

Heinemann

361 Hanover Street

Portsmouth, NH 03801–3912

www.heinemann.com

Offices and agents throughout the world

The material presented in this book is based on work supported by the National Science Foundation under Grant No. 0554651 and Grant No. 9554605, awarded to Seattle Public Schools. Any opinions, findings, and conclusions or recommendations expressed in this material are those of the author and do not necessarily reflect the views of the National Science Foundation.

Library of Congress Cataloging-in-Publication Data

Fulwiler, Betsy Rupp.
   Writing in science in action : strategies, tools, and classroom video / Betsy Rupp Fulwiler.
       p. cm.
   Includes bibliographical references.
   ISBN-13: 978-0-325-04211-4
   ISBN-10: 0-325-04211-X
   1. Science—Study and teaching (Elementary).   2. English language—Composition and exercises—Study and teaching (Elementary).   3. Video tapes in education.   I. Title.
LB1585.3.F855 2011
372.35'044—dc22   2011008839

EDITOR: Katherine Bryant
PRODUCTION: Victoria Merecki
COVER AND INTERIOR DESIGNS: Jenny Jensen Greenleaf
STILL PHOTOGRAPHY: © 2011 by Julie McMackin Photography
VIDEO PRODUCTION AND VIDEO PHOTOGRAPHY: True North Studios
TYPESETTER: Publishers' Design and Production Services, Inc.
DVD TECH DEVELOPER: Sherry Day
WEBSITE DEVELOPER: Nicole Russell
MANUFACTURING: Steve Bernier

Printed in the United States of America on acid-free paper

15 14 13 12 11 VP 1 2 3 4 5

In memory of Lynn Barnicle

Contents

Foreword

The use of science notebooks in science teaching and learning has, over the past decade, become almost a fad. There are many different kinds of notebooks you can buy in quantity to use with students. There are many books available on how to include science notebooks in the classroom. There is even a new word that has crept into the jargon—*notebooking*. But few if any of the people who talk and write about notebooks bring to their work the depth of experience, expertise, and thought that Betsy Rupp Fulwiler does. I am a regular user of her book *Writing in Science*, published in 2007. I assign it to my preservice students, I give it out in teacher development workshops and courses, and I recommend it to many others. It was therefore with great anticipation and delight that I looked forward to *Writing in Science in Action*. I was, of course, not disappointed. Once again, she has provided us with a rich resource for deepening our understanding of students' writing in science and a wealth of ideas and practices for use in the classroom. And this time it is not just a book but also a series of wonderful classroom videos and a website.

There are many reasons to explain why Fulwiler's work is so important and received so well. This is not the place to list them all. But I have several favorites. Perhaps foremost among them is the fact that Fulwiler is a rare literacy expert who has spent years to truly understand the nature of inquiry-based science. Her work is not about practicing writing in science, too often the view of the literacy world; it is about the importance of writing for science learning. At every turn she insists on the primacy of experience and the role writing plays in drawing meaning from that experience. This is not about simply connecting science and literacy programs; it is about the authentic use of writing in science learning as the important tool it is.

Another favorite reason is Fulwiler's deep understanding and respect for the work teachers do. What she writes about is an approach and practices that have been honed in the classroom by real teachers with real children. You feel their presence throughout and see them in the videos. Fulwiler also acknowledges the time it takes to learn to do something new—three years for inquiry science and the writing. This is not a quick fix or new gimmick—it is not a scripted curriculum. Rather, Fulwiler's science-writing approach is a deep and powerful way to teach children.

And a third favorite reason I value Fulwiler's work so highly is her insistence on the practical and useful. This book grows out of the questions, needs, and requests of the teachers with whom she worked. Her first book presented the approach and its foundations in detail before moving into practice. This book is mainly about classroom practice. In it she has responded to teachers who tell us over and over again that the most powerful help comes in the form of classroom examples and the experiences of practicing teachers. For each of the instructional strategies she highlights, she uses carefully interconnected video segments, student work, detailed classroom vignettes, and a website to illustrate and to take the reader into the richness and complexity of individual classrooms and the practices of skilled teachers.

I was particularly delighted with the descriptions of suggestions for interacting with children. Fulwiler not only shares the work of individual students but she also suggests how one might interact with that student around the work. This is unusual and very welcome. Too often teachers are given a first step—"have students write about. . . ." or "talk with students about. . . ."—with no guidance and support for what to do next. We are told what to say and do but not how to take the next step and respond to children.

I want to mention one more gift in this book that I value enormously. Part 2 is on assessment. It is now many years since research findings began to suggest that unless teachers assess and respond to students' notebooks, the impact of their use is minimal. But, of course, not just any kind of assessment has the power to enhance learning. In *Writing in Science*, Fulwiler provided a chapter to set the stage. In this book, a whole section provides extensive guidance on how to assess notebooks in multiple ways so that teachers and students are part of the process and learn from their work.

I look forward to dipping into this book, the video segments, and the website over and over. It will be a wonderful resource for me and those with whom I work. And, as Fulwiler herself says, it is not a book about a static approach. It is a book that starts the creative and interested teacher down a pathway with clear guidance and structures but also encourages teachers, particularly those working together, to go beyond and make this work their own.

Karen Worth
Wheelock College

Acknowledgments

I began developing what became this science-writing approach almost fifteen years ago. In *Writing in Science*, I acknowledged the many organizations and individuals who helped to support and develop the work. Since that book was published in 2007, other individuals and organizations have provided additional support to further develop the project, building on what the first supporters had done.

First, I want to thank the National Science Foundation (NSF), which has funded the last five years of this work as we developed the materials to help educators across the country implement the *Writing in Science* approach. I particularly want to thank our program officer, Bob Gibbs, for his guidance, support, and visit to classrooms, where the students were thrilled that he had come to see them working as scientists.

I also am grateful to the Nesholm Family Foundation, which, through the years, has provided funding for the Expository Writing and Science Notebooks Program in Seattle Public Schools. This program has enabled us to provide professional development for the district's teachers, which, in turn, has informed our work with teachers elsewhere. We are honored to assist them in their mission of helping underachieving students reach their full potential.

I am especially thankful to have worked for the last fifteen years with Elaine Woo, the program manager of the PreK–12 Science Program in Seattle Public Schools. Elaine is a remarkable visionary who also has incredible skills in turning ideas into real programs that positively impact all students. Due to her tireless efforts and leadership, we have been able to continuously develop our elementary science and science-writing programs for more than a decade, thereby allowing the district's teachers to benefit from high-quality professional development and their students to learn science through inquiry throughout the school year.

The science team and the district's teachers could not accomplish their work without Penny Knutzen's intelligent, efficient management of the program's complex administrative details. I personally am extremely grateful for her sense of humor, helpful advice, and generosity.

Over the years, my fellow coaches in the elementary science program have provided their expertise and guidance in developing this program. For more than a decade, Kathryn Show, who was my mentor as I began to learn about inquiry-based science, has helped hundreds of teachers learn to provide high-quality science instruction for their students.

As I began developing the science-writing program, I spent many hours in teachers' classrooms. Four of the master teachers who greatly affected the development of the program later became science coaches. I want to acknowledge and thank Ana Crossman, Kirsten Nesholm, Paula Schachtel, and Mindy Woodbury for their countless invaluable contributions to the program, including their pivotal work in this book, the video episodes, and the Stories from Schools section on the website. To be able to feature their work in *Writing in Science in Action* fills me with great joy.

In developing the video episodes for this project, I called on other master teachers to whom I will be forever indebted for putting themselves on the line in front of the cameras in order to show other teachers across the country how to implement this approach. These stellar teachers are Nani Castor-Peck, Dan Jordan, Stephanie McPhail, Christine Patrick, Joni Pecor, and Deb Schochet (who also contributed to the Stories from Schools section on the website).

In the video episodes that feature the science-writing group meetings and the teacher-student conferences, Katie Renschler (who began developing the writing approach with me in 1996) and Mindy Woodbury are fabulous as facilitators and commentators, presenting a picture of the value and the substance of these meetings. They were supported by their knowledgeable and insightful colleagues: Althea Chow, Dan Jordan, Jeannie Revello, Matthew Snyder, Ana Crossman, Shelly Hurley, Joe Kunkel, and Elyse Litvack. Dan and Joe also showed us how we can have meaningful conferences with our students.

I also have been honored to have worked since 2000 with the Lead Science Writing Teachers team, a group of more than fifty teachers who meet almost monthly during the school year. Through the years, they have provided continual feedback that I have used in refining the program in Seattle and beyond. Those who have served on the team for at least three years during the current NSF project include all the teachers I already have mentioned as well as: Kamilah Abdul-Alim, Chantel Anderson, Lynn Barnicle, Lisa Boveng, Jim Buckwalter, Heather Christothoulou, Whitney Denney, Diane Eileen, Paula Eisenrich, Liz Filep, Erika Haberly, Tamra Hauge, Theresa Healey, Ann Kumata, Kathy Langhans, Vernon Larsen, Joan Lassiter, Shawn LeValley, Theresa Lourde, Bernie McDonough, Marilyn Mears, Huong Nguyen, Kit Norman, Doris Toy Patin, Lauren Porter, John Revello, Tim Salcedo, Karma Sawka, Ann-Marie Spata, Jessica Thomashow, Marian Wagner, Katie Weinmann, and Patsy Yamada. The team includes two valuable members from outside Seattle: Laurie Rich, Tukwila School District, and Nina Wolsk, Edmonds School District.

During our NSF-supported project these last five years, we have benefited greatly from a number of talented teachers who generously contributed their time and expertise in order to field-test the materials in this project. I would like to publicly thank the leaders in their districts for supporting this work: Susan Giessaking, Gilbert Public Schools in Arizona; Lynn Farrin, Maine Mathematics and Science Alliance; Dr. Betty Young and Sara Sweetman, Guiding Education in Math and Science Network at the University of Rhode Island; Pat Bobbitt and Stacy Hashe, Anderson School District One in South Carolina; Andrew Schwebke, Puyallup School District in Washington; Jane Goetz, Renton School District in Washington; and Mark Cheney and Julie Vavricka, Yakima Public Schools in Washington.

I also would like to honor and thank Pat Hunter, the phenomenal principal of Maple Elementary, a Blue Ribbon School in Seattle Public Schools. She not only has been an intelligent, ardent, longtime supporter of science education and science writing, but she also generously contributed her time to write a powerful testimonial for the Stories from Schools section on the website.

Seattle's elementary science program has benefited greatly for more than a dozen years from our relationship with Stamatis Vokos, a professor of physics at Seattle Pacific University, and his colleague, Lezlie deWater. They are the experts we go to when we need help with physical science concepts and inquiry instruction. Many of us also have had adult content instruction from them and learned through those experiences how excellent inquiry instruction can enable anyone to learn physics concepts.

From almost the inception of the science-writing program, we have had the privilege of working with the program evaluators, Inverness Research, Inc. Katherine Ramage, Laura Stokes, and Heather Mitchell have been extraordinarily generous, insightful, and supportive through all these years. This program never would have served students and teachers as well as it does without their invaluable contributions.

Susan Mundry of West Ed, as an advisor to our NSF project, also has been generous in sharing her extensive expertise, especially in terms of creating effective professional development resources for teachers.

I want to thank Karen Worth and Jeff Winokur of the Educational Development Center for their support and advice over the years as well as for the opportunities they have given me to share our work at conferences. They are an inspiration to anyone who believes in the paramount importance of high-quality science instruction.

One of the most rewarding professional experiences I have ever had is working with True North Studios to develop the video episodes that accompany this book. Michele Costa, the producer, is extraordinarily gifted, not only in all the mysterious details of production but also in quickly understanding what teachers need to see in order to understand how to implement this approach. Furthermore, she is a gracious and empathetic soul who put all the teachers at ease despite the fact that two large cameras were zooming in on their every move. Bill Purdy, who handled the technical aspects of making the DVD, is also a talented professional to whom I am grateful for helping make the video episodes such a stellar part of this project. I also want to thank Julie McMackin, another member of the team, for taking the wonderful photographs for this book.

I am deeply indebted to Katherine Bryant, the lead editor of Math and Science at Heinemann, for her brilliant help and kind support in the shaping of this book. I also want to thank Victoria Merecki, the production editor, not only for so carefully managing all the production details but also for her thoughtful comments. Kate Montgomery, the publisher, and the rest of the Heinemann staff I have worked with have been extremely generous and knowledgeable as well.

As I said in *Writing in Science*, I was an editor before becoming a teacher, and like most editors, I go to battle with every sentence I have to write. I want to thank the friends and family members who so patiently have supported me during this long project. I particularly want to thank Ana Crossman, who has been so gracious about listening to my concerns and questions and then providing thoughtful and wise counsel. My niece Kimberly, an aspiring conservation zoologist, is an unusually insightful eleven-year-old who has offered, from a student's perspective, much humorous and useful advice about teaching. Deb Easter has kindly acted as editor-at-large through countless phone calls that always result in humorous, intelligent, and pragmatic advice that I greatly value.

To my children—Derek, Jonathan, and Kate—I am deeply grateful for their ongoing patience, support, intelligent advice, and humor during the last few years as I have been immersed in this project. I am more proud of being their mother than of anything else in my life.

Finally, I want to pay tribute to Lynn Barnicle, to whose memory our work has been dedicated since her death from leukemia in 2009. She was a longtime, dedicated member of our science-writing team, a master teacher, an ardent proponent of science education as well as of the arts and social studies, and the kind of human being we value beyond measure when they grace our lives. In spirit, she remains with us as a poignant and urgent reminder that all students need to have a strong science education so they can participate knowledgeably in our increasingly complex world. Some of them will be inspired to study at the highest of levels to become the scientists who develop cures for diseases that take such gracious and radiant human beings from us long before their time.

Introduction

A teacher shared this story with me at a national conference: On the first day of school, a mother was telling the teacher about her son, who receives services in special education. She said, "You'll never be able to get him to write. It's such a struggle for him." At a parent-teacher conference several months later, the teacher shared the boy's science notebook with his mother. When the mother saw the amount and quality of the writing in her son's notebook, she burst into tears and said, "How did you get him to do this?" The teacher replied, "I never expected him not to."

This is not an uncommon story for teachers who have high expectations for each of their students and who teach inquiry-based science and science writing using the methods you will find in *Writing in Science in Action*. Because of the scaffolding and modeling described in this book and its predecessor, *Writing in Science*, students with all levels of academic skills move to higher levels of achievement in both science and expository writing.

When I wrote *Writing in Science* in 2006, I had spent a decade, first in my own classroom and then working with over a hundred teachers in Seattle Public Schools, developing an effective, meaningful approach to teaching scientific thinking and writing. Since then, I have spent five more years developing, field-testing, and refining new materials, including video episodes that show teachers as they implement the approach. The result of these efforts, *Writing in Science in Action*, provides strategies, tools, and resources to help you begin to implement the approach with your students or continue what you began as you read *Writing in Science*.

These books and materials have been developed and produced as part of a National Science Foundation (NSF) Teacher Professional Continuum (TPC) grant. Feedback from over 1,200 teachers and reports from the external evaluators of the grant, Inverness Research, Inc. (who interviewed teachers, observed classrooms, and analyzed student work), helped inform the development of the science-writing program and resources in Seattle Public Schools. Evaluation studies of this approach indicate that students whose teachers use this approach have higher scores on standardized state assessments (Herman 2005), produce more sophisticated writing about science, and spend more time doing science than students whose teachers do not use this approach (Stokes, Hirabayashi, and Ramage 2003).

During the current NSF grant, from 2006 through 2011, teachers from Washington, Maine, South Carolina, Arizona, and Rhode Island field-tested the new materials produced after *Writing in Science* was published in 2007. This second book thus reflects eleven years of implementation by teachers in Seattle, which is a diverse, urban school district where students speak over a hundred different languages and about 40 percent of the students receive free or reduced-price lunches, as well as the experiences of other teachers in diverse settings in five states.

Why Does This Approach Matter?

This approach to science and science writing helps develop students' understanding of science concepts, scientific thinking, and writing in four key ways:

1. *The learning begins with concrete materials as students are actively engaged in "doing science."* This removes the obstacles that many students face in school because of their language skills, special needs, and other issues. All students start at the same place. This increases their interest, motivation, and, ultimately, their self-esteem and skills in science and writing.

2. *Literacy skills are acquired in a meaningful context.* Students do not learn different forms of writing in isolation, apart from authentic experiences. For example, they learn how to write a conclusion after they have completed a scientific investigation and need to share their results with other scientists. This makes the writing meaningful, which increases students' motivation.

3. *Writing about science concepts and scientific thinking provides students with the opportunity to engage in thinking and types of expository writing that they typically do not encounter at other times in the school day.* For example, talking about and writing scientific conclusions after conducting investigations and analyzing test results involves high-level thinking and writing skills that fall into the categories of writing to persuade and writing to explain, two purposes of writing that the new Common Core State Standards for English Language Arts emphasize as a means of improving students' literacy skills as they prepare for college and careers (Common Core State Standards Initiative 2010).

4. *Students are able to become scientifically literate at the same time that they are developing valuable thinking and literacy skills.* The scaffolding and modeling that are central to this approach help students both construct understanding of science concepts and develop their skills in scientific thinking, scientific skills, and scientific writing.

What's in This Book and How Can It Help You?

I developed the additional resources presented in *Writing in Science in Action* based on what teachers have done, what they say has worked well for them, and what obstacles they have encountered. I have found that teachers typically have three major requests: they want to watch teachers implementing this approach with real students, they ask for help with assessment, and they want strategies and tools that they can use easily and effectively with their students. In order to meet these needs, this book is divided into three parts. An accompanying website provides additional resources.

Part 1: *Writing in Science* in the Classroom

- **Chapter 1:** "Overview" presents the basic components of this science-writing approach. If you have read *Writing in Science*, this will be a useful review; if you have not read the book, the overview will provide the basic information you need to implement this approach in your classroom.

- **Chapters 2 through 7:** Each chapter focuses on a video episode that features a science and a writing session in a different grade (from kindergarten through fifth grade). These chapters present important components of this science-writing approach and resources to help you implement those components.

  - **Chapter 2** explains how to use modeling and scaffolding to help students develop their abilities to work, think, talk, and write like scientists.

  - **Chapters 3 through 6** focus on different types of notebook entries, in roughly the order they might be needed in a scientific inquiry: scientific illustrations, data tables, and observations; scientific comparisons; simple claims supported with evidence; and predictions, graphs, and complex conclusions. Chapters 3, 4, and 6 include checklists that identify the characteristics of an exemplary entry of each type. You can use these checklists in planning instruction and assessing your students' entries.

  - **Chapter 7** includes strategies that support English language learners as they learn science content, scientific thinking, and the language they need to use in communicating about science.

Part 2: Assessment

- **Chapter 8:** "Meaningful Assessment and Effective Feedback" explains the characteristics of meaningful assessment (what do you assess in science notebooks and how do you assess them?) and effective feedback (what do you say to students that helps build their confidence as well as their thinking, content understanding, and writing abilities?).

- **Chapter 9:** "Group Critiquing and Teacher-Student Conferences" focuses on three video episodes that show how groups of teachers work together to plan their instruction and assess their students' notebook entries in productive ways.

Part 3: Teachers' Toolkit

This section focuses on specific areas in which teachers want and need support.

- **Chapter 10:** "Planning Instruction: Focus Questions and Meaningful Notebook Entries" guides you in developing questions that focus students' thinking during and after their investigations. The chapter also helps you plan notebook entries that will deepen students' thinking and content understanding as they write each entry.

- **Chapter 11:** "Sample Minilessons" gives you some lessons to use in teaching your students how to make specific types of entries (for example, scientific observations and conclusions).

- **Chapter 12:** "Emergent Writing" presents some tips and strategies for supporting emergent writers in any elementary grade.

- **Chapter 13:** "Frequently Asked Questions and Next Steps" addresses the most crucial of the broad questions that teachers ask about this approach, then offers suggestions for where to go next as you implement the approach.

Additional Resources

DVD

The **video episodes** on the DVD, which are an integral part of *Writing in Science in Action*, show how teachers implement this approach to teaching science and science writing in real classroom situations. As noted earlier, seven chapters feature a video episode so you can learn from both reading and watching.

Website

The website associated with this book, www.heinemann.com/wisia, provides resources related to both this book and *Writing in Science*. The website is divided into sections as follows:

■ **Checklists for Exemplary Notebook Entries**, which are shown in Chapters 3, 4, and 6 and included here in a compact, downloadable form for you to use in planning instruction and assessing notebook entries.

■ **Reproducibles** of each of the other forms that appear in the book, and some from *Writing in Science*.

■ **Student Notebook Entries, Pre-kindergarten Through Fifth Grade**, which are grouped by type of entry (for example, comparisons, conclusions) and include annotations that highlight different aspects of each student's entry.

■ **Guidelines for Science-Writing Group Meetings**, which are designed to support you and your colleagues over a series of meetings as you gradually implement different components of this science-writing approach and reflect together on your instruction and your students' learning. Two versions of the guidelines enable you to use either this book alone as a resource, or this book with *Writing in Science*. Teachers who have had the opportunity to work together in this way say that it profoundly and positively affects how they view their students' work and their instructional practice and increases their enthusiasm about their teaching of science and science writing.

■ **Stories from Schools**, which include a testimonial from the principal of a Blue Ribbon School explaining the value of inquiry science and science writing, and stories from four teachers who share their experiences, their insights, and the successes of their students, including those with special needs, English language learners, and students with highly developed academic and language skills.

■ **Background Information About the Video Episodes**, which includes answers to typical questions teachers ask after watching each episode (for example, demographics of the school, background of the teacher and students, specifics about the classroom setup).

This Book and *Writing in Science*

Writing in Science in Action provides enough basic information that you can implement the approach without having read *Writing in Science*. If you have already read *Writing in Sci-*

ence, you will find this second book useful because it provides new materials to meet the needs that teachers in the field-test sites identified. If you have not read *Writing in Science*, you probably will find, as you and your students gain skill and confidence, that you want more information. *Writing in Science* goes into more depth about certain aspects of this approach, providing detailed information about the stages of teaching and learning, additional ideas about teaching different forms of expository writing, and an in-depth look at the process of developing a science-writing curriculum for a complete science unit. It also includes more details about the development and components of the Expository Writing and Science Notebooks Program in Seattle Public Schools and research about its impressive, positive impact on student learning and teachers' practices. It features a complete notebook from a student in a class that is studying physical science, and includes captions that describe the teacher's instruction and students' work before they wrote each entry.

In a time when teachers lament that they do not have time to teach science because they are working so hard to develop their students' literacy and math skills, the approach that you learn in *Writing in Science in Action* and in *Writing in Science* enables you to meet your students' literacy needs and at the same time provide them with rich science experiences. Ultimately, this combination will help them develop into scientifically literate citizens in a global community and, perhaps, even become scientists who address the challenges of this complex modern world.

Writing in Science
in Action

CHAPTER 1

Overview

Writing in Science in Action is designed to help you begin or continue to learn how to teach science writing through a dynamic approach in which writing and inquiry-based science instruction are mutually beneficial. Through modeling scientific language and thinking and providing different types of scaffolding, you support students as they learn how to think and write about science.

This chapter summarizes the essential components of this science-writing approach. You will understand the kind of teaching and learning presented in Chapters 2 through 7 and 9 much more easily if you watch each video episode on the accompanying DVD as directed. Seeing other teachers implement this approach with students in real classrooms is key to developing an understanding of how to teach in this way.

As you read this overview of the essential components of this science-writing approach, keep in mind that it typically takes about three years of teaching an inquiry-based science unit and about the same amount of time teaching science writing before teachers feel confident about teaching in these ways. But we also have found that even as teachers take small, incremental steps in implementing different strategies, they see an increase, sometimes even substantial growth, in their students' learning.

Before continuing, watch the Introduction Video Episode. It will give you a broad look at how this approach to science writing works before you read about the details. As you watch, think about your own approach to science and science writing. What similarities and differences do you notice?

The Three Key Elements of This Approach

The foundation of this science-writing approach is its focus on the Three Key Elements:

1. *Science concepts*—the ability to construct understanding of concept(s) or "big idea(s)" as scientists do when they explore and investigate objects, organisms, or events

2. *Scientific thinking*—the ability to think as scientists do (for example, making a distinction between what they observe and what they infer from that observation; making claims, then supporting them with appropriate evidence and/or reasoning; interpreting test results to determine if they answer a question scientists have been investigating)

3. *Scientific skills*—the ability to work as scientists do (for example, knowing how to use tools in scientific investigations; make detailed, accurate, objective observations; plan and conduct controlled investigations)

In our earlier work, we included expository writing as a fourth element (as discussed in *Writing in Science*). But over the last few years, we have realized that the Three Key Elements are so intrinsic to the writing that we cannot consider writing as a separate element.

The Structure of This Science-Writing Approach: Science and Writing Sessions

Early in the development of this science-writing approach, we tried to combine science investigations, science-writing instruction, and the students' writing of notebook entries (other than making observation notes, diagrams or illustrations, and recording data) all in one session. The results were disastrous. Students did not have enough time and energy for either the science or the writing, and everyone was frustrated. So we teach the science and the writing separately. We also have found that students make greater gains in learning science and science writing when we teach science at least twice a week and science writing at least twice a week. The sections that follow describe these sessions, which we generally refer to as the science session and the writing session.

Science Session

During the science session, students experience inquiry-based science, actively engaging in open explorations, controlled investigations or experiments, and discussions through which they construct an understanding of science concepts and practices. The 1996 *National Science Education Standards* explain scientific inquiry as follows:

> Inquiry is a multifaceted activity that involves making observations; posing questions; examining books and other sources of information to see what is already known; planning investigations; reviewing what is already known in light of experimental evidence; using tools to gather, analyze, and interpret data; proposing answers, explanations, and predictions; and communicating the results. Inquiry requires identification of assumptions, use of critical and logical thinking, and consideration of alternative explanations. (National Research Council 1996, 23)

The Three Key Elements reflect this multifaceted nature of inquiry. *A Framework for Science Education*, the document that will guide the development of the new K through 12 science standards, points out that inquiry is more than "engagement of students in experimentation or hands-on activities." The *Framework* uses "the term 'practices' instead of a term like 'skills' to emphasize that engaging in scientific inquiry requires coordination of both knowledge and skills simultaneously. This is to avoid the interpretation of skill as rote mastery of an activity or procedure" (NRC 2010, 1–13). Students need to be sharing their ideas with each other, testing those ideas using scientific skills and thinking, and continually refining their models and theories as they encounter new information.

In over a decade of work, we have found that using inquiry-based science units provides rich learning experiences for students when those units are implemented throughout the year. During the first year of applying this science-writing approach, we recommend that teachers teach all the lessons in at least one unit. Doing so helps students experience the full "conceptual story" that the lessons tell about specific science concepts. In the second year, teachers teach at least two full units, and preferably three. Their students then have deep and meaningful experiences with scientific inquiry and learning throughout the school year, which increases their excitement about science and their achievement in both science and science writing. In our program (as shown in the lesson examples and notebook entries in this book), we use inquiry-based units published by Science and Technology for Children (STC), Full Option Science System (FOSS), and Insights.

A typical science session generally lasts from forty-five to sixty minutes, depending on the lesson and the grade level of the students. Each session includes four stages.

1. Engagement: During this stage, you engage the students and connect them with their prior knowledge or previous investigations. This is also the time to introduce the focus question for the lesson (see the section "Science Notebooks in This Approach" that follows), and to have students set up their notebook entries by writing the date and the focus question (or, for younger students, pasting in a preprinted focus question). As needed, you also model how to make and use data tables, draw scientific illustrations or diagrams, and record data.

2. Active Investigation: During this stage, students work with concrete materials or organisms. The only writing they do in their notebooks is to record data, take notes, and/or make scientific illustrations or diagrams. As students work, check in with the groups, monitoring and supporting students' progress by asking questions and modeling the language and thinking that students need to know and use at this point in the science unit.

3. Shared Reflection: During this stage, you lead a class discussion, asking questions that help students make meaning of their investigation as they talk with their partner and together as a whole group. You and the students also create class data tables or graphs of the students' observations and/or test results as well as other visual organizers (for example, charts and diagrams) that help students visualize and remember new concepts and terms. These become visual records to which you and the students can refer during class discussions and during the writing session. At this time, you also add words to the science word bank and model how to think and talk as scientists do. (See "Modeling and Scaffolding," later in this chapter, for more about the strategies you can use during this stage.) Students refer to their notebooks to provide data and evidence for what they are contributing to the discussion.

4. Application: During this stage, you and the students connect the lesson to further investigations and/or make meaning of the investigation in terms of the real world.

Writing Session

The writing session should take place later in the day that you have the science session, or sometime the next day. You will lose momentum if you wait longer than that between the two sessions. The writing session generally lasts twenty to thirty minutes, depending on the lesson and the grade level. Like the science session, the writing session includes four stages.

1. Shared Review: This stage is the bridge between the science session and the writing minilesson. During the shared review, engage the students in remembering what they investigated and what they figured out in their shared reflection discussion about their investigation.

2. Shared-Writing Minilesson: During this stage, you provide the *structure* for the writing and thinking the students will do, while the students provide the *content*. Using the students' input, model how to write an appropriate entry, such as a comparison or a conclusion. (See "Modeling and Scaffolding," later in this chapter, for more about this stage and the next.)

3. Scaffolding: After the shared-writing minilesson, remove the shared writing so students cannot copy it, and replace it with a writing frame or structure for students to refer to as they do their own writing.

4. Independent Writing: Students write their own entries, using the writing frame and other scaffolding that you have provided as you work with small groups and individual students to provide support as necessary.

Finding time to teach science and science writing in this way can be challenging, but making that time a priority becomes increasingly desirable as teachers begin to see the dramatic effects it has on students' learning and writing as well as on their general excitement about science. Furthermore, the kind of writing included in the writing session typically is not part of most writing programs, yet it has a profound impact on students' abilities to develop and write about their critical thinking and conceptual understanding. This time can be considered an invaluable part of literacy instruction.

Science Notebooks in This Approach

In this approach to science and science writing, the expectation is that students will make an entry in the notebook during every science session (as previously described), and they will refer to their notebook during the class discussions. During every writing session, they will write a particular form of entry (as explained in the next section and in Chapters 3 through 6).

What to Write

As you begin to plan your science and writing sessions, and are thinking about what your students should be writing in their notebooks, consider this fundamental question: How will writing this notebook entry help develop my students' understanding of science concepts, their scientific thinking, and/or their scientific skills? Emphasizing the Three Key Elements means that students should focus their attention and energy on writing about what they are investigating and what they are figuring out in the course of their investigations and discussions about them. The types of notebook entries that accomplish this goal include scientific observations, scientific illustrations and diagrams, comparisons, cause and effect, predictions with reasoning, data tables, graphs, claims supported with evidence and/or reasoning, and basic and complex conclusions. (The video episodes and the chapters about them feature these types of entries, and other chapters provide additional information and materials for teaching your students how to write in these ways.)

Students should *not* be writing about what they *did*. This procedural writing is at the lowest level of both thinking and writing and does not help students deepen their conceptual understanding or their scientific thinking. Nor does it help them learn more complex forms of expository text that do deepen their understanding and thinking. Learning the scientific skills of planning and conducting investigations is important, but students can learn these skills by working together and writing class lists of different components of their controlled investigations (for example, the variables they all must keep the same in order for the test results to be valid).

Format for Notebook Entries

Teachers often ask, "What format should we use for a science notebook?" Because of the emphasis on the Three Key Elements in this science-writing approach, the answer to this question is quite different from what other programs recommend. In this approach, each entry has the following parts:

1. *The date* written in numerals.

2. A *focus question* that the class uses to keep everyone focused on something important about the investigation (see the next section about focus questions). A good focus question helps lead students to construct understanding of the science concept or concepts in an investigation and to develop scientific skills and thinking. Sometimes, a lesson may have more than one focus question; at other times, a single focus question may cover multiple sessions.

3. A *form of notebook entry*, or several forms (for example, a scientific illustration in the science session and a written observation in the writing session) that will engage students most meaningfully in communicating and deepening their understanding of science concepts and their scientific thinking. (Chapters 10 and 11 include suggestions for planning these entries.)

Teachers also may ask whether students should make a table of contents. As with procedural writing, making an entry for each lesson in a table of contents is time-consuming and takes time away from more meaningful thinking and writing. The one exception is with older students, who authentically *need* to have a contents page in order to find specific entries because their science units are longer and more complex than the units in the primary grades.

Focus Questions

In this approach to teaching science and science writing, every science lesson (or sometimes, a sequence of lessons) has a focus question that students think about as they conduct their investigation and make meaning of it. Introduce the question during the discussion in the engagement stage of the science session. Students circle the important words in the question and the class discusses them. This process serves several purposes.

It helps students learn to deconstruct a question, which is especially important with older students who are dealing with complex questions. It also helps students of all ages learn to read questions carefully, and to refer back to words in a question as they are writing responses in their notebooks. (See Chapter 10 for information about how to create and use focus questions.)

Assessment of Notebook Entries

Notebook entries in this science-writing approach are considered rough drafts. So, in this stage of writing, you are looking for what the entry reveals about the Three Key Elements: the student's understanding of science concepts, his scientific thinking, and his ability to use scientific skills.

- Do not assess, or discuss with the student, conventions (for example, grammar, spelling, punctuation), sentence fluency (the flow and the variety of the structure of sentences), voice (writing as a scientist, in this case), or handwriting and neatness (as long as it is legible enough for another scientist to read). Address these writing traits only if a student revises the rough draft in order to "publish" it as an article or report.

- When you discuss an entry with a student, begin by pointing out specific strengths in terms of the Three Key Elements. When you need to address weaknesses, discuss them by asking the student a question or questions that a scientist would have about the entry. Making scientists the audience for these entries teaches students to write to an audience outside the classroom, a valuable skill in both thinking and writing. Chapters 8 and 9 provide different assessment strategies and examples of critiqued notebook entries.

The Teacher's Science Notebook

Many teachers greatly value and benefit from making entries in their own science notebooks. Some choose to make entries just like their students'. So, for example, when a teacher wants to model how to make a data table and record observation notes, he might make such an entry in his own notebook. This is particularly effective if you use a document camera to project an image of what you are writing onto a large screen. Others use their science notebooks for planning and reflecting on their lessons. In either case, when you plan a writing session, write an entry yourself using your planned writing frame so you can discover where students might have trouble with the frame, then revise it as needed.

Modeling and Scaffolding

Modeling and scaffolding are critical components in successfully implementing this science-writing approach in your classroom. Students need to see and hear how to act, think, talk, and write when they are working as scientists. You show them these behaviors by modeling them and by providing three types of scaffolding—visual, oral, and written—that students then use as they learn specific ways of working and writing as scientists.

Visual Scaffolding

Visual scaffolding consists of all the things that students can see in the classroom that help them learn and remember new terms, concepts, and scientific ways of thinking, talking, and writing. This includes science word banks (see the next section) and anything you write and/or draw with the students (for example, class data tables, charts, scientific illustrations and diagrams, flow maps) and then display for everyone to refer to during discussions, investigations, and writing sessions.

Word Banks

Visual scaffolding is critical in helping students master scientific vocabulary. You provide this scaffolding for learning new science terms *after students have had concrete experiences* so that they already have begun to construct an understanding of a word's meaning. Giving students the meaning of science words before they have that concrete experience (sometimes called "front-loading") is not an effective strategy for building vocabulary understanding in science. As noted in *How Students Learn: Science in the Classroom*, published by the National Research Council of the National Academies, "Ideas develop from experiences, and technical terms develop from the ideas and operations that are rooted in those experiences. When terms come first, students just tend to memorize so much technical jargon that it sloughs off in a short while" (Donovan and Bransford 2005, 512).

To display new terms, make a word bank using a pocket chart (available from educational-materials catalogs). We have found that the most practical style has about ten horizontal "pockets" and is about thirty-three by forty-one inches, as shown on the left in Figure 1–1. (The teacher added a second chart because the unit was complex and she wanted to display the words together.)

- After students have been exploring and investigating a question using concrete materials, introduce new terms to connect with those experiences. Show a new term on a word card (made from tagboard or a sentence strip, with words printed using broad-tipped, dark markers so students can read the words from a distance), which you then place in the word bank.

- Include concrete materials, diagrams, and/or drawings with the word cards to help students recognize the words. For example, when young students are studying about wood, they begin by carefully observing different kinds of wood. As the class discusses each type of wood, you introduce the appropriate term (*cedar*, for example) and place the word card in the pocket chart along with a sample of the wood itself. Having this concrete reminder next to the word card helps students learn the new terms. It also makes both the word and the concrete object readily accessible for you to use during discussions and for students to see. Diagrams also can help remind students of the meaning of terms. For example, for the term *complete circuit*, you can write the words on a card and make a simple diagram that shows a battery or D-cell, a wire, and a lightbulb that is emitting light.

- If you have students who are learning English, introduce common words from daily life and place those word cards in the word bank before students conduct an investigation. For example, in learning about stream systems, erosion, and deposition, students use a model of a stream system. The model consists of a plastic tub, a cup with a hole in it, soil,

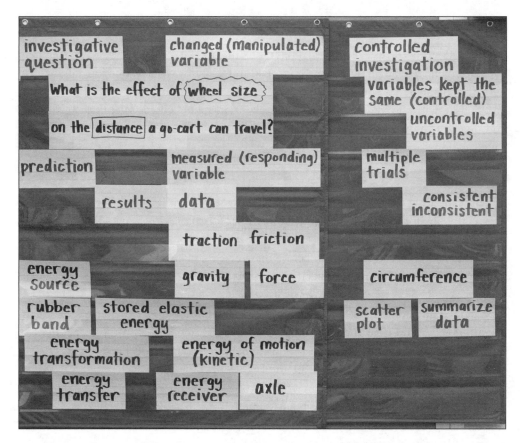

FIGURE 1–1 *Science word bank*

water, a plug, and a bucket into which the water drains. In preparing for an investigation with this model, show English language learners the word cards (with sketches) for the components of the model (for example, *tub, cup, soil, plug*). Then, during the class discussion *after* the investigation, introduce word cards for *model, stream system, channel, erosion,* or *deposition*. Having had the concrete experience, their minds are ready to connect the scientific terms with what they have experienced.

■ Students also need a second word bank where they can find more generic words they need to use in their science writing. The Useful Words and Phrases in Scientific Writing chart (see Figure 1–2) helps students learn to talk and write about their understanding and thinking about science.

■ Introduce different words and phrases from the chart as students have a need to know them. Initially, you can add some of these words and phrases (for example, *I observed, because*) to the science word bank. When the word bank becomes too full during the unit, move these generic words and phrases to another pocket chart or some other place where students easily can see the words. Figure 1–3 shows one classroom's pocket chart of useful words and phrases.

Diagrams, Scientific Illustrations, Graphs, Data Tables, and Other Graphic Organizers

Diagrams and scientific illustrations can help support students in learning and remembering terms for what they have been observing. Figure 1–4 shows a diagram of a go-cart that

Useful Words and Phrases in Scientific Writing

Questions	Observations	Contrasts	Sequence of Time, Cause and Effect, Reasoning
What is the effect of [*the changed variable*] on [*the measured, observed, responding variable*]? What do you think would happen if _____ ?	I observed _____. I noticed _____. When _____, After _____,	_____, but _____. _____ whereas _____. However, _____. In contrast, _____. At first, _____. But now, _____.	First, _____. Next, _____. Then, _____. Finally, _____. If _____, then _____. So, _____. This leads to _____ As a result, _____ Consequently, _____

Evidence	Reasoning and Metacognition	Adding Information, Evidence, Reasoning	Conclusions
_____ because _____. I think this because _____ For example, _____ For instance, _____ The evidence is _____ The data show _____ The data provide evidence that _____	_____ because _____. I think this because _____ I think this means _____ At first I thought _____ because _____. But now I think _____ because _____.	Also, _____. In addition, _____ Furthermore, _____	Therefore, I think _____ In conclusion, I think _____ Therefore, _____ In conclusion, _____

Note to teachers: To support students in becoming independent writers, continually model how to use the language in this chart. Make a language word bank or post the categories of a chart like this, adding words and phrases to the categories as needed. Include commas when needed to underscore where they are used with the words. Also teach students how to use words from questions, when applicable, to begin their notebook entries. Over time, you may want additional strategies for helping students develop more independent writing skills. Chapter 13 provides other strategies for moving students away from using sentence starters and writing frames. (This is a revised version of a chart featured in *Writing in Science*.)

FIGURE 1–2 *Useful Words and Phrases in Scientific Writing*

May be photocopied for classroom or workshop use. © 2011 by Betsy Rupp Fulwiler from *Writing in Science in Action*. Portsmouth, NH: Heinemann.

FIGURE 1–3 *Word bank of useful words and phrases*

a teacher made as her students told her the different parts to add. The class diagram helps students remember the names for the parts and gives them a common visual organizer that they can refer to as they talk together and when they make notebook entries.

Scientific illustrations, which are especially useful in life science units, can be helpful in the same way. For example, if students are studying the parts of a flower or of an animal cell, being able to look at a large illustration during class discussions and writing sessions can support students as they learn the terms for what they have been observing.

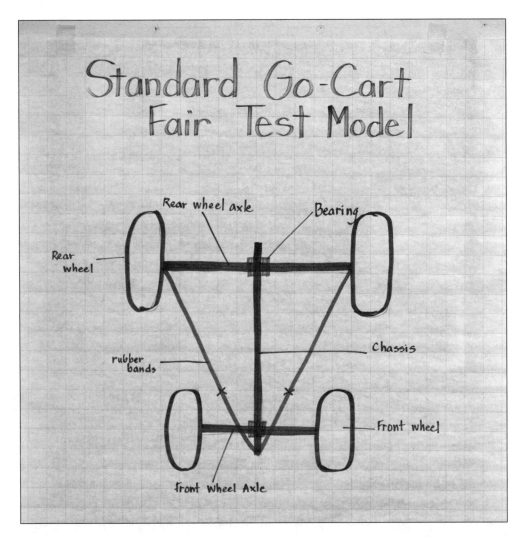

FIGURE 1–4 *Labeled diagram*

Figure 1–5 shows another type of visual scaffolding—a class graph. This class scatter plot displays the averages or means of the students' test results, which makes it easy for the class to discuss their data. When you discuss data in a graph or in a data table, you introduce vocabulary as the students make sense of their data. In this example, the teacher has added the words *only* and *but* to the graph to help students learn to use comparative language when interpreting, explaining, and summarizing data.

Depending on the unit, you may need to use other graphic organizers as well. The most common are T-charts, flow maps, and system-parts or tree maps.

Oral Scaffolding

The second of the three types of scaffolding is oral scaffolding, which you provide in talking with students during whole-class, small-group, and one-on-one discussions. You need to model the language students need to use in communicating their scientific thinking and understanding. Modeling how to use language includes having students say words or terms with you. Using phrases such as "Say it with me" or "Read it with me" gives students the

FIGURE 1–5 *Scatter plot*

opportunity to use the words orally well before you expect them to use them in their writing. Continually modeling the words is critical for students to learn the language and develop an ear for the way it sounds. Students also need to repeat the words and phrases numerous times before they can internalize the language and eventually use the language naturally in their writing.

One important strategy for doing this is to give students a phrase or the beginning of a sentence that will help them talk about something together and, ultimately, write an entry in their notebook.

- For example, if you want students to talk about the results of a controlled investigation, you could tell them to turn to a partner during the class discussion and begin their discussion together by saying the words "I think" (for example, "I think the rubber ball is a better bouncer than the Ping-Pong ball."). Then they would use the phrase "I think this because" to support their thinking or claim with evidence (for example, "I think this because the rubber ball bounced twelve times but the Ping-Pong ball bounced only eight times.").

- In a discussion about an investigation, you could tell them to use the following structure: "At first I thought . . . because . . ." (for example, "At first I thought the small wheel would make the go-cart go farther than the large wheel because it is smaller and weighs less."). By modeling this structure orally and having the students use it as they talk together, you are modeling the language they can use orally and in their writing as well as providing a structure to develop their thinking and prompt them to include their evidence and/or reasoning.

- Later, they could use another frame for expressing the development of their thinking: "But now I think . . . because . . ." (for example, "But now I think the large wheel makes the go-cart travel farther because every time it makes one complete turn, it goes farther than the small wheel does."). This language structure helps students think about

Writing in Science in Action

and express the change in their thinking, which is important in their metacognitive understanding of how their own thinking and understanding are evolving.

Oral scaffolding also includes your modeling of appropriate scientific vocabulary and language use. When students use a common term instead of a scientific term, model how to use the scientific word. For example, if a student uses the word *dirt*, you can say, "The scientific word for *dirt* is *soil*." In discussions, model how to speak in complete sentences, use appropriate scientific terms, and use *because* and *I think this because* to provide evidence and reasoning. Then expect students to speak in those ways during discussions. This will help them use the language in their writing as well.

Written Scaffolding

The category of written scaffolding includes written phrases and sentences that you use in modeling how to write certain notebook entries during a shared-writing minilesson during the writing session. For a comparison, for example, you could provide this sentence starter for the first sentence to support students in writing about the similarities of two objects, organisms, or events: "The _____ and the _____ are similar because _____." Written scaffolding for a prediction might be, "I predict _____. I think this because _____."

Often, as in these examples, the three types of scaffolding are used together to structure the expression of the same concept or thinking. You show the *visual* scaffolding—the sentence starter or frame. Then you model how to use the scaffolding *orally* and the students use it in their speaking. Then, after the shared-writing minilesson during the writing session, you include the words in the *written* scaffolding.

Working with Other Teachers

Quite early in the process of implementing this approach, you will see gains in your students' science and writing abilities. If you are able to work with another teacher or teachers, you may find that the extra support helps you plan and reflect on your instruction and your students' learning even more efficiently and effectively. Teachers we have worked with over the years highly value being able to work with colleagues, especially at their own grade level, to plan and reflect on their instruction and assess their students' work. Most of them meet almost monthly throughout the school year following guidelines that you will find at www.heinemann.com/wisia. The positive impact of this collaboration is particularly evident when looking at student work because one teacher often can see strengths in a student's writing that another teacher might overlook as he concentrates on where the student needs to improve her skills. Chapter 9 features video episodes and information about these science-writing group meetings.

Beginning to Implement This Science-Writing Approach

Research on this project has shown that students at all levels of academic ability can be successful when they experience science through inquiry and when their teacher uses modeling and scaffolding to help support them as they learn new science concepts and scientific skills and thinking. But you cannot implement these strategies all at once. Start by showing your students how to use *because* and *I think this because*. This is a simple strategy that almost immediately improves students' scientific thinking, speaking, and writing, because using the word and phrase prompts students to provide reasoning and evidence, which is not something they naturally do. The reasoning and evidence will not necessarily be accurate, but it is an important part of the thinking, talking, and writing in science, starting in kindergarten.

As you read each subsequent chapter, you will learn about additional strategies and information to help you further implement this science-writing approach.

CHAPTER 2

Modeling and Scaffolding

Before You Watch

Thinking scientifically, and talking and writing about this thinking, are not skills that students naturally develop as they are conducting science investigations in the classroom. You need to model the thought processes and the language for them, and provide scaffolding that further supports their learning. The Soils Video Episode illustrates this modeling and scaffolding as the teacher helps his students become a community of young scientists who are learning to work, think, speak, and write as adult scientists do.

This episode shows a science session and a writing session at the end of a unit about soils. In the initial lessons in the unit, students conducted different tests on three separate soil components—sand, clay, and humus—to discover the properties of each one. Later, they conducted tests to identify which of these three soil components were in a "mystery mixture." In the final science sessions leading up to this video episode, students have been conducting the same tests on samples of local soil. By applying what they now know about the properties of the three soil components, they can interpret their test results to determine which soil components are in the local soil.

While You Watch

As you watch the video episode, consider the following questions:

1. How does the teacher use modeling and scaffolding in the science session and in the writing session?

2. What modeling and scaffolding do you think helped the students learn the behaviors they demonstrate during the sessions? (They did not think and work like scientists on their first day in this classroom.)

3. How does the physical setup of the classroom contribute to the students' learning?

After You Watch

The students in this video episode demonstrate complex scientific thinking and language in their speaking and writing. To help students reach this level of complexity, the teacher must be especially intentional about modeling and providing scaffolding that simplifies the learning process. Through *modeling*, he demonstrates the behavior and language of scientists. For example, in earlier lessons, he modeled how to conduct different tests on the soil and how to work collaboratively in pairs and small groups. In the videotaped lesson, he models how scientists talk and think.

The teacher also provides three types of *scaffolding* (explained in Chapter 1).

■ He uses *visual scaffolding* (for example, word banks and a class data table) to introduce and practice new terms and to display class data and other information so that everyone can see and discuss them. He keeps this scaffolding available as needed throughout the unit so he and the students can keep referring to it.

■ *Oral scaffolding* results from the oral modeling the teacher provides as he uses scientific language and thinking. This modeling becomes oral scaffolding over time as students begin to "hear it in their minds" because they have heard the teacher model it repeatedly.

■ Finally, the teacher uses *written scaffolding*, which consists of the sentence starters and writing frame he uses as the skeletal structure of a form of scientific writing (in this case, a conclusion).

During discussions (whole group, small group, and with individual students), the teacher asks questions that help students make connections between their testing of the local soil and the same tests they conducted at the beginning of the unit to discover the properties of sand, clay, and humus. This is a complex process that involves all the Three Key Elements:

1. *Scientific skills*. Students first need to learn how to conduct each test and how to collect and record appropriate observations and data.

2. *Science concepts*. These observations and data then help students learn the properties of sand, clay, and humus, which is part of the content learning in this science unit.

3. *Scientific thinking*. Students refer to their records in their notebook and their understanding of the properties of soil as they use scientific thinking to identify the soil components, first in a "mystery soil," then in the local soil.

Note that in the writing session, the teacher focuses his students on using scientific thinking to identify the soil components. He does not waste time having students write about what they *did*. Instead, they think scientifically as they write about their answer to the question they have been investigating, supporting their claims with specific evidence from their tests.

Strategies for Your Classroom

Modeling and scaffolding are key components of this science-writing approach and consist of a number of strategies, both simple and complex, that you can learn to implement incrementally over time.

Preparing for the Lesson

Before the lesson, make sure the physical setup of your classroom and the scaffolding materials encourage the kinds of behaviors and results you want.

- Group students' desks or tables so students can work and talk in pairs and discuss in groups of two or four. This facilitates their science conversations.

- Designate an area where students can gather for the group discussions and you can create class data tables and other written records used in discussions. Moving to this area gives students a few minutes of physical activity during the science session. Sitting together also facilitates student interactions and brings students closer to the teacher and to the class data table and other materials they will need to see clearly as they talk about their investigations.

- Display two word banks: one for the specific science terms in the unit you are teaching, and one for general words and phrases that students will need in their speaking and writing. Plastic pocket charts (available from educational supply companies) are perfect for word banks because you can remove specific word cards during discussions to reinforce the meaning and usage of the words, and students easily can see the words during discussions and writing sessions.

- Check to make sure that all students can see the word banks and any other visual materials from their seats. It is worth the extra few minutes it takes to stand at each student's seat and confirm that everything you want each student to see is visible.

- Make a large copy of the focus question for your lesson or a related group of lessons. (For more on developing strong focus questions, see Chapter 10.) Post the focus question in a place where all students can see and refer to it.

- Gather necessary materials for the science lesson and plan how students will manage them. In the classroom in this video episode, for example, a designated "materials person" from each pair of students gets the materials for the investigation and returns the materials at the end of the investigation.

Modeling Strategies

Good modeling, as the video episode clearly shows, is essential to effective implementation of this approach to science writing. For your students to learn how to work like scientists, you need to model how scientists think and talk about their observations and test results, how they provide evidence for their thinking, and how they write entries in their notebooks. The following list includes some effective modeling strategies.

- Model behaviors and scientific techniques and thinking you expect students to use.

  - Demonstrate and expect appropriate behavior for transitions, sharing and use of materials, and discussions. For example, to help students learn to distribute materials in a safe and orderly way, show them how to move in a line, all in one direction, up to and around the materials table.

  - Show students how to conduct tests or other parts of investigations as needed. In this video episode, the teacher does not model how to conduct any tests because students have performed the same kinds of tests during previous investigations. But earlier in the unit, he modeled how to do each step in a new test. If the steps required two students to work together, he chose a student to do the modeling with him.

  - Model how to make connections between investigations, interpret evidence from tests, and use evidence to support claims. The teacher in this video episode models how to make connections with test results from their previous tests. By modeling how to make these connections, he helps students interpret the data from their current tests. For example, he asks, "Does all this work [testing] we've been doing support your new data?" and "Do you remember when, in the settling test from before . . . ?" He also models how to use the results "as evidence of what is in our local soil."

- Model the scientific language you expect students to use.

  - To help students have effective discussions about their observations and ideas, model how to agree and disagree in nonthreatening ways. For example, model with a student how to say, "I agree with what you said about . . . I have a different idea about . . . because I think . . . "

  - Pull cards from the word bank during discussions, so that you *show* the word while *saying* the word. This reinforces understanding by providing both visual and auditory repetition of the word multiple times. For example, in the video episode, the teacher asks, "When you're talking about 'went to the bottom,' what's another word we can use that goes along with that test we were doing?" As he reaches for the word card for *settling test*, he asks, "When they went to the bottom, they . . . ?" Then the student connects her experiences with the term *settled*.

  - Provide word cards with key words and phrases such as *because, I think this because,* and *I think this happened because*. Students do not naturally provide evidence and/or reasoning for statements or claims that they make, but using *because* and *I think this because* prompts them to do so. Not only will students learn to explain their reasoning, but you also will have a much better idea what students are thinking and can adjust your instruction as needed to address misconceptions. At first, it may help you to keep another copy of the word card with your lesson notes so that you remember to hold it up every time students need to provide reasoning and/or evidence for what they are saying.

  - Repeat key phrases frequently. For example, the teacher in the video episode repeatedly, over several sessions, has modeled key phrases related to the soil tests the students have completed (for example, "like in the settling test from before"). Because students have heard the phrases frequently, they internalize the words and use them naturally in their discussions and in their writing.

- Use phrases such as "A scientist would say . . ." to introduce and reinforce the scientific language you expect students to use.

- Refer back to the focus question during the science session and the writing session. This helps keep students focused on their task and reminds them of important terms to use in their entries.

■ Model how you expect students to use their science notebook. Create a learning environment in which students regularly make an entry in their notebook and *use* their notebook as an integral part of their scientific investigations and discussions.

- Establish early on the expectation that students will record data, notes, and/or illustrations in their notebook during every science session and complete a written entry every science-writing session. Also expect them to refer to their notebook entries to provide evidence during reflective class discussions after investigations.

- Guide students in making their own data table. "Think out loud" and ask them questions as they determine what to include in each data table. To make each row, talk about how many lines to count down on the lined notebook paper before drawing a horizontal line. For the columns, model how to make each vertical line. (For more on data tables, see Chapters 3 and 11).

- Have students record test results and observations (using data tables, box and T-charts, or other organizers as appropriate) on a left-hand page, leaving the facing right-hand page blank (as shown in the video episode). This way, students do not have to flip pages back and forth when they refer to observations and data as they write about them.

- Model how students can use a data table while writing a notebook entry. One useful strategy for many students is to check off in their data table what they include in their writing (see the sample entries from the video episode later in this chapter). Using their data table as an organizer in this way helps students write detailed, organized conclusions and other types of notebook entries.

Scaffolding Strategies

■ Make and display visual scaffolding, such as records of student questions or other material that the class needs to use in discussions (for example, the class data table that shows the students' test results and the list of the students' questions about soils shown in the video episode). Even if you have access to a document camera or white board, keeping copies of this scaffolding displayed in the room allows you and your students to refer to them easily in later sessions.

■ As you do a shared-writing minilesson with your students, provide a *structure* for their writing and ask them to provide the *content*. For example, as you begin each sentence during the minilesson, suggest one way that students could begin that sentence in their own conclusion. Once students have had experience with a particular phrase or structure, you can have them suggest sentence openers, such as in the video episode when one student begins a sentence with "My evidence is." That is not a phrase that students typically would know and use, but the teacher has modeled its use in previous lessons.

- Once you have finished the shared-writing minilesson, remove the shared, modeled writing from students' view so that they cannot copy it. Replace it with a writing frame that students may use as they write independently.

- When you first begin using this approach with your students, use the same writing frame in the shared writing and the independent writing so that the frame is totally familiar to your students when they use it in writing their own notebook entry. As students become more familiar with the process, you can move them toward more independent work. Use students' language in your shared-writing session, and then provide a writing frame for the independent session. This shows students that there is more than one way to write scientifically. Some students will use the frame, while others may choose to use other language for their notebook entry.

Sample Notebook Entries from the Video Episode

The reflections on student notebook entries that follow give examples of both the results of the approach described here and how to model scientific thinking and language when discussing entries with students.

Notebook Entry: Mar'Jon

Mar'Jon's data table is shown in Figure 2–1. He clearly has benefited from the teacher's modeling and scaffolding. For example, he has written accurate observations and test notes, which are, for the most part, written as notes rather than sentences, just as his teacher had modeled at the beginning of the unit. Mar'Jon's thinking about which soil components might be in the local soil is logical. For example, his observation that the local soil sample is black and has medium and small particles would support his thinking that humus is in the sample because those are distinctive properties he noticed in his earlier observations of humus.

In talking with him about his data table, you would point out these specific strengths and how scientists value them. Even when this is just a brief interchange, your comments are a form of modeling that helps students understand specific scientific skills, thinking, and concepts. For instance, because his notes about the smear test are less detailed, and the light color would not be the most distinctive property of sand that would show up in the smear test, you might ask Mar'Jon, "Another scientist might wonder about your entry for the smear test. You wrote that the smear is a little light, which apparently is evidence that the soil is maybe sand and humus. Are they both light? What other properties did you observe in the smear test that could be evidence that both sand and humus are in the local soil?" Your modeling of this scientific thinking would help Mar'Jon realize that scientists need to see evidence to support each part of a data table. These details also are important when scientists write conclusions.

In his conclusion in Figure 2–2, Mar'Jon has used parts of the writing frame to structure his conclusion, as modeled by the teacher. He also has checked off items in the data table as he has addressed them. Focusing on evidence from one test, he has written an organized, substantiated conclusion. The next step in Mar'Jon's science-writing development will be to work on adding the results of another test in his conclusion. (Perhaps he had planned

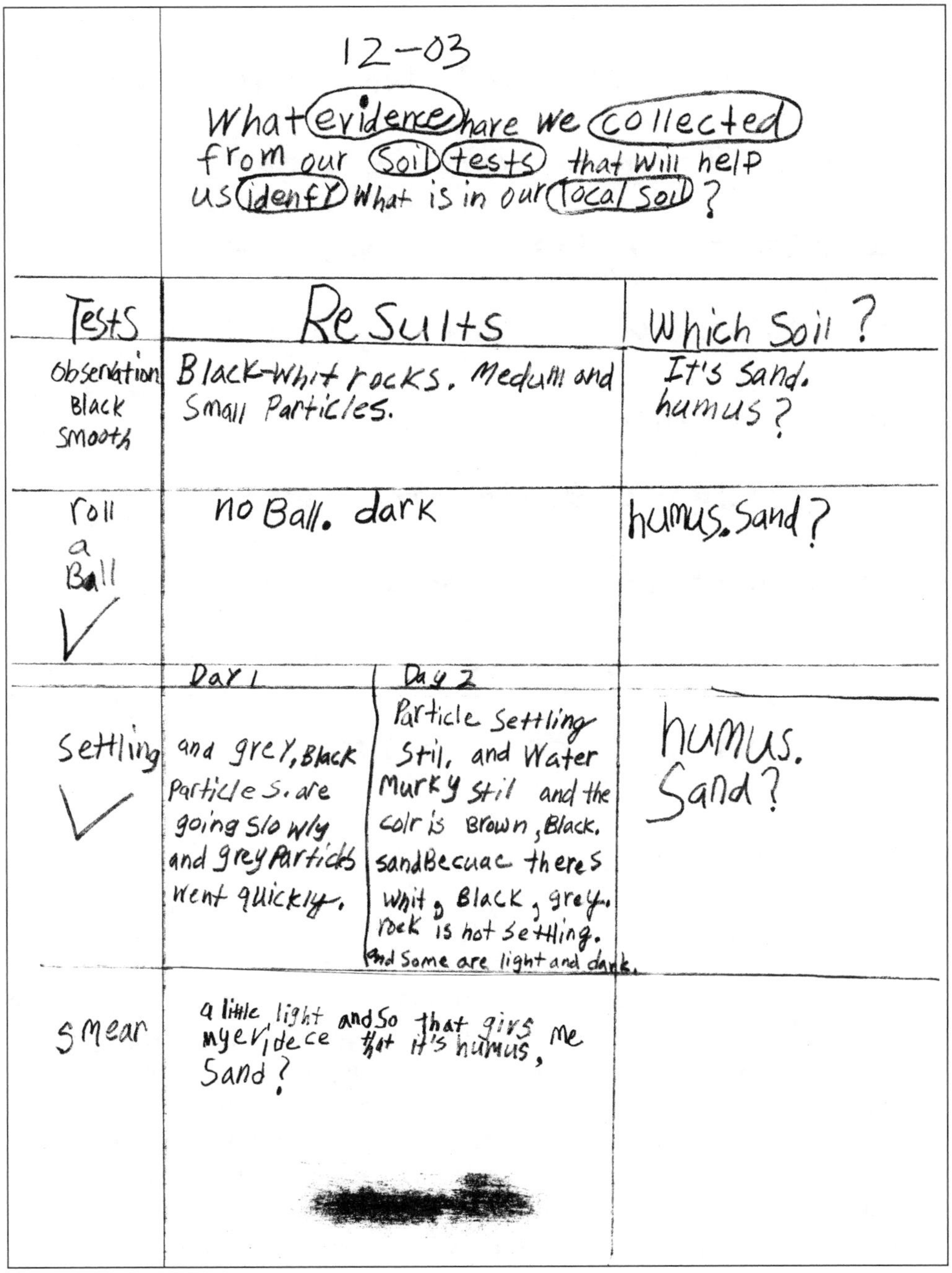

The handwritten data table contains:

12-03

What evidence have we collected from our soil tests that will help us identify what is in our local soil?

Tests	Results	Which Soil?
observation Black smooth	Black-whit rocks. Medum and small Particles.	It's sand. humus?
roll a Ball ✓	no Ball. dark	humus.Sand?
Settling ✓	**Day 1** and grey, Black Particles are going slowly and grey Particls went quickly. **Day 2** Particle settling stil. and water murky stil and the colr is Brown, Black. sand Becuac theres whit, Black, grey, rock is not settling. And some are light and dark.	humus. Sand?
smear	a little light and so that girs me evidece that it's humus, sand?	

FIGURE 2–1 *Mar' Jon's data table*

on adding test results from the roll-a-ball test when he checked that off on his data table, but then ran out of time.)

Notebook Entry: Jonah

Figure 2–3 is Jonah's data table from this same episode. He has included many accurate, important details in the Results column of his data table, and his thinking that humus and sand are in the local soil makes sense given the properties he has included in the table. In

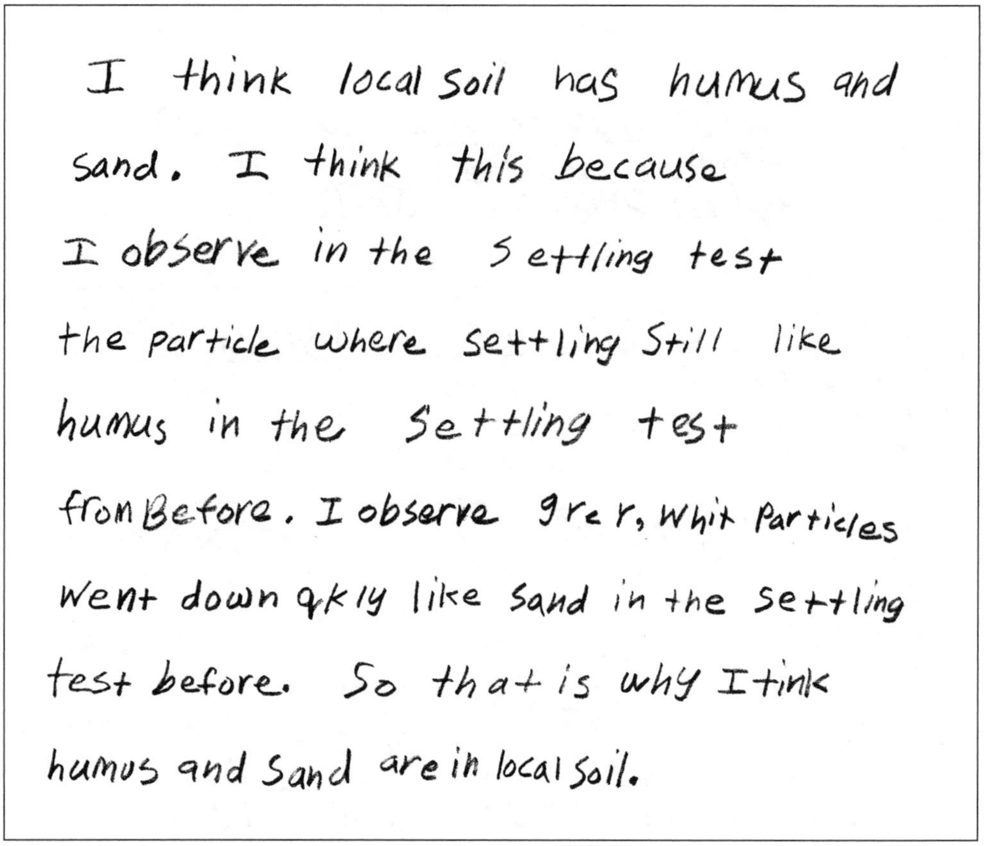

I think local soil has humus and
sand. I think this because
I observe in the settling test
the particle where settling still like
humus in the settling test
from Before. I observe grer, whit particles
went down qkly like sand in the settling
test before. So that is why I tink
humus and sand are in local soil.

FIGURE 2–2 *Mar' Jon's conclusion*

talking with Jonah about his entry, you first would point out the specific strengths in his data table. Although these are his own notes and they presumably make sense to him, you also might say, "Another scientist might wonder which properties indicate sand and which ones indicate humus. Did you write the notes randomly as you made observations or did you write *sand* and *humus* across from their properties? Would the table make sense to her?" The teacher had modeled how to organize notes. Having Jonah reread his notes should make him realize why notes are organized in the way that the teacher had modeled.

In Jonah's conclusion in Figure 2–4, he provides accurate evidence from all three tests, keeping organized by checking off each test as he writes about it in his conclusion, just as the teacher had modeled. One question a scientist might have concerns some details in Jonah's conclusion that he has not included in his data table. Given how detailed his data table is, it is not surprising that he does not include every detail that he observed in the tests. To make a point about the usefulness of a scientist's data table, you might ask, "Scientists record detailed observations in their data table, just like you have, so they can rely on that table if they have to think about the investigation weeks or months after they make their notes. A scientist might ask how you know that in the roll-a-ball test, there were particles falling off and pieces of wood because he wouldn't see those notes in your data table. What would you tell him?" It is possible that Jonah did not have time to write all the observations he made during each test. It also is possible that he did not know that he needs to include everything if he is going to include it in his conclusion.

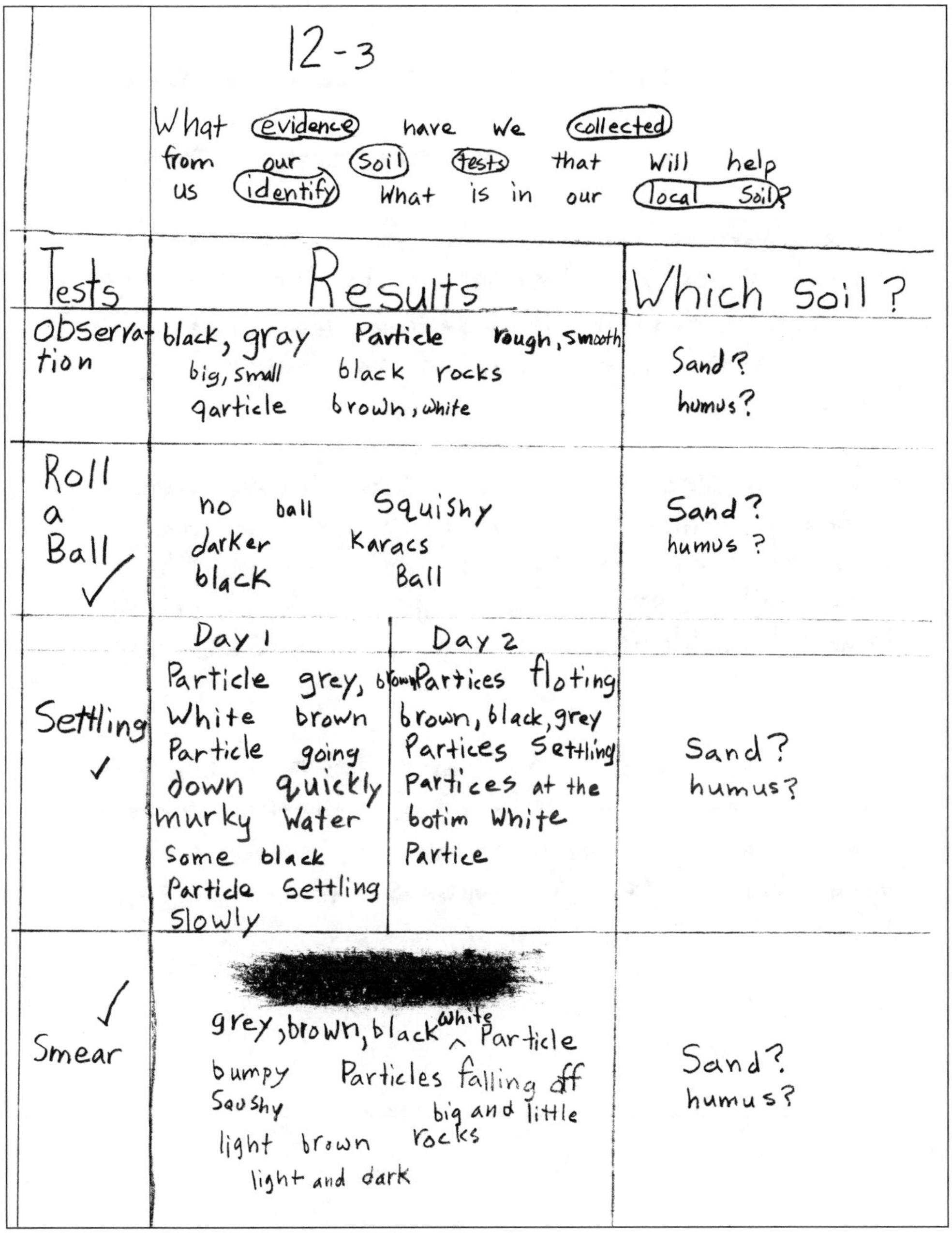

12-3

What (evidence) have we (collected) from (our) (Soil) (tests) that will help us (identify) what is in our (local Soil?)

Tests	Results		Which Soil?
Observation	black, gray Particle rough, smooth big, small black rocks garticle brown, white		Sand? humus?
Roll a Ball ✓	no ball Squishy darker Karacs black Ball		Sand? humus?
Settling ✓	**Day 1** Particle grey, brown White brown Particle going down quickly murky Water Some black Particle Settling Slowly	**Day 2** Particles floting brown, black, grey Partices Settling Partices at the botim White Partice	Sand? humus?
Smear ✓	grey, brown, black white Particle bumpy Particles falling off Saushy big and little light brown rocks light and dark		Sand? humus?

FIGURE 2–3 *Jonah's data table*

Benefits of Modeling and Scaffolding for Students with Special Needs

Shelly Hurley is a teacher in the Special Education Program in Seattle Public Schools where she has a class of high-performing fifth-grade students with autism. She provided the following insights about using this scaffolded approach to teaching science writing with students who have special needs, particularly autism:

> All my students have a hard time writing. They can't find a way to start, and have a hard time coming up with ideas to write about. The best way to teach students

I think local soil has sand and humus.

My evidence is in the settling test

Some partices at the bottom were grey
settled quickly like sand in the settling
test before. Also in the settling test some partice
were floting like humus in the settling test
before.

Also in the Roll a ball test. There were
partices falling off like sand in the
Roll a ball test before. In addition in the
Roll a ball test there was wood making
kracs like humus in the Roll a ball test
before.

Also in the smear test. There were
particle falling off like sand in the smear
test before. In addition in the smear test
wood fell off like humus in the smear test
before.

So that is why I think sand and
humus is in local soil.

FIGURE 2–4 *Jonah's conclusion*

who have special needs like this is to model and teach the writing skills in mini-lessons. Then you have time to focus on teaching things they don't yet understand. The writing frames are extremely helpful, too. I use them all the time and keep them up as prompts for the students.

Using the handout [see Figure 6–2 in Chapter 6] as a guide for writing each part of a complex conclusion was wonderful for the kids I work with in my classroom. Kids who have special needs, especially those with autism, are so literal. The way they have to write about their data and their thinking in this conclusion is abstract, so this kind of writing is especially hard for them. We used the handout, this frame, and it was great because all I had to say was, "Just go down the list and write one paragraph answering each one of these questions." That way they actually could think, in a linear way: What am I going to write for this question? What am I going to write for this next question? And go down the list. When they were done, I knew they had included all the data and the other parts. A lot of times, they can talk it to me, but getting it from this verbal form to a written piece is really, really hard for them. So having these wonderful frames to scaffold the writing for them is a great thing.

Other Highlights of the Video Episode

■ This video episode underscores a fundamental component of scientific thinking, discussion, and writing: When students, of any age, make a claim or statement, they must know that they have to provide evidence for that claim. The evidence might be something they have observed (qualitative data), such as how a soil component settles in water, or something they have measured (quantitative data), such as the amount of water that is absorbed by different soil components. The sample notebook entries discussed here demonstrate how Mar'Jon and Jonah have begun to learn this critical skill. (For more on scientific claims and evidence, see Chapter 5.)

■ In science, students should learn that the words *prove* and *proof* are not appropriate. Instead of asking them how they can *prove* something, ask, "What evidence do you have for your thinking?" or "What data from your investigation would support your claim?"

Related Material

Chapters

■ Chapter 3: "Scientific Illustrations, Data Tables, and Observations"
■ Chapter 5: "Scientific Investigations and Supporting Claims with Evidence"
■ Chapter 6: "Predictions, Graphs, and Complex Conclusions"
■ Chapter 10: "Planning Instruction: Focus Questions and Meaningful Notebook Entries"
■ Chapter 11: "Sample Minilessons"

Website

■ Student Notebook Entries, Pre-kindergarten Through Fifth Grade
  • Read examples from your own grade level as well as samples from a grade above and below your level.

■ Stories from Schools: "Reflections and Suggestions from a Science Coach"
■ Background Information About the Video Episodes: Soils

CHAPTER 3

Scientific Illustrations, Data Tables, and Observations

VIDEO EPISODE: PLANTS

Before You Watch

The Plants Video Episode features a science session in which the teacher models how to make a scientific illustration and collect and record both quantitative (measured) and qualitative (observed) data in a data table. The science session is followed by a separate writing session in which the teacher models how to write a scientific observation using a data table and other scaffolding to organize both the thinking and the writing. The sessions were done back-to-back for videotaping purposes, but this teacher, like others who use this science-writing approach, teaches science in one session, then teaches the science writing later that day or the next day.

While You Watch

As you watch the video episode, think about the following questions:

1. What modeling does the teacher do during these two sessions, first to teach observational skills and scientific thinking, and then to show students how to write scientific observations?

2. What scaffolding does she provide that students can use during the lessons and as they make entries in their own data table and write observations of their own plant?

3. How does she use the focus question—"What can we observe about the plant's growth and development over time?"—in both sessions?

4. How could the modeling and scaffolding help support students who are at very different places on an academic-skills continuum, especially in writing?

Modeling how to make, record, and write scientific observations is a critical component of this approach to science writing. Yet it can be a tricky balance to provide enough modeling to allow students to work independently and be successful but not end up essentially copying what you have written or drawn.

One way of finding that balance in a unit like this is to have a class plant. The teacher in the video episode uses the class plant to model how to make scientific illustrations and observation notes as well as how to measure, record, and graph the growth of the plant. She thinks out loud as she models how she makes these entries, letting students hear the thinking process that underlies the way she makes her entries. She also engages them in discussing their observations so that the experience is shared rather than merely demonstrated.

After the teacher models how to make these entries, students observe their own plant (each student has a plant) as they make a scientific illustration, measure and record the height of the plant, and write their observation notes in their data table. (The teacher modeled how to make such notes in earlier lessons.) Because of the teacher's modeling and the way she has added to the class data table, her students now can use their own table for three purposes: as a place to collect and record their data; as scaffolding to remind them what they need to include in their table and how they should organize that information; and as an organizer for writing their scientific observation.

Strategies for Your Classroom

Strategies for Supporting Students at All Levels

The careful modeling and different types of scaffolding the teacher provides help students at all levels of academic skill succeed with their observations. Furthermore, the hands-on nature of conducting science investigations (in this unit, planting a seed and observing their plant develop over time) motivates students to draw and write about what they are observing.

The following strategies can provide additional support to meet students' different needs:

- Students who struggle with getting started with their writing may benefit from telling either a partner or the teacher about what they want to write or draw just before they start a notebook entry.

- Students who have difficulty completing a written observation may need a reminder to keep referring to the sentence starters or writing frame. They also can look at their science notebook, the class data table, and the word banks.

- Students who have more developed language and the writing skills to use their own words benefit from having support for organizing their observations and learning how to focus on details. They also frequently need to learn how to describe their observations rather than jumping ahead and making inferential statements. For example, "The plant is dead" is a common inferential statement. A scientific observation of the same plant is, "I have observed that all the parts of the plant are brown and the stem is bent to the ground." To combine the two and write a strong scientific entry, a student could write,

"*I have observed* all the parts of the plant are brown and the stem is bent to the ground. *I think this means that* the plant is dead."

Strategies for Making Scientific Observations and Illustrations

Students need guidance in making scientific observations and illustrations.

- Model how to make an observation and an illustration in a focused, organized way. For example, the teacher in the video episode models how to observe and draw the class plant by starting at the bottom of the plant and observing and drawing each part as she moves upward. If you were drawing an object or a different organism, you would start by drawing the outside contour, and then you would focus on different parts as you asked the students what details they had observed in each part.

- When possible, provide scaffolding to serve as a visual reminder of how to organize an observation. The teacher in the episode lists the plant parts, in order, to the side of the class data table.

- For drawing smaller objects or organisms that do not move, teach students the quadrant strategy. Show them how to fold a small, square piece of blank paper in fourths, then draw a line down each crease. Place the object in the center of the paper so that part of the object is in each quadrant. Repeat the folding process with a second piece of paper, then draw a line down each crease. Model for students how to focus on just one quadrant at a time as they observe the object on the first piece of paper and draw the object on the second sheet. This process enables students to notice and draw more details than if they just were told to observe and draw without the quadrants. The process also helps reluctant illustrators develop confidence because it breaks the drawing process into smaller, manageable steps. Figure 3–1 shows an illustration that a student made using the quadrant strategy.

- If students are not making observations of something over time, then you might have only one chance to model how to make and write an observation. You can do this in at least two ways. During the engagement stage of the science session, before students use the materials, model how to make a scientific illustration or diagram and/or take observation notes before students start their own investigation. Model by using a *different* organism or object than the one that students will be observing so as not to diminish their discovering things on their own. Another option is to do the modeling during the shared reflection stage of the science session when the class is discussing the investigation together. As students share what they have observed, you can model how to draw and label a scientific illustration or diagram and make notes. After the discussion, remove this drawing. Students then can make their own entries in their notebook, looking again at the organism or object they had been observing earlier.

Chapter 11 includes minilessons for making and writing scientific observations and drawing scientific illustrations.

Strategies for Using Data Tables

In helping students develop an understanding of how something changes over time, create data tables that not only include student data and observation notes but also show changes that have occurred.

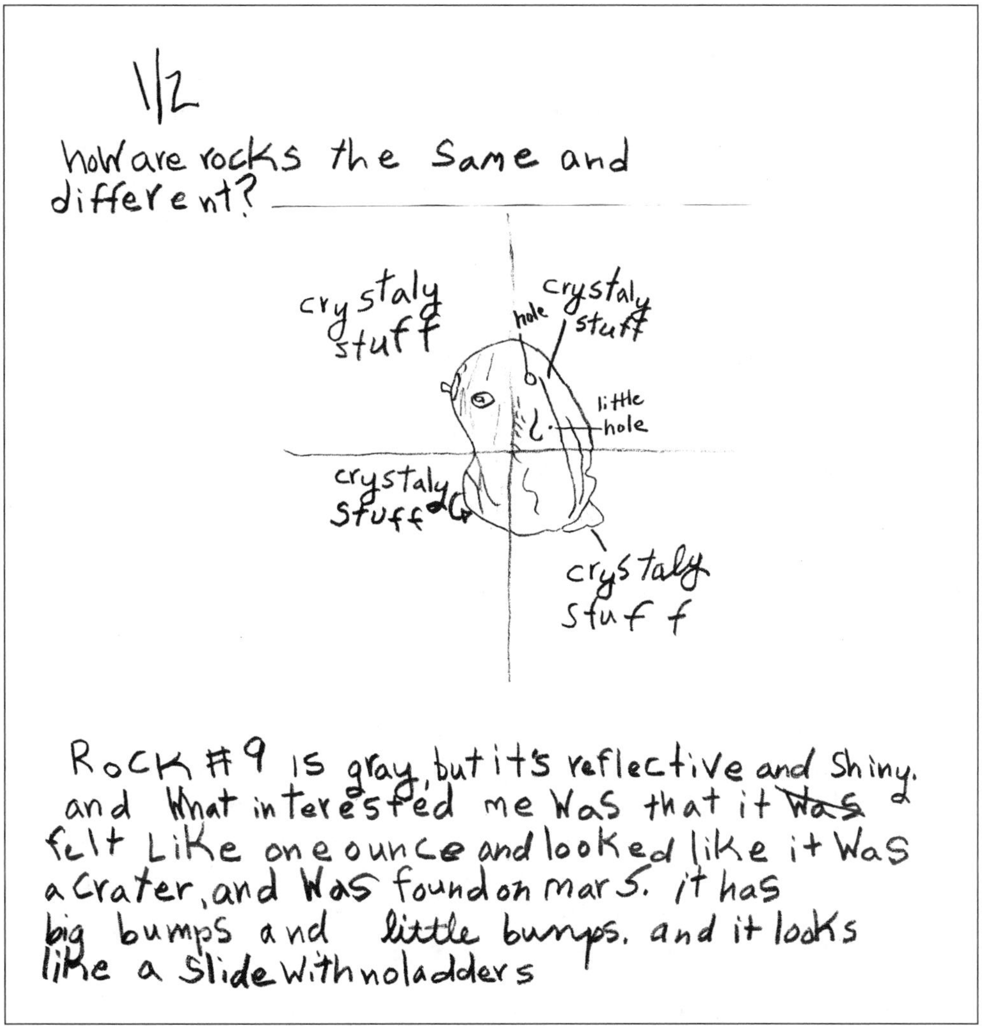

FIGURE 3-1 *Quadrant strategy and observation*

- Help students learn the scientific skill of creating a simple and effective data table. Model how to make the different parts, thinking out loud and asking students for suggestions for each. It will take students some time to learn this skill, but after making several tables, they will be much more independent and will have a valuable tool.

- For more complex data tables or those that require more space, use eleven-by-seventeen–inch sheets of paper. As shown in the video episode, the larger paper allows students to draw successive illustrations side by side, and makes comparing them easier than if the drawings were displayed vertically.

- Have students tape the data table to a left-hand page in their notebook. They then can tape a corresponding graph, if they have made one, to the facing page, so they can see all their illustrations, data (in the table and the graph), and observation notes in one place without flipping pages back and forth in their notebook.

- When students write about their observations, they use a separate sheet of notebook paper so they can write as they are looking at all the information they need from their

Scientific Illustrations, Data Tables, and Observations

investigations. After they finish writing their observations or conclusion, they glue that page onto the next blank page in their notebook.

- Use the science sessions as an opportunity to model how students should record observations in their data table. Students can refer to the models made during whole-class sessions as they make scientific illustrations, measure and record quantitative data (such as the height of the plant in the video episode), and write their observation notes in their data table.

- Even if you have access to a document camera, the advantage of making entries on a large piece of chart paper is that the entire data table (or graph) is always visible. When you use a document camera, parts of large images like data tables often are cut off on the screen. In addition, creating class records like this on chart paper and posting them in the classroom ensures that you and the students can refer to them whenever you need to during discussions, investigations, and independent writing times.

Strategies for Writing Scientific Observations

In scientific writing, students need to be as specific as possible about what they actually observe. In creative writing and personal writing, students can expect readers to use their imaginations and make their own meaning of the writing. In scientific writing, however, the readers are scientists and they want to know exactly what another scientist has observed and tested. This is a difficult idea for many students to grasp, especially if most of their writing has been in genres that have a great deal of personal voice and rely on feelings and opinions rather than on empirical data as evidence. We have to be explicit about teaching them the differences between the writing and the thinking behind it.

One strategy for teaching the difference is to do the following:

- On the top half of a piece of paper, have students draw an *artistic* drawing of a flower. Then have them observe a real flower and draw a *scientific illustration* of the flower on the bottom half of the paper. Have the class discuss the differences they can see between the two types of drawings.

- Next, give students copies of the written scientific observation in Figure 3–1. Ask students to talk with a partner about which parts of the observation are scientific and which are not. During a class discussion, ask students to identify the scientific observations (the rock's color, reflective and shiny properties, relative weight, and surface texture or features), making a list as students talk. Make a separate list together of the creative, or nonscientific, writing ("it felt like one ounce," "looked like it was a crater, and was found on Mars," and "looks like a slide with no ladders").

- Tell students, "A scientist would want to know what the student *actually observed* that made him write those words. And she also would want to know more about what he thinks an ounce feels like. What could the student do to make those parts of his observation clearer to the scientist?" Then discuss how to write about actual observations and use measuring instruments when needed.

In general, elementary students should not use analogies in their science writing because to write effective analogies they would need to have a deeper understanding of abstract concepts than they do at this age. However, students do need to make connections to other investigations (for example, "The short ruler is like the short tuning fork because they both have high pitches and fast vibrations."). Students also need to use similes when describing most smells and sounds. The English language does not have many adjectives for those properties, which is why we make observations such as, "It smells like a rose."

Using Checklists for Instructional Planning and Assessment

In the following sections, you will find checklists of the characteristics of exemplary scientific illustrations, data tables, and written observations. You can refer to the checklists when you read the sample notebook entries later in this chapter.

Planning Instruction and Assessing Scientific Illustrations

In thinking about scientific illustrations and what you need to consider in terms of instruction and assessment, the following questions, which target each of the Three Key Elements, can be helpful. What does the scientific illustration reveal about the student's:

1. Ability to use *scientific skills* (for example, makes accurate, objective, clearly labeled, detailed, and complete illustrations)?

2. Ability to *think scientifically* (for example, draws only what is observable, recognizing the differences between an observation, an inference, and fanciful thinking)?

3. Understanding of one or more *science concepts* (for example, accurately identifies the properties or characteristics of an object or organism by labeling parts and/or making lists)?

The Three Key Elements can be hard to separate in assessment. For example, an accurate and complete scientific illustration or diagram indicates that the student has developed the *scientific skills* of making accurate observations and drawing what is observable. It also indicates that the student has constructed, or is constructing, an understanding of the properties or characteristics of what she is observing, which is crucial in developing understanding of the *science concepts* in the unit of study.

Consider these Key Elements as you use the checklist shown in Figure 3–2.

Planning Instruction and Assessing Data Tables

In planning your instruction and, later, assessing your students' data tables, consider these questions. What does the data table reveal about the student's:

1. Ability to use *scientific skills* (for example, collects and records observations and/or data in an organized way; includes accurate, complete observations and/or data; jots down notes, not complete sentences)?

2. Ability to *think scientifically* (for example, includes detailed, organized, complete observations and/or measured data; distinguishes between an observation and an inference)?

3. Understanding of one or more *science concepts* (for example, includes only relevant and accurate observations)?

Characteristics of an Exemplary
Scientific Illustration and Diagram

Both scientific illustration and diagram:

☐ *Title*

☐ *Accurate representation of what can be observed (i.e., not inferred or made up)*

☐ *Parts clearly, accurately labeled*

☐ *Lines from label clearly, accurately point to the appropriate place; arrows used only to show direction*

☐ *Caption or explanation (where necessary) clearly, accurately explains what the illustration or diagram shows*

Illustration:

☐ *Large, but not so large that it requires unreasonable time to draw it*

☐ *Detailed/complete*

Diagram:

☐ *Often smaller than a scientific illustration, which should be more detailed*

☐ *Includes only essential details. For example, in a unit on electric circuits, a diagram of a circuit needs to include only a rectangle with a + and – sign to represent a D-cell or battery. In contrast, in a unit about plant development, students need to make a detailed scientific illustration in order to observe carefully, record, and remember the parts and overall structure of a plant.*

FIGURE 3–2 *Checklist for Characteristics of an Exemplary Scientific Illustration and Diagram*

Now look at the checklist that shows the characteristics of an exemplary data table (Figure 3–3).

Planning Instruction and Assessing Written Scientific Observations

An accurate written observation indicates that the student has developed scientific skills, scientific thinking, and content understanding. For example, if a student makes a connection between the color of each plant part and the health of the plant, she is demonstrating the ability to report her observations (the color of each plant part) and her understanding of what those observations indicate (the condition of the plant). When planning instruction and assessing scientific observations, consider the following questions. What does the written observation reveal about the student's:

1. Ability to use *scientific skills* (for example, makes and records accurate, detailed, complete, and objective scientific observations)?

2. Ability to *think scientifically* (for example, distinguishes between an observation and an inference; provides appropriate data or reasoning to support a statement or claim)?

3. Understanding of one or more *science concepts* (for example, includes accurate, relevant properties or characteristics of an object or organism)?

Think about these Key Elements as you go over the checklist in Figure 3–4.

Sample Notebook Entries from the Video Episode

The following notebook entries from students in the videotaped classroom are critiqued in terms of the Three Key Elements and the appropriate checklist for each type of entry.

Notebook Entry: Lilabeth

Scientific Illustrations and Data Table

Looking first at the scientific illustrations shown in Lilabeth's data table (Figures 3–5a and 3–5b), we can see that she quite accurately has drawn all the parts. She also has added accurate labels, with the lines from the labels clearly pointing to the correct part. The seed leaves are heart shaped and have smooth edges whereas the true leaves have jagged edges and a more oval shape. The only small inaccuracy is on day 14. One of the true leaves has the smooth edges of a seed leaf.

Lilabeth also has been recording the plant's height and growth regularly. The measured (quantitative) data appear to be accurate and complete in terms of typical plant growth patterns in this class. She has accurately calculated the growth of the plant on days 11 and 19. On days 9 and 14, she has made errors in her calculations, probably because the task required subtraction skills that she has not developed yet, which is true for many of her classmates and will be addressed in further whole-class instruction.

In her notes, Lilabeth appears to have made quite accurate and complete observations, which she has organized following the list on the left-hand column of her data

Characteristics of an Exemplary
Table of Observed and/or Measured Data

☐ *Main title, and a heading for each column and row*

☐ *Observations (qualitative* data, not measured data) if applicable:*

- *notes (not complete sentences)*

- *accurate*

- *observable, not inferred*

- *complete*

- *organized*

- *legible (not necessarily neat)*

☐ *Measured (quantitative**) data if applicable:*

- *accurate*

- *complete*

- *organized*

- *legible (not necessarily neat)*

Qualitative data: *observed, not measured (e.g., color, condition of a plant—"The plant has yellow leaves and the stem is bending down to the soil.")*

Quantitative data: *measured (e.g., measured height or growth of a plant—"The plant is 13 cm tall and grew 2 cm over the weekend.")*

FIGURE 3–3 *Checklist for Characteristics of an Exemplary Table of Observed and/or Measured Data*

Characteristics of an Exemplary
Written Scientific Observation

☐ *Accurate*

☐ *Detailed/complete*

☐ *Organized*

☐ *Made with all applicable senses (except taste) to note important characteristics/properties, which may include size, shape, color, lines, patterns, texture, weight, odor, sound, behavior*

☐ *Describes what is observable—e.g., "I observed that the plant's leaves and stem are brown and dry." If an inference is included, uses a phrase such as "I think this means" to introduce the inference—e.g., "I think this means the plant is unhealthy and dying."*

☐ *Scientific—no personal feelings or opinions; no fanciful thinking or creative-writing analogies*

Also may include the following:

☐ *Explains what the object, organism, or event reminds student of in prior knowledge or earlier investigations*

☐ *Describes how object/organism acts or behaves in different situations when something happens to it (cause and effect—e.g., "When . . . , then . . . [happened]")*

☐ *Describes how object/organism changes in one situation (e.g., oil dropped into water) or over time (e.g., plant growing over time)*

☐ *Explains how observation or investigation has helped build his understanding of what he is investigating*

☐ *Poses question(s) to investigate*

FIGURE 3–4   *Checklist for Characteristics of an Exemplary Written Scientific Observation*

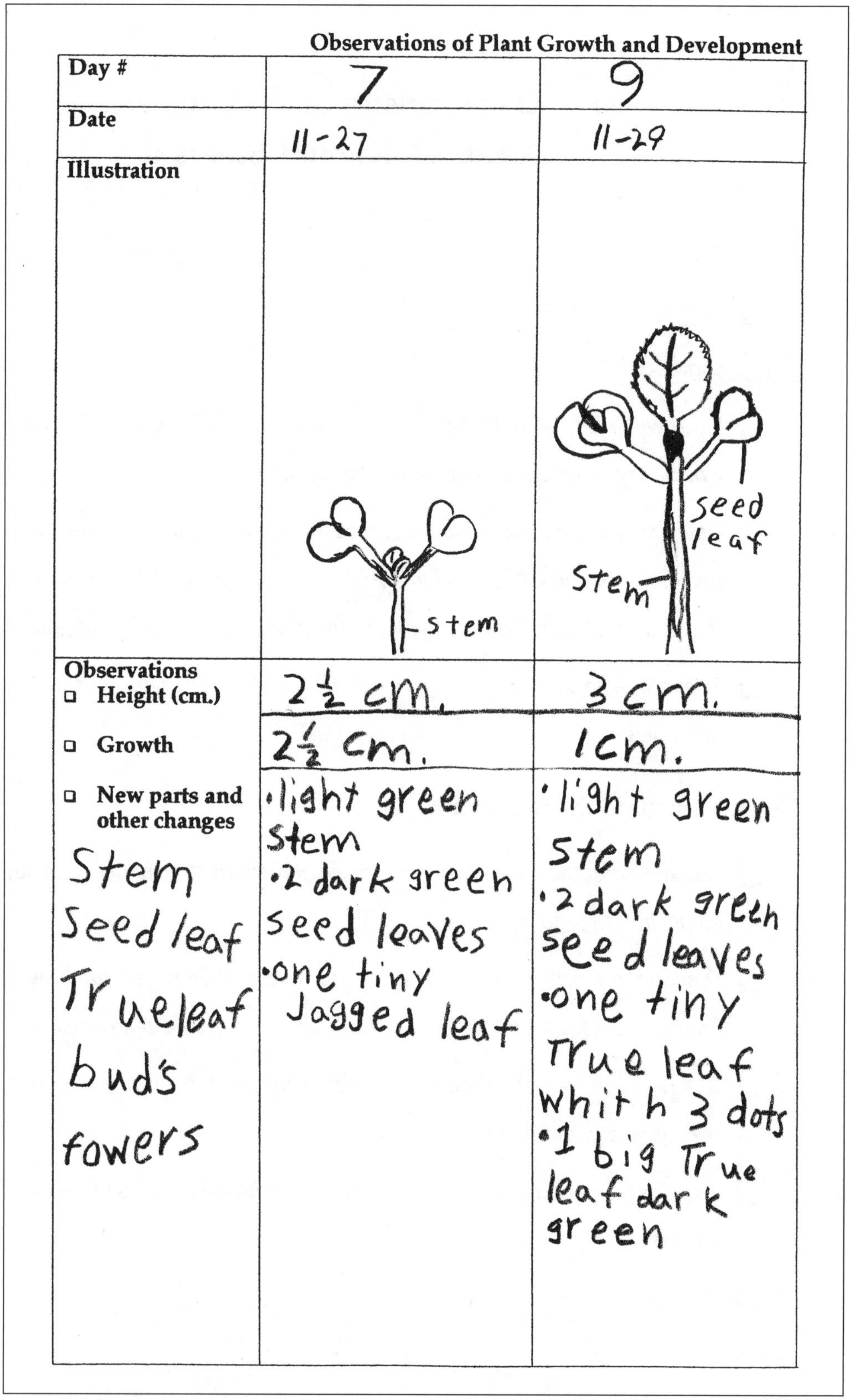

	Observations of Plant Growth and Development	
Day #	7	9
Date	11-27	11-29
Illustration	—stem	seed leaf Stem
Observations ❑ Height (cm.)	2½ cm.	3 cm.
❑ Growth	2½ cm.	1 cm.
❑ New parts and other changes Stem Seed leaf True leaf buds fowers	•light green stem •2 dark green seed leaves •one tiny Jagged leaf	•light green stem •2 dark green seed leaves •one tiny True leaf whith 3 dots •1 big True leaf dark green

FIGURE 3–5a   *Lilabeth's data table*

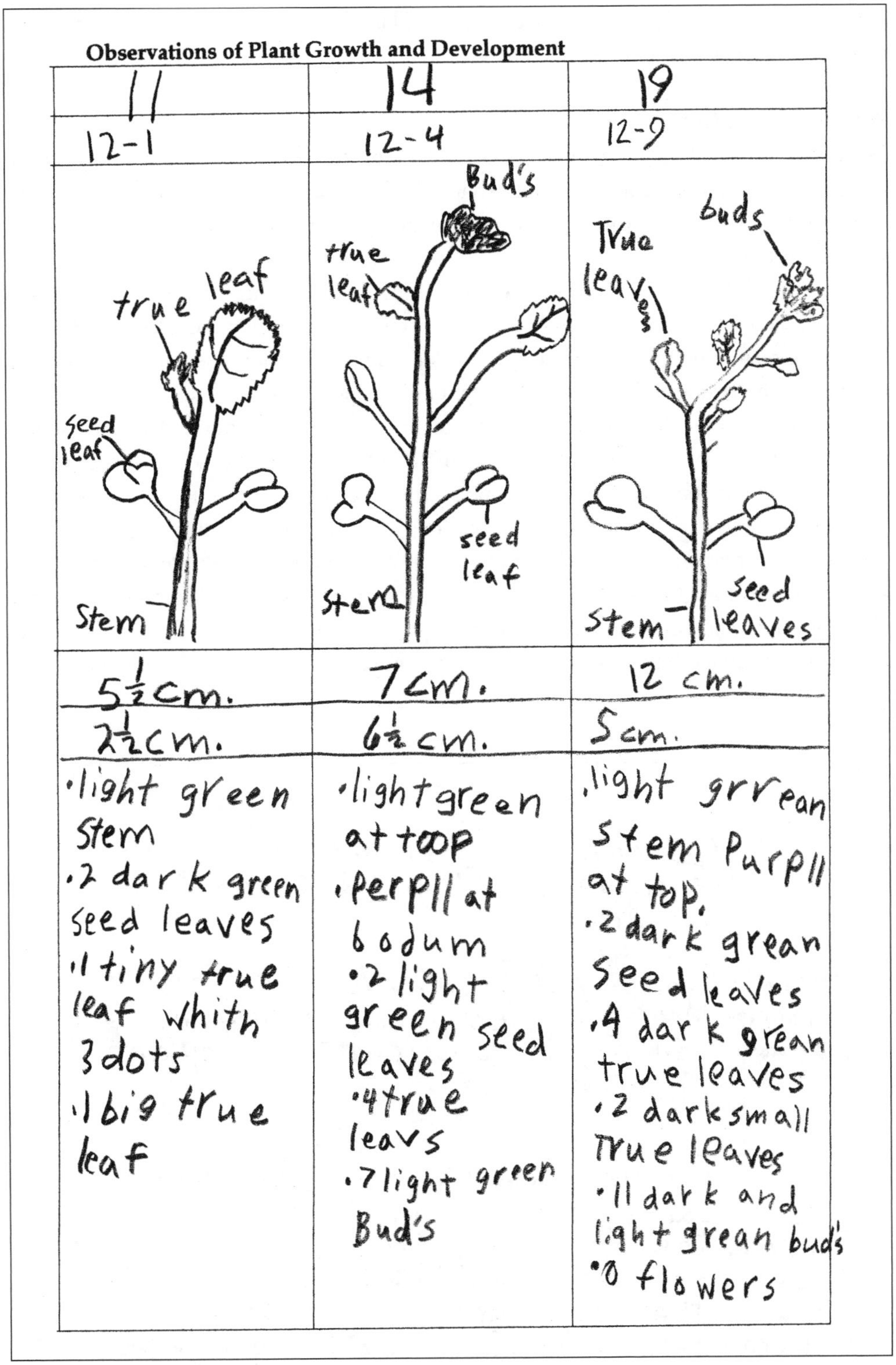

Observations of Plant Growth and Development

11	14	19
12-1	12-4	12-9
true leaf seed leaf Stem	Bud's true leaf seed leaf Stem	buds True leaves seed leaves Stem
$5\frac{1}{2}$cm.	7cm.	12 cm.
$2\frac{1}{2}$cm.	$6\frac{1}{2}$ cm.	5cm.
•light green Stem •2 dark green seed leaves •1 tiny true leaf whith 3dots •1big true leaf	•lightgreen at toop •perpll at bodum •2 light green seed leaves •4true leavs •7light green Bud's	•light grrean stem Purpll at top. •2 dark grean seed leaves •4 dark grean true leaves •2 darksmall True leaves •11 dark and light grean bud's •0 flowers

FIGURE 3–5b *Lilabeth's data table continued*

table. Consequently, it is easy to see how the plant has developed over time. She has made observations rather than inferences.

Written Observation

Before writing her observation (Figure 3–6), Lilabeth writes her teacher's scaffolding in the margin of her notebook entry, a strategy that helps her remember to include the important components of the observations. She also makes a check mark next to each part she includes in her entry.

She begins her written observation by describing the plant's height as well as its growth and speed of growth, which she has calculated accurately. She then includes, in a detailed and organized way, observations about each of the plant's parts. Her observations are focused on what is observable and do not include fanciful or personal statements.

Lilabeth has some discrepancies in her notes and written observation. A positive, effective way to help her work with these discrepancies is to say, "Another scientist might wonder about the differences in your notes and your written observation. Here you write, the 'top of my stem is dark green and the batum [bottom] is purple.' In your notes for Day 19, you write, 'light grrean stem purpll at top.' This is different from your notes on Day 14. So another scientist might ask, 'I'm confused by the observations in the data table and in the observation. Could you give some more information about the color of the stem?'" This would prompt Lilabeth to look at her plant again and compare notes with her science part-

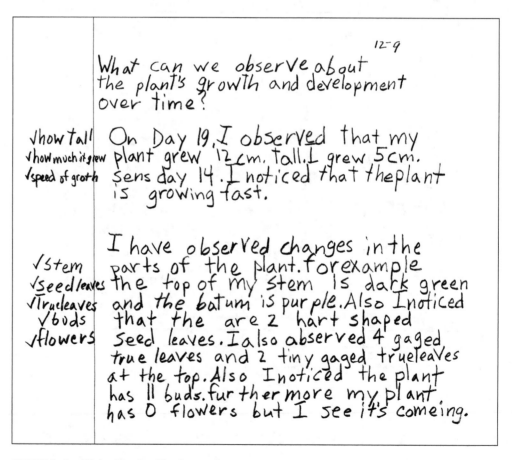

FIGURE 3–6   *Lilabeth's scientific observation*

Writing in Science in Action

ner to see if she can clarify her notes and written observation. You also could say, "A scientist might wonder what you mean by '0 flowers but I see it's comeing.' What exactly did you observe that made you write those words?"

Overall, Lilabeth's written observation is quite accurate, detailed, complete, and organized. Her success is due in part to her experiences observing her own plant, her conversations with her science partner as they have observed their plants, and the modeling and scaffolding in the science and writing sessions.

Notebook Entry: Rose

Written Observation

The first paragraph of Rose's scientific observation (Figure 3–7) is accurate as well as complete in that it includes the plant's height on that day, the amount of growth since the last measured height, and a qualitative statement about the speed of growth—"is groin [growing] fast."

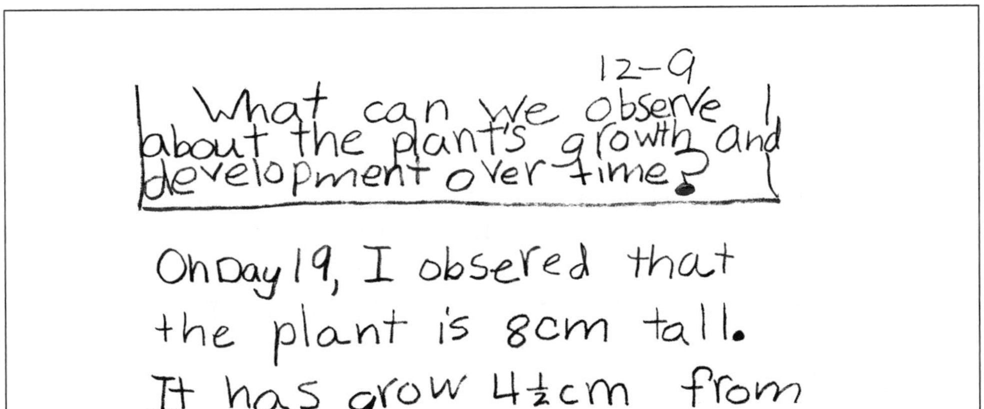

FIGURE 3–7 *Rose's scientific observation*

In the second paragraph, she includes accurate descriptions of the color of each part: "The stem coler [color] is gren [green]. Also the seed leves or gren [leaves are green]. Also the troleffs or litt gren [true leaves are light green]. Also the dods or gren ish yeloish [buds are greenish yellowish]." So she has written a good observation in terms of describing all the parts in terms of color, which is an important indicator of the health of the plant. She organizes her observation by moving up the plant, from the stem to the buds, and includes only what she can observe. Her written observation also is scientific in that she has not included personal feelings or opinions, and has not used fanciful images or analogies.

In talking with Rose about her entry, you first would identify, from the perspective of a scientist, these strengths in her scientific observation. Then you might say, "A botanist might want to know what else you observed about the shape of the leaves, the condition of the stem, and the number of buds. What would you want to share with her about your other observations?" This student receives services in special education for writing, so we might have her talk rather than write about what else she would like to share. On the other hand, Rose already has written quite a strong entry and in the video episode, she makes important contributions to class discussions and conversations with her science partner, so she probably is ready to add more details to her written observation.

Notebook Entry: Sophie

Written Observation

In the first paragraph of Sophie's observation (Figure 3–8), she includes accurate data about the plant's height and the growth as well as fairly advanced calculations (approximate growth per day). This part of the entry is accurate, complete, and organized.

In the second paragraph, she uses the parts of the plant as her organizer, and includes detailed observations about different characteristics of each part (for example, both color and condition of the stem; changing size and color of leaves). Some of the details in her written observation are not included in her data table. (Her table is not included here.)

In giving Sophie positive, constructive feedback, you would note the strengths first, saying how this observation includes useful and varied information about the plant's characteristics. For example, you might say, "Sophie, your observation is strong because you included accurate data about your plant's growth, even calculating its approximate growth per day. That's very strong scientific thinking. You also described details about each part of the plant in an organized way. That is an important scientific skill."

Then you might say, "Another botanist might wonder about some of the details in your written observation. Does your data table include the same information?" This helps her consider her observation in terms of her notes, which will establish the importance of including more notes in a data table. This is an important lesson because scientists rely on their notes after they no longer have access to the object, organism, or event they have been observing. You also would need to point out to Sophie that even when a scientist makes exciting observations, she does not include exclamation marks in her scientific writing. Sophie has well-developed writing skills and an important part of her growth as a writer of expository text is to learn the difference between creative or personal writing and scientific writing.

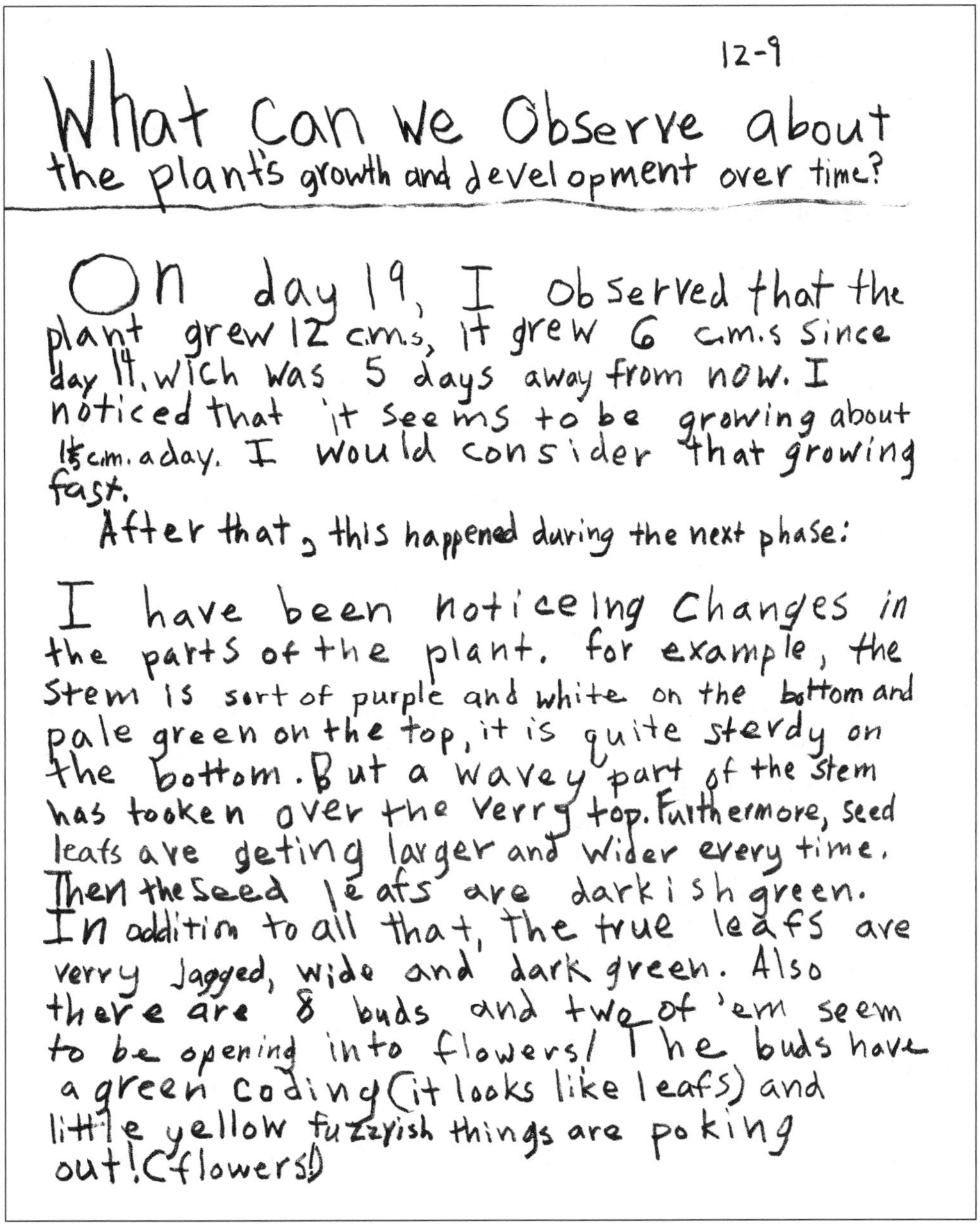

> 12-9
>
> What can we Observe about the plant's growth and development over time?
>
> On day 19, I observed that the plant grew 12 c.m.s, it grew 6 c.m.s since day 14, wich was 5 days away from now. I noticed that it seems to be growing about 1.5cm. a day. I would consider that growing fast.
>
> After that, this happened during the next phase:
>
> I have been noticeing changes in the parts of the plant. for example, the stem is sort of purple and white on the bottom and pale green on the top, it is quite sterdy on the bottom. But a wavey part of the stem has tooken over the verry top. Furthermore, seed leafs are geting larger and wider every time. Then the seed leafs are darkish green. In addition to all that, the true leafs are verry jagged, wide and dark green. Also there are 8 buds and two of 'em seem to be opening into flowers! The buds have a green coding (it looks like leafs) and little yellow fuzzyish things are poking out! (flowers!)

FIGURE 3–8 *Sophie's scientific observation*

Other Highlights of the Video Episode

Introducing Vocabulary

The teacher in this video demonstrates effective strategies for developing students' scientific vocabulary. In inquiry-based science, teachers introduce new terms *after* students have had a concrete experience and thus are ready to attach new words to different aspects of that concrete experience. For example, a student in this episode refers to "a green, sticky thing." Appropriately, the teacher at this point does not tell him the correct term (*stigma*) because she knows that in the next science session, students will observe a larger flower.

After closely observing the flower, students will discuss what they have observed and the teacher will introduce the term for each plant part as she models how to draw and label each part. Then students will draw and label an illustration of their own plant. Sometime after the modeling, the teacher will put a word card for each new term in the word bank.

Using the Focus Question

The teacher also uses the focus question to support students' development of scientific skills and vocabulary. Before the students began observing the plants, they wrote the focus question for the first time in their notebook. During a class discussion, they talked about what they thought were the important words in the question. The teacher underlined those important words—*observe, growth, development, over time*—on the class copy of the question posted in the front of the room. Students circled the words in their own focus question in their notebook. The teacher repeatedly brings the students back to the focus question, which becomes a scaffold for remembering what they need to be thinking about as they investigate and write.

Reading Shared Writing

The teacher in this video episode models the rereading of the shared writing after they have finished writing the entry together. This is an essential skill and habit for students to develop. Although this teacher mentions that they need to reread the writing for "flow" or sentence fluency, students should be thinking about whether their entry would make sense to a scientist. Thus, they should focus on the writing traits of content, organization, and word choice.

Related Material

Chapter

- Chapter 11: "Sample Minilessons"
  - Includes minilessons for scientific observations, illustrations, and data tables

Website

- Student Notebook Entries, Pre-kindergarten Through Fifth Grade: Scientific Observations, Illustrations, and Diagrams
  - Look at entries above and below your grade level.

- Checklists for Exemplary Notebook Entries
  - Includes the checklists in this chapter as well as checklists for other types of notebook entries (for example, comparisons, basic and complex conclusions)

- Stories from Schools
  - "Success for All: A Story of Inquiry Science and a Student with Special Needs" was written by the teacher who is featured in this video episode.

- Background Information About the Video Episodes: Plants

CHAPTER 4

Making and Writing Scientific Comparisons

VIDEO EPISODE: ECOSYSTEMS

Before You Watch

The process of making scientific comparisons deepens students' understanding of the organisms, objects, or events that they are observing and studying. For example, when a student observes sand, she will notice certain properties of that soil component. Then when she observes clay, she not only will notice properties of that soil component but also will discover additional properties of the sand because of the differences between sand and clay. Thus, the process of observing two components broadens the student's comprehension of each one.

In the Ecosystems Video Episode, the teacher chooses to have her students compare and contrast a model ecosystem and a real ecosystem. She knows that when students use models to help them construct an understanding of science concepts, they often do not make connections between the model they are observing and what the model represents in the real world. In this video episode, students go outside to observe a real ecosystem after they have spent several weeks observing models they have made of ecosystems. They then compare the model and real ecosystems and write their comparisons.

While You Watch

As you watch the Ecosystems Video Episode, think about the following questions:

1. How does a class chart like the one the teacher creates with the students in this episode help support students' learning of complex concepts?

2. How does using the box and T-chart strategy help students organize their thinking and develop their conceptual understanding of ecosystems and models?

After You Watch

Some science units, particularly life science units, require students to learn a great deal of information, including new science terms. Visual scaffolding is particularly critical in teaching these units, especially for students who are learning English or who have special needs. As they learn new information, the class makes entries in their class chart, which serves as an organized community record of the important things that the students have observed and learned. In addition, the terms students need to remember are displayed in organized ways (for example, the words that relate to the concept of *producers* are grouped together).

The box and T-chart is another critical visual scaffolding method because it helps students think about their observations and the information they have learned and then organize that information into similarities and differences—in this case, between real and model ecosystems. This then leads to greater understanding of the models and ecosystems.

Overuse and Misuse of the Box and T-chart Strategy

The box and T-chart strategy is a simple and effective way to make comparisons. When used with the Compare and Contrast writing frame (see Figure 11–3 in Chapter 11), all students can be successful at making and writing comparisons. As a result, teachers tend to overuse, and sometimes misuse, the strategy.

In a science unit, use the box and T-chart no more than two or three times. After that, have students *discuss* comparisons during the shared reflection discussion at the end of an investigation, but then have them *write* about something else, such as the relationships they have observed, cause and effect, or what variables they had to keep the same or control in order to make a controlled investigation.

The box and T-chart also can be misused. For example, the following question in a unit about electric circuits would not lead to meaningful writing: "How are conductors and nonconductors similar and different?" The important concept here is how conductors and nonconductors are *different*, because it is some of their distinctive properties that define their function. It is not important that conductors and nonconductors are similar because they are both materials. Having students spend time making an organizer and writing a comparison of the two would not result in a meaningful and, therefore, productive notebook entry. The important thing to consider in planning notebook entries is this question: How will writing this entry deepen the students' conceptual understanding and/or scientific thinking? Using the box and T-chart strategy to compare and contrast conductors and nonconductors will not deepen scientific thinking and/or understanding of science concepts of the unit. Elementary students have limited time, energy, and attention spans. You need to maximize their opportunities for meaningful learning when planning the types of notebook entries they will make.

Strategies for Your Classroom

Notebook Organization Strategies

For many students, it is easier to write a comparison when they can see their notes without flipping pages back and forth. The teacher in this video episode knew that students would need to have their observation notes about the outdoor ecosystem on a left-hand page and their box and T-chart on the facing right-hand page so that students could see their observation notes as they wrote similarities and differences in their box and T-chart. When it was time for students to write a comparison, the teacher had them write it on a loose sheet of notebook paper because she wanted students to be able to read the box and T-chart while they were writing their comparison. When they were finished writing, they taped the sheet of paper on which they had written their comparison onto the next left-hand page.

Strategies for Making Comparisons over Time

When students are observing things that change over time, they actually are comparing characteristics or properties at one point in time with characteristics or properties from another point in time. When observing how a plant has grown and developed, for example, students can look at their data table much as they do a T-chart to compare their observations and measured (quantitative) data about the plant's height and growth on one day as compared with another day.

Figures 4–1a and 4–1b give an example of this kind of comparison. When students investigate how different soil components behave in water, they observe (and draw) the soil and water on one day, then make more observations and drawings a day or more later, in order to discover the settling properties of different soil components.

In Figures 4–1a and 4–1b, Romain has recorded his observations in his drawings of three settling tubes. Such drawings are a kind of data table in which students can record their test results and refer to them as needed. (The settling tube drawings for the first day of these settling tests are on a previous page in his notebook.)

To scaffold the students' entries, the teacher gave them this frame: "Last time, _____, but now _____." She also told the students to report their observations of the soil *and* the water in each tube, and to check their drawings as they wrote. This entry is a good example of supporting students in writing more independently (telling them to report about the soil *and* water, and to check their drawings) while also giving them a very simple scaffolding or writing frame to help them organize and provide details in their writing. The scaffolding enables students to focus on contrasting the last observation (recorded in the earlier set of drawings) with the current observation. This is a highly effective strategy to teach students when they are determining what changes, if any, have occurred over time.

Strategies for Planning Instruction and Assessment

To be able to write an effective comparison, the student must develop a box and T-chart with strong content and organization and must be able to use that organizer with the appropriate language. To focus your planning and assessment on the Three Key Elements, consider the following questions. What do the box and T-chart and written comparison reveal about the student's:

1. Ability to use *scientific skills* (for example, uses accurate, detailed, complete, and objective scientific observations in comparing and contrasting objects, organisms, or events)?

2. Ability to *think scientifically* (for example, notices accurate similarities and differences; organizes them appropriately; distinguishes between an observation and an inference; for example, "I notice the cricket is motionless and headless. I infer it is dead.")?

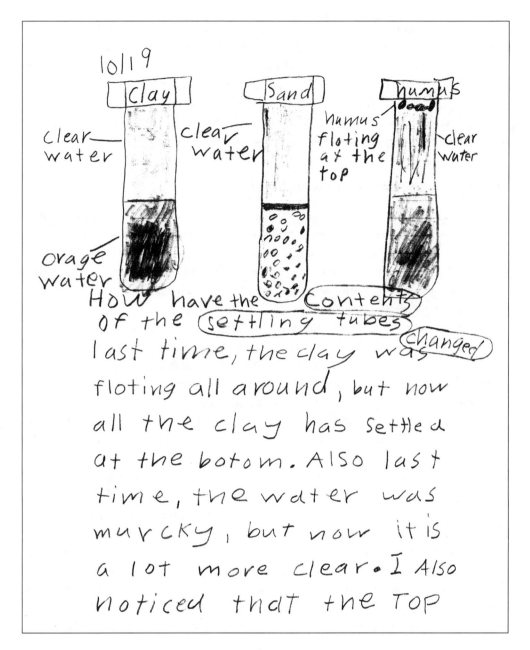

FIGURE 4–1a *Romain's settling tube drawings and conclusion*

3. Understanding of one or more *science concepts* (for example, includes relevant similarities and differences in the properties or characteristics of an object, organism, or event)?

   The checklist shown in Figure 4–2 can be helpful both in planning your instruction and in assessing your students' entries.

Sample Notebook Entries from the Video Episode

Refer to the checklist in Figure 4–2 as you read the sample notebook entries and critiques here.

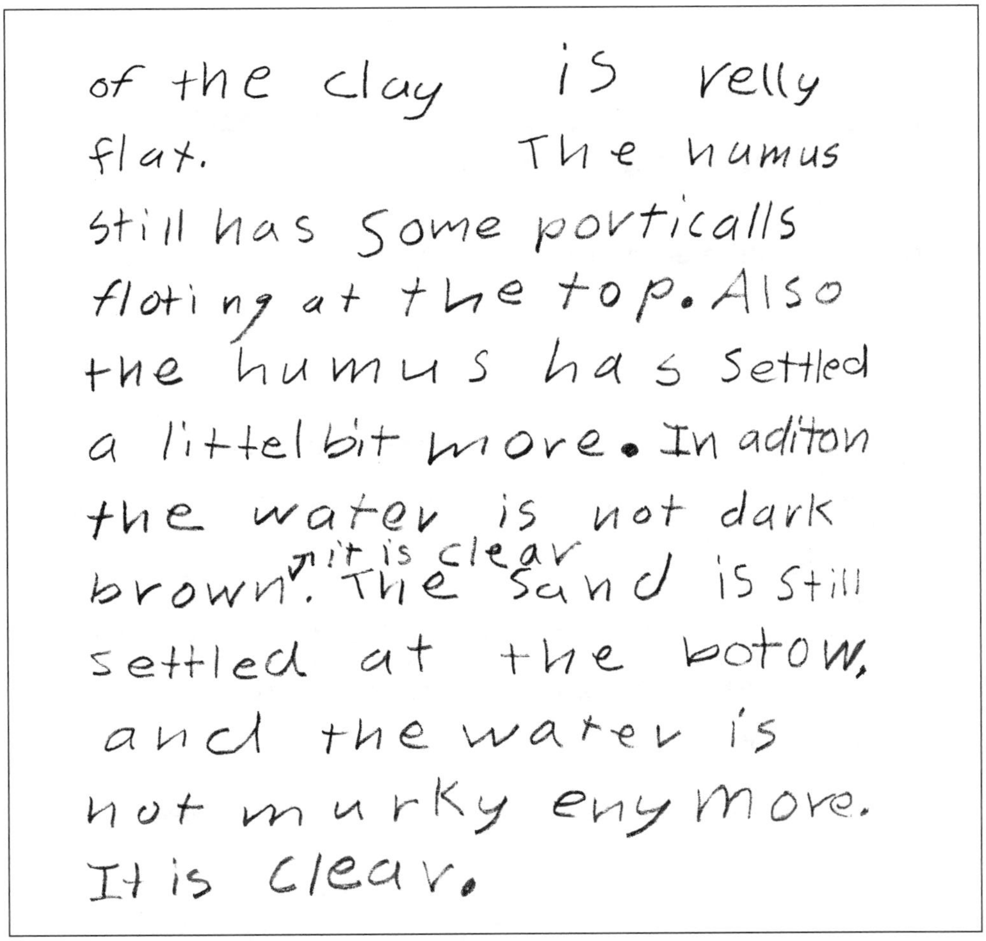

of the clay is relly
flat. The humus
still has some porticalls
floting at the top. Also
the humus has settled
a littel bit more. In aditon
the water is not dark
brown, it is clear. The sand is still
settled at the botow,
and the water is
not murky eny more.
It is clear.

FIGURE 4–1b *Romain's conclusion continued*

Notebook Entry: Annie

Annie has a good understanding of the science in the *Ecosystems* unit, but because English is her second language, she does not find it easy to express herself in writing. She apparently has copied the class box and T-chart during the class discussion (Figure 4–3). She also may have copied the first part of the paragraph in Figure 4–4 during the shared writing that the class wrote with the teacher.

When the teacher talks with Annie during the independent writing stage of the writing session, Annie feels stuck. But once the teacher reminds her about the phrase *In addition* and gets her focused on the Compare and Contrast writing frame (Figure 11–3), Annie completes the paragraph and the rest of the entry on her own. The scaffolding helps her express her understanding of the science concepts.

Although it certainly is preferable for students to do their own writing, the fact that Annie completed the rest of the comparison independently indicates that she probably lacks confidence in her writing abilities but is able to write independently once she gets going, with a little support from her teacher. This is a fairly common occurrence with students, including those who are learning English, who are not yet sure of their writing skills. Note also that on her own, Annie uses an effective organizational strategy, putting an X next to each part of the organizer as she includes it in her writing.

Characteristics of an Exemplary Box and T-chart and Written Comparison

Similarities in the box and differences in the T-chart are:

- *accurate*

- *complete*

- *organized, so that each row refers to the same category of information, just as in a data table (e.g., one row includes differences in color; another row includes differences in size)*

- *observable, not inferred*

- *relevant, not extraneous (e.g., the color of a plant's leaves is important because it reflects the health of the plant; the color of a ball is not important because it is not a property that affects the behavior of a ball)*

  Note: *Early in a unit, students might not yet have had enough experiences to determine what is relevant.*

Written comparison includes:

☐ *descriptions or explanations that are:*

- *accurate*

- *complete*

- *organized*

- *objective (observable, not inferred)*

☐ *relevant similarities and differences*

FIGURE 4–2 *Checklist for Characteristics of an Exemplary Box and T-chart and Written Comparison*

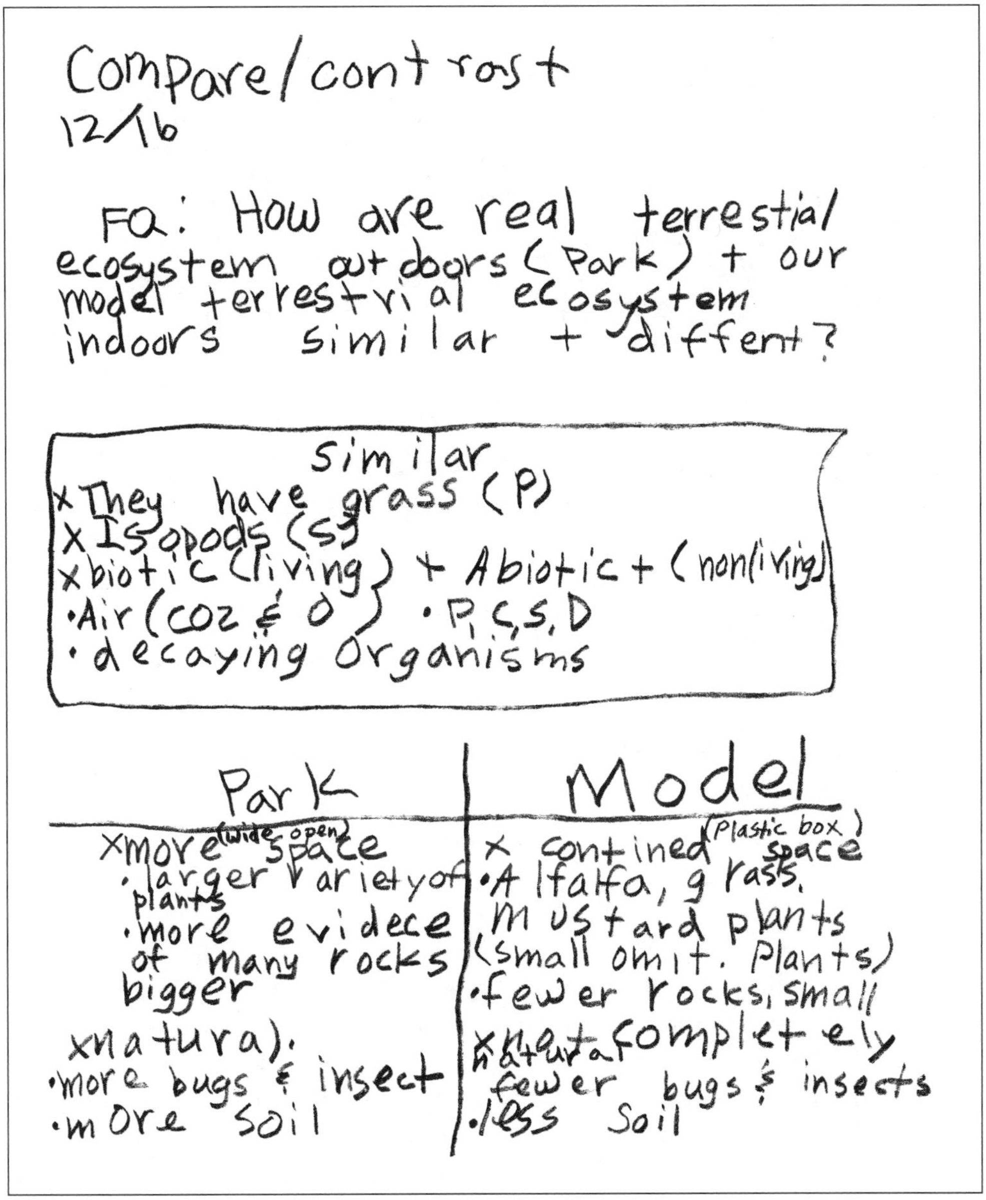

Compare/contrast
12/16

FQ: How are real terrestial ecosystem outdoors (Park) + our model terrestrial ecosystem indoors similar + different?

Similar
x They have grass (P)
x Isopods (S)
x biotic (living) + Abiotic + (non living)
• Air (CO2 & O) • P,C,S,D
• decaying Organisms

Park	Model
x more (wide open) space	x contined (Plastic box) space
• larger variety of plants	• Alfalfa, grass,
• more evidece of many rocks	mustard plants (small omit. Plants)
bigger	• fewer rocks, small
x natura).	x Not completely
• more bugs & insect	• natura fewer bugs & insects
• more soil	• less soil

FIGURE 4–3 *Annie's box and T-chart*

In her box and T-chart, Annie has included similarities and differences that are accurate and complete. The similarities are listed in the box. The differences are included in the T-chart and organized horizontally by category as they would be in a data table. All the characteristics are observable except for the presence of air. But this characteristic is appropriate to include because the class has learned about oxygen and carbon dioxide as they have been observing their model ecosystems over time. The class data table had "P, C, S, D" listed (for "producers, consumers, scavengers, and decomposers"). Scientists reading this entry would wonder what the initials mean, so Annie and other students would need to make the meaning clear either in the box or in the written comparison.

In her written comparison, Annie apparently copied the first sentence from the shared writing the class did with the teacher. But from "In addition" on, she does her own writing. The similarities are accurate, organized, and objective. The information could be

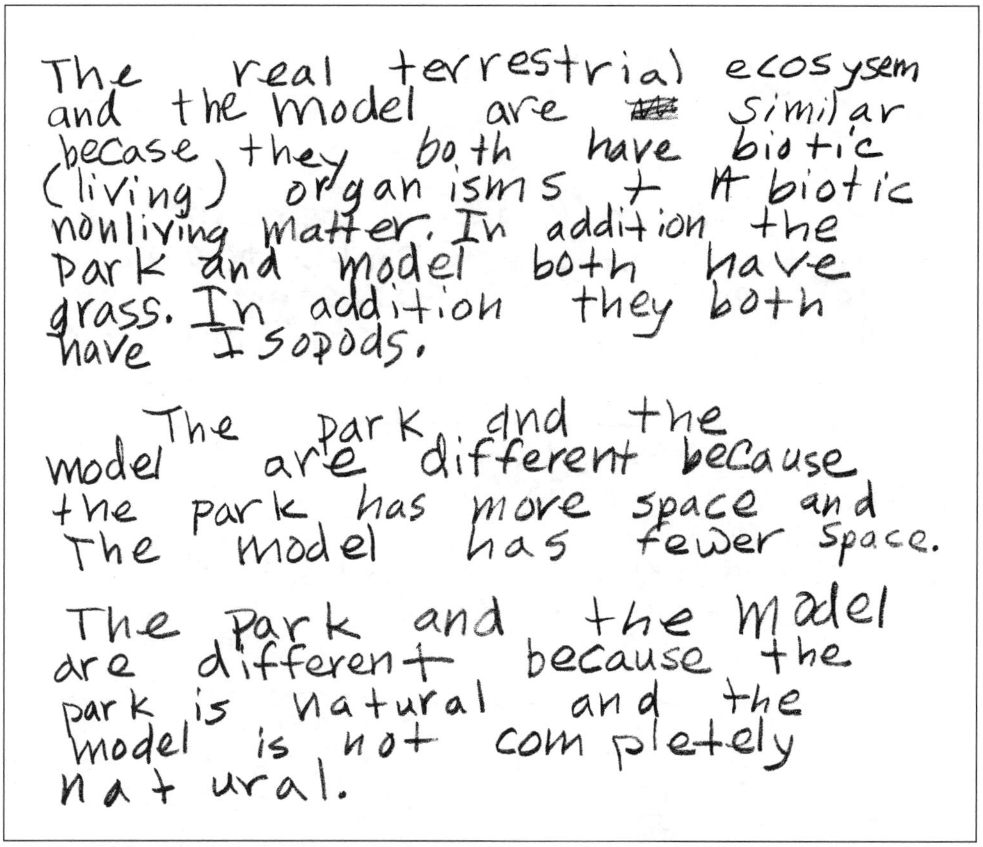

FIGURE 4–4 *Annie's comparison*

more complete if she had written *producers* instead of just *grass*, which is only one type of producer, and *scavengers* instead of just *isopods*, which are one example of scavengers. A more complex sentence would be, "In addition, the park and model both have producers (for example, grass), consumers (for example, crickets), and scavengers (for example, isopods)."

In the second paragraph, Annie chooses to write about two important differences, both of which are accurate, complete (she would not be expected to include every difference), organized by category, objective, and relevant. "Fewer space" is not grammatically correct, but the teacher (and another scientist) would know what she means. Clarity is more important in this rough draft stage than grammar. And since she is learning English and needs to build her confidence as a writer, the teacher would point out the many strengths in the entry and overlook the grammatical weaknesses, which are a natural part of her language acquisition.

Notebook Entry: Kyra

Kyra, another student in the videotaped classroom, has strong conceptual understanding and strong writing skills. She includes her own ideas in her box and T-chart (Figure 4–5), which she creates during her team's discussion of their model and the park. During the writing session, she chooses to use some of the scaffolding as she writes independently (Figure 4–6).

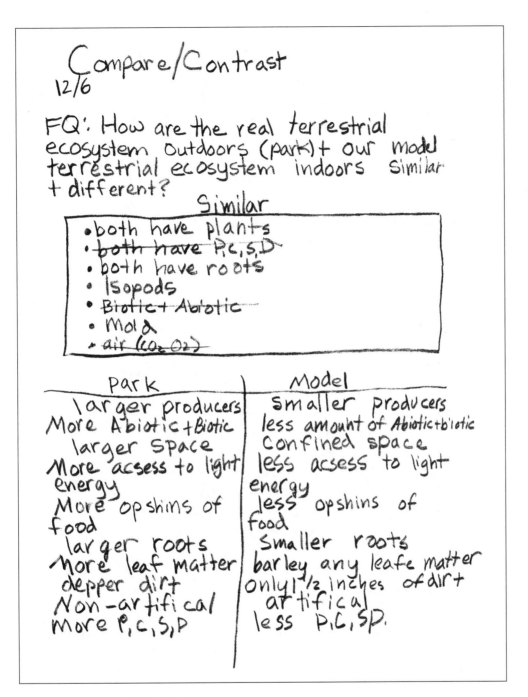

Compare/Contrast

12/6

FQ: How are the real terrestrial ecosystem outdoors (park) + our model terrestrial ecosystem indoors similar + different?

Similar
- both have plants
- ~~both have P,C,S,D~~
- both have roots
- Isopods
- ~~Biotic + Abiotic~~
- Mold
- air (CO₂, O₂)

Park	Model
larger producers	smaller producers
More Abiotic + Biotic	less amount of Abiotic + biotic
larger space	confined space
More acsess to light energy	less acsess to light energy
More opshins of food	less opshins of food
larger roots	smaller roots
More leaf matter	barley any leafe matter
depper dirt	only 1½ inches of dirt
Non-artifical	artifical
More P,C,S,P	less P,C,S,P.

FIGURE 4–5 *Kyra's box and T-chart*

Her entries in her box and T-chart are accurate and she includes most of the important characteristics. (Students are not expected to include every characteristic because there are so many.) The characteristics are organized, in that the similarities are in the box and the differences are organized by category in the T-chart. Except for "air (CO_2, O_2)," she can observe everything, but her inference about air is appropriate, as explained earlier.

The characteristics are mixed in terms of their importance, but that is because the students create the organizer as they are making their observations of their model ecosystems, so they would not be placing each characteristic in order of its importance in the ecosystem. They use that level of thinking when they are writing the comparison.

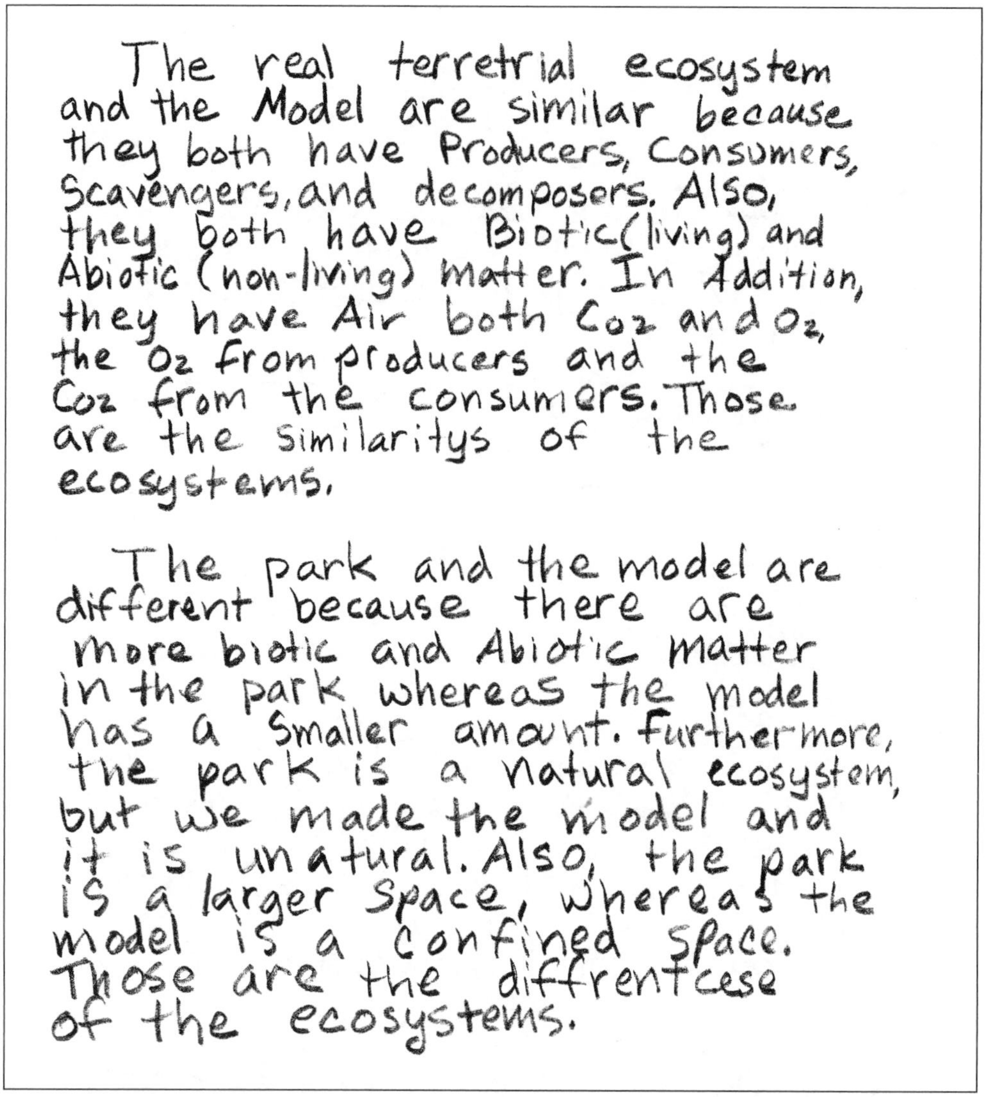

The real terretrial ecosystem and the Model are similar because they both have Producers, Consumers, Scavengers, and decomposers. Also, they both have Biotic (living) and Abiotic (non-living) matter. In Addition, they have Air both CO_2 and O_2, the O_2 from producers and the CO_2 from the consumers. Those are the similaritys of the ecosystems.

The park and the model are different because there are more biotic and Abiotic matter in the park whereas the model has a Smaller amount. Furthermore, the park is a natural ecosystem, but we made the model and it is unatural. Also, the park is a larger Space, whereas the model is a confined space. Those are the diffrent cese of the ecosystems.

FIGURE 4–6 *Kyra's comparison*

In writing her comparison, Kyra includes similarities that are accurate and complete in terms of the most important characteristics of the ecosystem. In the box, she writes other similarities (for example, *plants, roots, mold*). But those specific characteristics are in the more general categories she writes about in her paragraph instead: *producers* include plants that have roots, and mold is a *decomposer*.

She writes the second paragraph from a similar perspective, focusing on the relevant but more general differences. For example, she writes about the park's having more biotic and abiotic matter than the model rather than writing that there is more leaf matter and deeper dirt in the park or real ecosystem.

Note that she crosses out the three similarities that she chooses to include in her written comparison. She does not cross out or put an X next to what she includes for differences. She has written a strong comparison nonetheless. Learning to use the checking-off strategy more consistently, however, would help her better organize and keep track of details she wants to include in her writing—often a challenge for students who have strong language and thinking skills.

Other Highlights of the Video Episode

■ In this science-writing approach, visual scaffolding is essential to helping students develop their understanding of science, their scientific thinking, their scientific skills (such as making scientific observations), and their abilities to write scientifically. At the same time, however, it is important not to have too much visual scaffolding in the classroom because many students either will overlook what is there or become distracted by it.

■ In watching this video episode, some teachers comment about the amount of time and space it takes to create and display all this visual scaffolding. Making word cards and other visual supports is time-consuming the first time teachers teach a unit. But once the scaffolding is in place, teachers need not spend the time again. Many teachers laminate the master chart or table so they can reuse it each time they teach the unit.

■ Teachers who do not have a lot of wall space can use flip charts and/or a rolling chart holder. Teachers also put other charts and tables on the white board only during the science and science-writing sessions. Some who teach in open-concept classrooms with no walls put up clotheslines and hang charts and writing frames from them.

Related Material

Chapters

■ Chapter 3: "Scientific Illustrations, Data Tables, and Observations" (Plants Video Episode)
  • A prerequisite to being able to make an effective box and T-chart and write a strong comparison is to develop the *scientific skill* of making accurate, detailed, and organized scientific observations.

■ Chapter 11: "Sample Minilessons"
  • This chapter includes a sample minilesson on making a box and T-chart and writing a comparison.

Website

■ Student Notebook Entries, Pre-kindergarten Through Fifth Grade: Box and T-charts and Scientific Comparisons
  • Read examples of comparisons from your own grade level as well as samples from a grade above and below your level.

■ Checklists for Exemplary Notebook Entries
  • Includes checklists for different types of notebook entries (for example, observations, scientific illustrations, and conclusions)

■ Background Information About the Video Episodes: Ecosystems

CHAPTER 5

Scientific Investigations and Supporting Claims with Evidence

VIDEO EPISODE: BALLS

Before You Watch

For students to be able to think and write like scientists, they need to learn how to work like scientists. In this video episode, the teacher uses modeling, class plans, and rules of behavior to establish a positive classroom environment in which students can work productively—and excitedly—to plan, conduct, and make sense of a scientific investigation. A fundamental part of such an investigation is making claims or statements and supporting them with evidence and/or reasoning. In this video episode, the young students write a simple kind of conclusion: make a claim that answers the question that has been investigated, then support that answer with evidence from observations and/or test results. Building on this basic structure, they will learn to add inferences (for example, "I think this happened because . . .") and generalizations (for example, "I think that the higher the ramp is, the faster the ball will move.").

While You Watch

As you watch the Balls Video Episode, think about the following questions:

1. In what ways does this teacher model how to plan and conduct a fair test? What is effective about this modeling?

2. What kinds of scaffolding does the teacher provide in both the science and writing sessions to help students learn to plan fair tests and write claims that are supported with evidence?

3. Which of this teacher's strategies do you typically use in your inquiry-based science and science-writing instruction? Which ones do you think you could implement more often and/or more effectively than you do now?

After You Watch

Students need to develop their scientific skills so that they know how to plan and conduct a fair test. Going through the process as a class and creating a written plan on chart paper so everyone can easily refer to it is an effective and worthwhile learning experience. With younger students or students who are learning English, reading the plan together also helps deepen their understanding of the plan and the words in the plan, and develops their oral language skills and reading fluency.

In planning the test, the teacher refers students to the focus questions. (Occasionally, a science lesson will have two or three focus questions.) The first question is, "How can we measure the bounciness of balls to find the best bouncer?" Exploring this question is important because students need to understand testing and evidence, and that as scientists, they cannot make claims or statements without supporting those claims with scientific evidence, such as measured test results. The students have begun to answer this question in their earlier, initial explorations with the balls.

The question for the investigation that the students are planning is, "Is the Ping-Pong ball or the rubber ball a better bouncer?" As the teacher guides students in making their plan for testing the property of bounciness in the two balls, she models different parts of the testing procedure using concrete materials. For example, when a student mentions that the balls should be dropped from the same height, the teacher works with another student to model what "dropping the balls from the same height" means (see Figure 5–1). Giving students a

FIGURE 5–1 *Modeling a fair test*

concrete, visual model like this is important in working with elementary students, and it is essential with students who are learning English and/or have special needs.

Strategies for Your Classroom

Strategies for Planning and Conducting Investigations

■ Students need concrete experiences to help them understand what a "fair test" is and how to conduct it. Use concrete materials to help students visualize and plan their tests.

■ In modeling techniques for students to use in their investigations, such as counting the ball bounces in this video episode, it is important to be clear but not to preempt students' discoveries. In the video episode, the teacher models how to count and record the number of bounces using different balls than the ones the students will be using. She chooses a larger ball so that everyone can easily count the number of bounces. Without this careful modeling, the students would not count the balls' bounces in the same way, which would result in meaningless data. Using different balls also allows students to make their own discoveries with the Ping-Pong ball and the rubber ball.

■ Articulate and model rules for working like scientists (for example, moving in the same direction to pick up materials and treating materials appropriately). To help students work effectively in groups, you may want to assign different "scientist" roles to students (for example, "Number Ones" report and record test results for their team; "Number Twos" get materials for their team).

■ Planning and making data tables are important in many investigations. Engage the students in helping you think about making each part of the table. For example, the teacher in the video episode asks the class what another scientist would need to see as titles in their data tables in order for him to understand that they are collecting data about the two balls.

• When data tables are more complex and have multiple columns, model how to crease the pages in the notebook to make the columns of the table and then show students how to draw lines down the creases. Students need to make the table functional, not perfect. (You can find a minilesson on creating and interpreting data tables in Chapter 11.)

• Some data tables are so complex that it would take too long for students to make them. In those cases, give students a blackline master. But be sure to talk about how the table is set up.

Strategies for Writing: Supporting Claims with Evidence

The fundamental point of this kind of writing is that when students, of any age, make a claim or statement, they must provide evidence for that claim. The evidence might be something they have measured (quantitative data), such as the number of bounces, or something they have observed. For example, when investigating what a plant needs in order to be healthy, students report their observations of the color of the stem and leaves. Supporting claims with evidence is a key part of writing scientific conclusions (see Chapter 6 for more on conclusions, including checklists to help you assess your students' work).

To help students write about the data they have recorded in graphs, you need to provide different forms of scaffolding. For students with well-developed independent writing skills, the scaffolding can take the form of a list such as the following, from the video episode:

1. Tell what the line plot shows.

2. Report (tell) the number of bounces each ball had.

3. Then, answer the question, "Which ball is a better bouncer?"

You can adapt this list to match the content of your own units. By including each of these components, students can write a complete entry without following a detailed writing frame.

For students who need more support, provide a more detailed writing frame. This kind of scaffolding provides students with a structure for writing about the data that also serves as a structure for thinking about it.

- Begin by having the students identify the general content of the graph (such as, in the video episode, the number of bounces of balls). Use a frame such as "Our line plot shows _____" during your shared writing session.

- The next step is to report the data, in this case the quantitative (measured) data, for each ball. For example, in the video episode, the teacher writes, "The _____ ball bounced _____ times and the _____ ball bounced _____ times."

- The frame then ends by having students answer the question and state what the data tell them about that answer: "The numbers show that _____ is a better bouncer than _____ because _____." So a student might write, "*The numbers show that* the Ping-Pong ball *is a better bouncer than* the rubber ball *because* the Ping-Pong ball bounced more times than the rubber ball."

You also could use a slightly different approach, in which students write a simple kind of conclusion. Students would begin the entry by answering the question they have been investigating: "Is the Ping-Pong ball or the rubber ball a better bouncer?" To begin the conclusion, a student might write, "The Ping-Pong ball is a better bouncer than the rubber ball." (Note that students should include both balls that are in the question.) Then students would provide data or evidence to support that answer or claim: "The Ping-Pong ball bounced ten times, *but* the rubber ball bounced *only* eight times." Teaching students to use *but* and *only* supports them in making sense of the data. Otherwise, students tend simply to list the numbers without showing any understanding of whether the numbers are larger or smaller than others. Finally, students would end with a concluding statement: "So the data show that the Ping-Pong ball bounces more times than the rubber ball, which means that the Ping-Pong ball is a better bouncer." Students might then add their inferential thinking about why they think that happens: "*I think* the Ping-Pong ball is a good bouncer *because* it is hollow and the material it is made of makes it able to bounce well."

Notebook Entry: Keeto

Figure 5–2 shows Keeto's entry on a left-hand page in his science notebook. He has glued in the focus question for the lesson as well as the question for the investigation of the two balls. He uses inventive spelling to write titles for two T-chart data tables in which he later records the results of each test that he and his partner conduct. He has recorded the data clearly. In talking with Keeto about this page of his notebook, you would point out that these parts of the entry show that he has strong scientific skills. Then you could say, "Another scientist might wonder what the X means in your test results for the rubber ball.

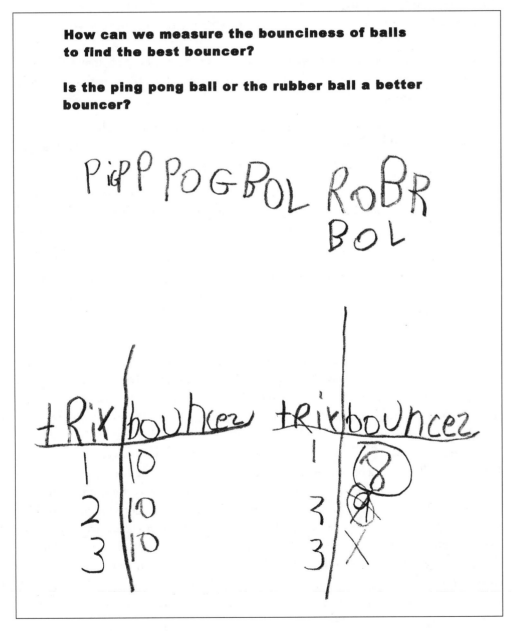

FIGURE 5–2 *Keeto's data table*

What would you tell her?" Keeto has a good understanding of the science he is learning and probably has a plausible reason for putting an **X** instead of a number in his data table.

In Figure 5–3, he writes about what the class test results show. He begins with the writing frame that his teacher provided, "Our line plot shows . . ." Then he writes, "how mine bowsis av bols [how many bounces have balls]." This is an accurate statement.

Then he goes on to write, "the peg pog bol bows ulot uv tims [the Ping-Pong ball bounces a lot of times]." This is a qualitative statement that tells another scientist that that ball bounced many times. Then Keeto supports his claim with quantitative (measured) data: "it bows 10 tims [It bounces 10 times.]" He then provides the quantitative data for the other

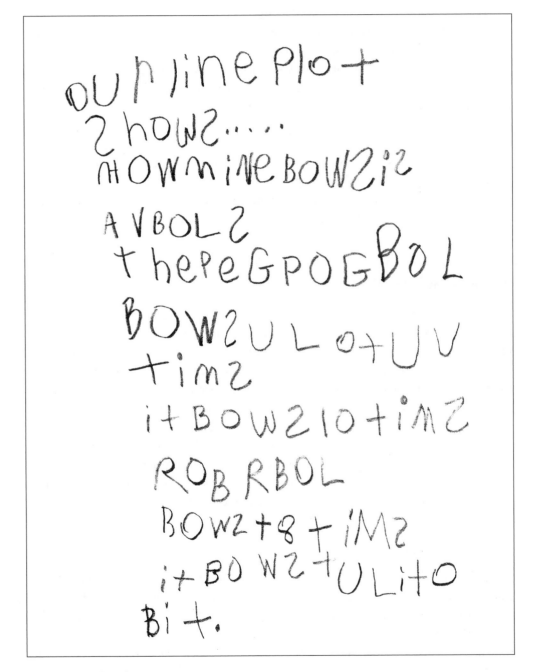

FIGURE 5–3 *Keeto's entry*

ball: "robrbol bowzt 8 tims [rubber ball bounced 8 times]," then makes an appropriate qualitative statement: "it bowzt ulito bit [It bounced a little bit.]"

Many adults would look at this entry and see only the weaknesses in spelling and other conventions. But notebook entries are rough drafts, so what matters at this stage of the writing process is the content of the writing, the organization, and the word choice. Keeto has written a strong entry. He accurately states what the line plot shows. He then writes independently, without using the rest of the writing frame. And what he includes is important, accurate, complete, and quite sophisticated for his age.

Students of all ages often report data about only the object or organism that "answers the question" (in this case, the Ping-Pong ball because it is the "better bouncer"). Students also typically report only the measured data or the comparative statement (for example, it is the *better* bouncer or it bounces *a lot more* times). But Keeto reports both the comparative statement and the test results for *each* ball.

The only thing he has left out is the answer to the question. After pointing out specific strengths in his entry, you could ask him, "So you have included all this important information in your entry. What could you do to help another scientist know the answer to the question you have been investigating? Is the Ping-Pong ball or the rubber ball the better bouncer?"

By focusing on the significant strengths in this entry in terms of Keeto's scientific thinking and his understanding of what is important to include in the entry, a teacher's feedback can positively affect both his motivation and his self-confidence. And engaging with him as a scientist communicating with other scientists also makes his work meaningful and exciting to him.

Notebook Entry: Jazmin

In Figure 5–4, Jazmin has copied much of the frame accurately and appears to understand that the Ping-Pong ball bounced ten times and the other ball bounced eight times. She knows and reports the test results, the quantitative data, for *each* ball. This is an important aspect of providing evidence. Interestingly, even though she is learning English and her copying indicates that she does not understand all the words that she is copying, she does report the data for each ball, something that many students do not do.

In talking with her, you would emphasize these strengths. Then you could reread the first sentences with her to help develop her understanding of the language, and then show her how scientists edit their entries by making deletion and insertion marks. She needs to know that it is appropriate to revise notebook entries (as long as students do not change anything that would change the meaning of their results, such as the data or their predictions).

Notebook Entry: Katie

In writing her entry about what the line plot shows about the investigation (Figure 5–5), Katie follows the writing frame, completing it accurately. In the most independent part of the writing frame, after *because*, she supports her claim: "becase [because] pingpong ball bouncer [bounced] more then rubber ball." So she is making a comparative or qualitative statement (bounced *more* than the rubber ball) to sum up the test results she has provided earlier.

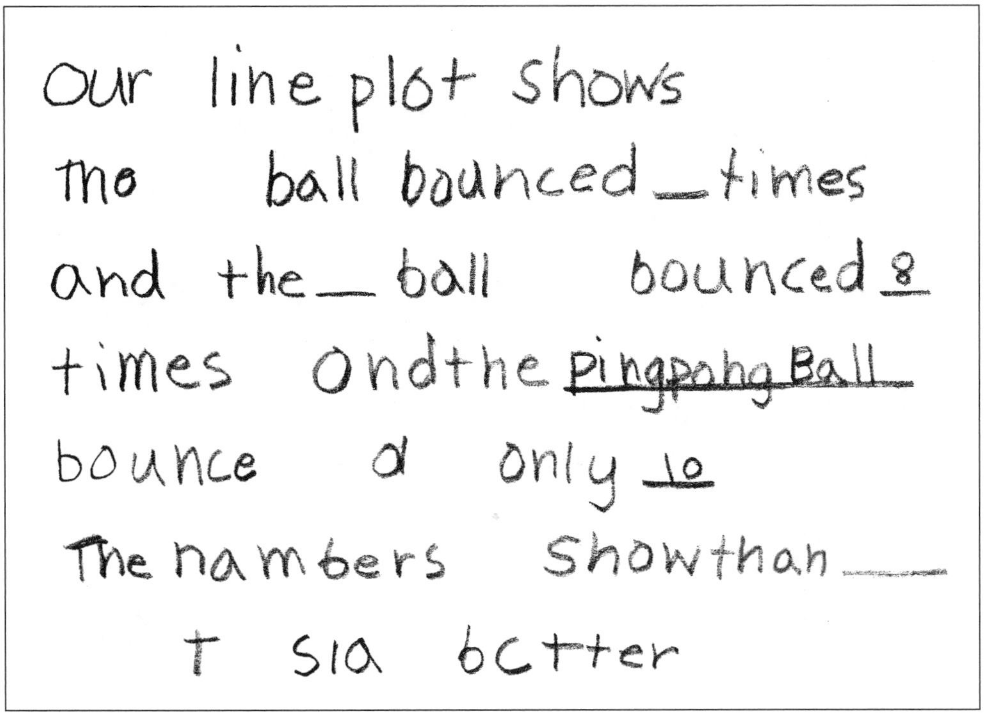
Our line plot shows
tho ball bounced __ times
and the __ ball bounced 8
times Ondthe Pingpong Ball
bounce d only 10
The nambers showthan __
T sia bctter

FIGURE 5–4 *Jazmin's entry*

Katie needs to hear about these strengths in her entry. Then you might ask her, "Another scientist might be confused because the class line plot showed that the rubber ball bounced eight times. What could you tell her about the data you have reported here?" Katie probably either has made an error in writing the data or she is using data from her own data table. As a young scientist, she needs to clarify that one part of her entry.

Sample Notebook Entry from Another Lesson: Mary Margaret

This sample comes from a later, more complex investigation to answer the question, "How does the speed of the ball affect how far a ball moves an object?" Students write a prediction, make a data table, record data from their tests, then write a basic conclusion to the investigative question.

In Figure 5–6 Mary Margaret writes the question and makes her prediction: "the ball on the 2 block ramp will move fast." She then supports the thinking with her reasoning: "Because wen we tested it togather it rold faster." So she is focusing her prediction on how fast the ball will move, basing that prediction on earlier experiences with balls and ramps.

She does not address how the speed of the ball is going to affect how far the ball moves an object, perhaps because her experience so far has been in comparing speeds of balls. This also is a complex investigative question in which students have to consider the relationship between the steepness of the ramp (one ramp rests on one block; the other ramp rests on two blocks) and the speed of the ball. They also have to think about the speed of the ball and the distance the ball can push a carton.

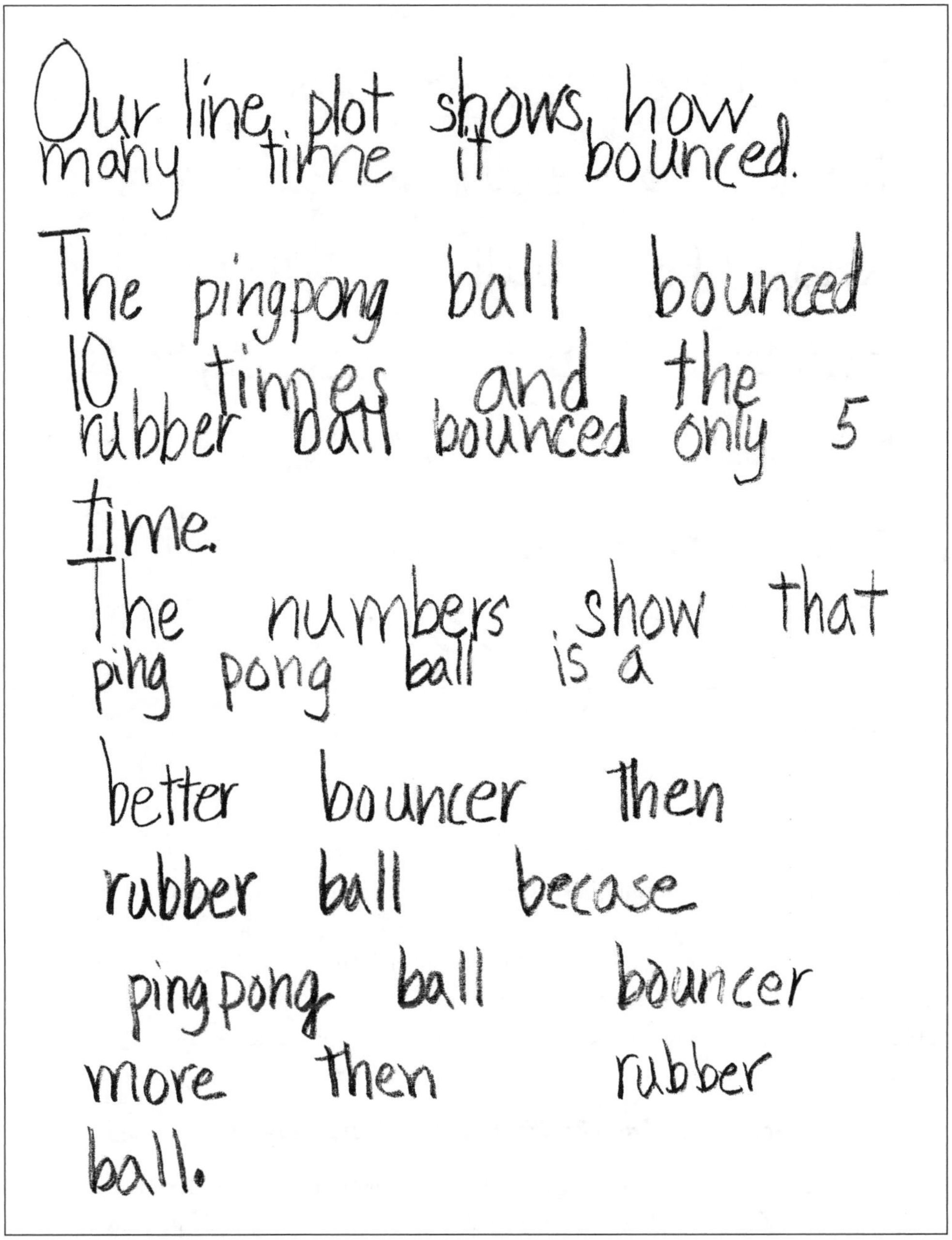

Our line plot shows how many time it bounced.
The pingpong ball bounced 10 times and the rubber ball bounced only 5 time.
The numbers show that ping pong ball is a better bouncer then rubber ball becase pingpong ball bouncer more then rubber ball.

FIGURE 5–5 *Katie's entry*

In her data table, Mary Margaret uses a method of crossing out, in each column, the lowest number, then the highest number, then the lowest number, and so on, circling the remaining number in each column as the "middle number." Students put their "middle numbers" on the class graph.

In her conclusion in Figure 5–7, Mary Margaret begins by answering the question: "The 2 block ramp pusht the carton farther." This is a shorthand way of saying that the *ball* on the two-block ramp pushed the carton farther. She then supports that claim or statement with her evidence, the quantitative data or test results for each ramp: "The 2 block ramp poosht it to 17 cm. And the 1 Block ramp only pusht it to 12 cm." Note that she uses the word *only* to emphasize the relative difference between the two distances.

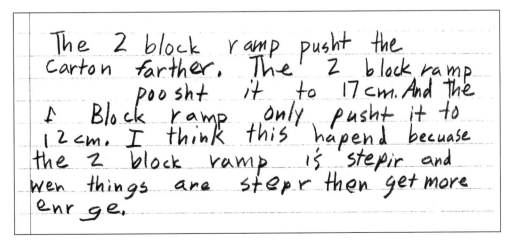

3-12

How does the (speed) of the ball affect
how far a (ball) (moves) an (object?)

I predict the ball on
the 2 block ramp Will move fast.
Because wen we tested it togather
it rold faster.

1 block	2 block
1. 14 cm	1. 18 cm
2. 12 m	2. 20 cm
3. 7 cm	3. 10 cm
4. 13 cm	4. 17 cm
5. 8 cm	5. 15 cm

FIGURE 5–6   *Mary Margaret's prediction and data table*

She then makes an inference about why she thinks this happened: "I think this hapend becuase the 2 block ramp is stepir [steeper] and wen things are stepr then get more enr ge [energy]." Presumably, she thinks that with more "energy," the ball is able to push the carton a farther distance than when the ball rolls down the less steep ramp.

After discussing all the strengths of the entry, you could say, "When you write that when things are steeper, they get more energy, a scientist would ask what you mean by *energy*. What would you say to her?" Students, especially those who have a great deal of

The 2 block ramp pusht the
Carton farther. The 2 block ramp
        poosht it to 17 cm. And the
1 Block ramp only pusht it to
12 cm. I think this hapend becuase
the 2 block ramp is stepir and
wen things are stepr then get more
enr ge.

FIGURE 5–7   *Mary Margaret's basic conclusion*

Scientific Investigations and Supporting Claims with Evidence

background knowledge, will use words like *energy* and *gravity* without fully understanding the meaning of the words. Asking them, "What do you mean by . . ." prompts students to explain their thinking and understanding. For example, in this case, Mary Margaret might be thinking that *energy* is synonymous with *speed*. By asking the question, you gain insight into her understanding and misconceptions and can plan further instruction accordingly.

Other Highlights of the Video Episode

This video episode shows the teacher using effective questions to help build students' facility with all three Key Elements. Questions such as "Can you tell me more about that?" or "What else would you tell another scientist about that?" encourage students to expand their understanding. "How do you know? What did you observe?" and "Because . . . ?" prompt students to provide their reasoning or data. "If another scientist looked at your data table, what would she need to know?" is a way to help students identify information they may have left out, while maintaining a positive approach.

Related Material

Chapters

- Chapter 6: "Predictions, Graphs, and Complex Conclusions"
- Chapter 11: "Sample Minilessons"
- Chapter 12: "Emergent Writing"

Website

- Checklists for Exemplary Notebook Entries: Basic or Complex Conclusions
- Student Notebook Entries, Pre-kindergarten Through Fifth Grade: *Because* and *I Think This Because*; Scientific Conclusions
  - Read examples from your own grade level as well as samples from a grade above and below your level.
- Stories from School
  - "Young Students' Science Writing: Raising the Bar"
- Background Information About the Video Episodes: Balls

CHAPTER 6

Predictions, Graphs, and Complex Conclusions

 **VIDEO EPISODE: GO-CARTS**

Before You Watch

The Go-Carts Video Episode focuses on the shared reflection and writing session after students have conducted an investigation about the effect of wheel size on the distance a go-cart can travel. Students need to interpret data from their testing, answer their investigative question, and reflect on what they think has caused the outcomes and why. As students conduct investigations like this and try to communicate complex thinking and conceptual understanding, they continue to need modeling and scaffolding that help them think through, as well as talk and write about, their learning. Without this scaffolding and the shared reflection, most students would not be able to write a complex conclusion.

In the writing session, the modeling and scaffolding for writing a complex conclusion begins with the structure of the simplest form of a conclusion: the answer to the investigative question and evidence to support the claim. After that, students need to learn how to add layers of evidence and reasoning that subsequently lead them to deeper reflections of their ideas.

While You Watch

As you watch this video episode, consider the following questions:

1. What evidence do you see of students using scientific skills and thinking as they conduct their investigations, interpret their data, reflect on their predictions, and discuss and write their complex conclusions?

2. What modeling and scaffolding for interpreting data and making and writing complex conclusions do you observe in this classroom and this teacher's instruction that would meet the learning needs of students who:

- are learning English?

- are served in special education programs?

- meet state academic standards?

- exceed state academic standards?

After You Watch

In an investigation like this, students need to apply many different scientific skills and use sophisticated scientific thinking in order to reach a conclusion. The skills and thinking include:

- planning a controlled investigation

- making a prediction, including reasoning

- conducting tests according to the plan

- collecting and recording data

- calculating means of the data

- creating a scatter plot

- interpreting what the data in the graph mean

- recognizing and thinking about the effect of many variables

- coming to a conclusion about the test results

- writing a complex conclusion that answers the investigative question, includes supporting data, and discusses the student's reasoning and metacognition (how she thinks she knows what she knows)

Whether students are conducting simple investigations or more complex investigations like the one in this video episode, it is critical that you have a separate science-writing session later in the day or sometime the next day after the science session. Begin the writing session by leading a class discussion to review what you all had discussed in the science session. Separating the two sessions results in better notebook entries because the students can be more focused and productive than they would be at the end of an hourlong science session.

Strategies for Your Classroom

Strategies for Interpreting and Talking About Data in Graphs

During the shared reflection, as students are making sense of the data they have collected, introduce words and phrases that help them talk and write about their test results. Use visual and oral scaffolding to support students as they learn to make and interpret graphs.

- Model the use of words such as *only* and *but* when presenting comparative data. Otherwise, students typically will report just the numbers without using comparative language to indicate the relationship between two numbers.

- Provide visual scaffolding directly on the class graph. For example, during the class discussion in the video episode, the teacher places word cards next to key data points: the word *only* next to the smallest number and *but* next to the highest number. This provides a language structure that prompts students to compare the data: "The small wheel made the go-cart travel *only* 140 cm, *but* the large wheel made the go-cart travel 283 cm." The teacher also models the use of the words *In fact* to help students elaborate on their results. Placing the word cards on the class scatter plot gives the students visual scaffolding, not only for remembering the words but also for actually doing the thinking that helps them make sense of the data in the first place.

- Make the "story" of the graph easy to see. For example, the teacher in the video episode uses brightly colored dots to indicate the mean distances that students calculated for the three wheel sizes, based on the class scatter plot. Using green dots to show the mean distances helps students focus on just the three numbers. The line connecting the three dots makes a clear picture of a line going upward, which helps students see the "story" the graph tells: the distance the go-cart travels increases with each larger wheel size.

- Model how to summarize the data in the graph. When students write about data in graphs (or data tables), they usually include all or most of the data rather than summarizing the results. In the video episode, the teacher and students discuss all the data as they begin to interpret the graph. Later, the teacher directs students' attention to the mean distances for just the smallest and largest wheels so they learn to summarize data by reporting only the highest and lowest data points. Although including the middle data point (for the medium wheel) would not be cumbersome in this case, students should learn that when there are multiple data points, they include only the highest and lowest points in the summary (unless inconsistent or inconclusive data make it impossible to derive a conclusion from the test results, in which case students' summaries should address these results).

- Also model how to calculate differences and make other comparisons with the data. For example, either on a class graph or the class data table, show students how to subtract the lowest number from the highest number, writing the numbers next to the graph or data table. Have students perform similar calculations with their test results, writing the calculations next to their data table or graph in their notebook. Model how to talk about the data starting with the phrase *In fact*: "In fact, the largest wheel made the go-cart travel 143 cm farther than the smallest wheel. That's almost twice as far."

Strategies for Planning Instruction and Assessing Graphs

The checklist in Figure 6–1 identifies the characteristics of an exemplary graph. To make an effective graph, students need to use the *scientific skill* of constructing a graph that has the correct parts put together in an effective way. *Scientific thinking* and *content understanding* are involved when the student later interprets the data in the graph and writes a conclusion.

Characteristics of an Exemplary Graph

☐ *Type of graph appropriate for data (e.g., line plot for growth, temperature, and other things that change over time; bar graphs to show discrete things, such as the number of days for each kind of precipitation—rain, hail, snow, no precipitation—in a month)*

☐ *Main title, and a title for each axis of the graph. In a controlled investigation, the manipulated (changed) variable is shown on the x-axis, the responding (measured) variable is shown on the y-axis.*

☐ *Reasonable intervals, numbered and labeled accurately, for each axis*

☐ *Data recorded:*

- *accurately*

- *completely*

- *clearly*

FIGURE 6–1   *Checklist for Characteristics of an Exemplary Graph*

Strategies for Writing Complex Conclusions

The thinking and writing that students must do in writing a conclusion to the go-carts investigation are complex. In this case, a writing frame to guide students in writing this complex conclusion would be too cumbersome. The handout in Figure 6–2, which students are following in the videotaped writing session, guides students as they write and check off each component of the conclusion. (Students write their conclusion in their science notebook, not on the handout.) You can use this as a template for your own handout for writing a complex conclusion.

■ A complex handout requires you and the students to do the thinking and use the wording during the whole-class reflective discussion after the investigation. For example, the following scaffolding would be difficult to understand if a student just read it and tried to follow it as a template for his thinking and writing: "At first, I thought _____ because I thought _____. Then I revised my thinking when _____. Now I think _____ because _____." But when you use these frames during discussions, particularly during similar discussions throughout a school year, students understand what the frame is prompting them to think and write.

■ One response using that scaffolding might be: "*At first, I thought* the small wheels would make the go-cart travel farther than the large wheels *because I thought* the small wheels would make the go-cart less heavy so it would go farther. *Then I revised my thinking when* our data showed that the larger wheels made the go-cart go farther. *Now I think* the large wheels make the go-cart go farther *because* every time they turn [make one revolution], they go farther than the smaller wheels go every time they turn. So with the same number of turns, the larger wheel would cover more ground." By using the phrases and the word *because*, the student communicates his reasoning in a way that makes him think about how he knows what he knows now. This communication lets you know what he understands and what kind of further instruction you might need to plan for him or the whole class.

■ With a conclusion this complex, you may find it helpful to split the modeling of the writing into two parts. During the shared-writing minilesson, write the first part of the conclusion (sections 1 through 3 on the handout). After the lesson, have the students write that first part independently. Then interrupt the independent writing time to do an oral shared-writing lesson on how to begin writing about their prediction and how their thinking has or has not changed. This keeps the shared-writing lesson from being too long and complex, and students will remember what to do in each part of the complex conclusion.

■ To develop your own effective handout, keep each part as simple as possible. For example, in the class discussion, students begin to learn how to provide supporting data. Then, when they are writing their conclusion and they get to number 2 in the handout, they are reminded of the language to use in providing data for the 7.5 centimeter wheels. Scaffolding for the second set of data, for the 11.5 centimeter wheels, purposely is minimal because students should be able to write that part on their own. (Class discussion is crucial here, so that students understand what they are being asked to include.) As students' proficiency grows throughout the year, you can provide increasingly less scaffolding in each handout.

Investigative question:

What is the effect of the size of the wheels on the distance a go-cart can travel?

1. Answer the question:

2. Include supporting data (evidence) from the *Wheel Size vs. Distance Traveled* scatter plot:

The data show that _____ [include "only" and ", but"]

☐ *the 7.5 cm wheels make the go-cart travel* _____ *cm.*

☐ 11.5 cm wheels—distance in cm

☐ *In fact,* _____ . [use numbers you computed to the right of your data table]

3. Write a concluding statement:

Therefore, the [smaller/larger] *the wheels, the* [shorter/longer] *the distance the go-cart travels.*

_____ .

**4. Reread your prediction. Think about your reasoning for your prediction.
   Then write about how your thinking has changed:**

At first, I thought _____ *because I thought* _____ .

Then I revised my thinking when _____ .

5. Explain why you think the wheel size does affect the distance the go-cart travels:

Now I think _____ *because* _____ .

**6. If your group's test results were inconsistent, explain why you think your group got
   different results than other groups did:**

My group's test results were inconsistent. I think this happened because _____ .

7. Write what you would like to investigate next time:

Now I want to investigate what would happen if _____ .

FIGURE 6–2   *Handout for the independent writing session in the video episode*

Writing in Science in Action

- To ensure that the handout will provide appropriate scaffolding, use it to write your own complex conclusion to the investigation while you are planning the science and writing sessions. This will help you anticipate where your students might have difficulty with the writing or be confused by parts of the handout.

Strategies for Planning Instruction and Assessing Complex Conclusions

In this science-writing approach, the first two components of a *basic* conclusion are the answer to the question and the evidence or data that support the answer. The third component is a general statement about what the data indicate (for example, "As the wheel size increases, the distance the go-cart travels increases."). The fourth component, when it is included in a basic conclusion (young students typically do not write this part), addresses whether the student's prediction is accurate based on the test results.

A *complex* conclusion has all four of these components (as shown in Figure 6–3). It also includes components that help students think and write about the development of their scientific thinking and understanding, inconsistent or confusing data and what might have caused those outcomes, and other questions they want to investigate.

When planning your lesson for teaching students how to think and write about the conclusion to their investigation, then later assessing their notebook entry in terms of the Three Key Elements, consider the following questions. What does the written conclusion reveal about the student's:

1. Understanding of one or more *science concepts* (for example, uses appropriate evidence and reasoning that indicates she understands the concept or concepts)?

2. Ability to *think scientifically* (for example, chooses and provides appropriate data and/or reasoning to support the answer or a claim; reaches a conclusion that makes sense based on the data; recognizes when data do not support a prediction and when reasoning, the student's hypothesis, does not make sense)?

3. Ability to use *scientific skills* (for example, has accurately collected and recorded observations and/or quantitative data on which the conclusion is based)?

Strategies for Making and Writing Predictions with Reasoning

Students in this video episode wrote a prediction for their investigation well before the videotaping, so the instruction is not shown in the episode. But reflecting on their prediction and initial reasoning is an important part of developing students' conceptual understanding and ability to write a complex conclusion, so you will need to use some strategies to help students learn to write their predictions and provide reasoning for them.

- In this approach to science writing, the term *prediction* means what a student *thinks will happen* in a given situation. The part that follows the prediction begins with *because* or *I think* (or *I predict*) *this because*. The part that follows *because* is the student's reasoning for *why* she thinks that outcome will happen. This reasoning is based on ideas the student holds based on prior investigations and experiences. In this approach, the student's reasoning is considered her *hypothesis*.

Characteristics of an Exemplary
Basic (#1–4) or a Complex (#1–7) Conclusion

1. **Accurately answers the question the student has been investigating.**

2. **Provides evidence to support answer:**

   ☐ *Observations (qualitative data)—i.e., what student has observed, such as the color of a plant's leaves (rather than what he has measured, such as the height of a plant).*

   and/or

   ☐ *Comparison of test results (e.g., "The largest wheels made the go-carts go farther than the smallest wheels.").*

   ☐ *Summary of measured (quantitative) data (i.e., reports specific measured data from the lowest and highest ends of the range, not all data: e.g., "7.5 cm wheels . . . went only 140 cm, but 11.5 cm wheels . . . went 283 cm.").*

   ☐ *Comparative data (e.g., "In fact, the 11.5 cm wheels made the go-cart travel 143 cm farther [and/or "about twice as far"] as the 7.5 cm wheels.") if needed.*

   ☐ *Other data, if inconclusive test results make it impossible to reach a conclusion.*

3. **Makes concluding statement that answers the question in a more generalized way (e.g., "Therefore, as the wheel size increases, the distance the go-cart travels increases." Or "So, the larger the wheels, the farther the distance the go-cart travels.").**

4. **Discusses whether results of investigation support student's prediction (i.e., *what* he thought would happen).**

5. **Addresses initial reasoning (inference or hypothesis) that was the basis for the prediction. Explains how thinking has or has not changed since making the prediction.**

6. **Points out inconsistent or confusing data, if applicable, and what might have caused those results.**

7. **May include question(s) student wants to investigate because of the results.**

FIGURE 6–3 *Checklist for Characteristics of an Exemplary Basic or a Complex Conclusion*

- Modeling these language structures is critical because it gives students scaffolding for understanding and explaining the development of their thinking. It also provides a window into their thinking process. Without using such scaffolding, students typically will write only the prediction of *what* they think will happen in the investigation without explaining the reason for that prediction.

- Additional words can prompt students to include more reasoning when they need to explain more complex thinking. *So that means* is another useful phrase, as in, "*I predict* the smaller wheels will make the go-cart go farther *because I think* the small wheels are closer to the ground. *So that means* that they are more stable, *which means* that they are less likely to wobble than the large wheels." Even though this reasoning is based on a misconception, it indicates that the student is thinking like an engineer. (Because of all the testing students have done in designing their own go-carts, the student knows that large wheels can make the go-carts less stable than small wheels. The "so that means" structure allows you to see the sophisticated reasoning behind the student's prediction.)

- Students often think that the goal of making a prediction is to be "right." They do need to determine if their data support their prediction (and thus whether the prediction is accurate). But they should value the reasoning they use in making their prediction and how their hypothesis evolves as they test their ideas, just as scientists do.

Strategies for Planning Instruction and Assessing Predictions

As always, the initial questions to ponder when planning instruction and assessing predictions with reasoning focus on the Three Key Elements. What do the prediction and reasoning reveal about the student's:

1. Ability to use *scientific skills* (for example, makes a prediction that relates to the question; if the question is for a controlled investigation, the student mentions both the manipulated and responding variables)?

2. Ability to *think scientifically* (for example, states what she thinks will happen based on previous investigations and/or prior experiences, not a wild guess; provides appropriate scientific reasoning for predicted outcomes)?

3. Understanding of one or more *science concepts* (for example, describes or explains cause and effect and/or relevant properties or characteristics of an object, organism, or event to the extent possible based on level of experience with the concepts)?

The checklist in Figure 6–4 identifies the characteristics of an exemplary prediction with reasoning. You can use it as you think about your instruction and assessment of your students' notebook entries.

Sample Notebook Entries from the Video Episode

The critiques in the following pages use the planning and assessment checklists shown in earlier sections of this chapter.

Characteristics of an Exemplary
Prediction with Reasoning

Prediction—*what the student thinks will happen*—answers the focus or investigative question.

☐ *In a controlled investigation, mentions at least two aspects of the manipulated (changed) variable as well as the responding (measured) variable. For example, if the investigative question were "What is the effect of wheel size on the distance a go-cart can travel?" the student might write: "I predict that the largest wheel will make the go-cart travel farther than the smallest wheel will . . . " Note that the student names both the highest and lowest parts of the manipulated variable in her prediction. Students typically write about only one, usually the one that they think will have the most effect. This student also includes the relative distance (farther), which is the responding variable.*

Reasoning—*why something will happen*—supports the prediction.

☐ *Usually follows because or I think/predict this because. For example, to add to the prediction above, the student might write, "because I think larger wheels have a larger circumference than smaller wheels and that makes them travel farther with one rotation of the wheel than a smaller wheel does with one rotation." Note that the student includes both parts of the manipulated variable and the responding variable in her reasoning.*

☐ *Reasoning makes sense at that point in the unit.*

☐ *Reasoning is not based on personal feelings or opinions.*

FIGURE 6–4 *Checklist for Characteristics of an Exemplary Prediction with Reasoning*

Notebook Entry: Anna

Prediction

A student's initial prediction and reasoning become an important part of her complex conclusion because they show how the student's ideas have changed or been supported with more data and further thinking. In Anna's entry (Figure 6–5), she predicts what will happen and mentions the three sizes of the wheels (the manipulated variable), not just the wheel she thinks will have the greatest effect on the distance the go-cart will travel. This is an important part of a strong prediction, although she did not need to include the medium wheel. Also, at this age, it is appropriate that students use a kind of shorthand. In this case, Anna writes that the "larger size wheels will go further" instead of using more accurate wording, "the larger sized wheels will make the go-cart go farther."

In the second part of that sentence, she provides her reasoning: "because the largest wheel has a bigger cicumference." Then in the second sentence, she elaborates on that idea, explaining that "the larger wheel would cover more ground because it is bigger and then travel farther." She could explain that reasoning a bit more, because another scientist would wonder what she means by "bigger." In that statement, she also mentions twisting the "rubber band on the axle 10 times." Since that is a controlled variable in the investigation (in

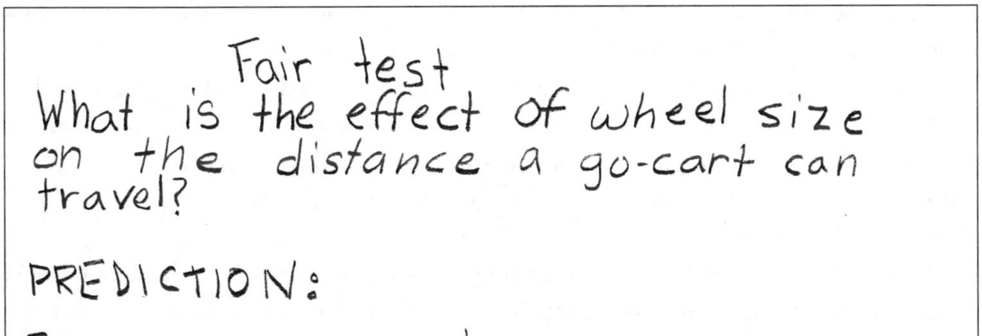

Fair test
What is the effect of wheel size on the distance a go-cart can travel?

PREDICTION:

I predict that the larger size wheels will go further than the smaller and medium wheel, because the largest wheel has a bigger cicumference. So, for example, if you twisted up the rubber band on the axle 10 times, the larger wheel would cover more ground because it is bigger and then travel farther. I think that it would take 2 revolutions with the small wheel and It would only take one revolution with the bigger wheel, but they would both cover the same ground.

FIGURE 6–5 *Anna's prediction*

other words, all the students should have twisted the rubber band ten times), she does not need to include that part.

Her last statement builds on her idea that the "bigger" wheels will go farther. Interestingly, she thinks that "it would take 2 revolutions with the small wheel" to cover the same ground. Students in the classroom have not measured the circumference of the wheels, so they cannot know how far each wheel goes with one revolution. (Many students had this reasoning, which may have been based just on observing the relative sizes of the large and small wheels.) So another scientist might wonder why she thinks the smaller wheel would go half the distance of the larger wheel.

Even though a scientist would question some of Anna's reasoning, she has written a strong entry because she answers the question, addressing both the smallest and largest wheel and the relative distance for both. She includes *because* and then provides her reasoning in enough detail to support her prediction. If she had written a prediction that the test results did not support, the entry still could be considered strong if the prediction included all the parts and her reasoning was clear and made sense given where she could be expected to be in her conceptual understanding at this point of the unit.

Graph

Anna's scatter plot is shown in Figure 6–6. The teacher had given students a few guidelines but otherwise expected students to work together to make their own individual scatter plot in their science notebook using the data from their data table. (Anna's data table is not shown here.) Their biggest challenge was to determine the intervals for the y-axis.

Anna has chosen intervals that work well because they are consistent and far enough apart that the resulting graph shows the increase in distance with each wheel size. A scientist would question the placement of the mean for the large wheel because it is placed above 284.

After students help create the class scatter plot, Anna may realize that her graph would be easier to read if she did not include the trials and their numbers or the abbreviated unit of measure (cm) for each data entry. If she had not included those unnecessary labels, then she could have written the means at their actual data points rather than at the top of the graph. This process of trying to create a graph with less guidance, instead of just copying a graph, helps students understand what makes a graph effective and easy to read.

Complex Conclusion

We can assess Anna's complex conclusion (Figure 6–7) in terms of the seven components from the checklist. She begins by answering the question in a general way in her first sentence. She does not need to mention the small and large wheels because they both are implicitly included in the phrase, "The larger the wheel . . ." She accurately reports the evidence or data for both the small and large wheels, using *but* and *only* to compare the data. She uses the phrase *In fact* to state her calculation that the small wheel has "traveled only half the distance of the larger wheel."

In her concluding statement to this first part of her conclusion, she departs from reporting the data and instead states her inferences about what happens: "Therefore, the smaller wheel takes two revolutions to cover the same distance that the larger wheel would take only one revolution." Then she goes back to make a generalization about the actual data: "So, the larger the wheel, the farther it goes."

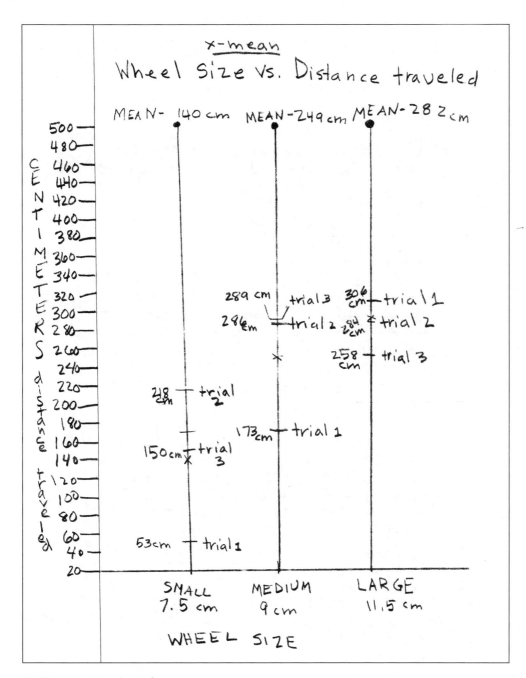

FIGURE 6–6 *Anna's graph*

Anna's conclusion and everything she reports about the data to support her conclusion are accurate and complete. The sentence about the revolutions is misplaced; it is not actual evidence or data, so she cannot use that inferential thinking to support her answer or claim. Just as in the most simple of conclusions, students should answer the question, and then support the answer with evidence or data. Organizing their conclusion in this way helps students make a clear distinction between evidence and inferential thinking.

In the next part of Anna's conclusion, she notes that her prediction was accurate. She does not need to revise her thinking except to make a generalization: "Now I think the larger

> What is the effect of the size of the wheels on the distance it goes?
>
> 3.10
>
> The larger the wheel, the farther the go-cart goes. The data show that the smaller wheel only traveled 140cm., but the larger wheel traveled 282 cm. In fact, the 7.5 wheel traveled only half the distance of the larger (11.5 cm. diameter) wheel. Therefore, the smaller wheel takes two revolutions to cover the same distance that the larger wheel would take only one revolution. ~~and they would both cover the same ground.~~ So, the larger the wheel, the farther it goes. At first, I thought that the larger wheel would go further than the smaller wheel because the larger wheel has a bigger circumference. I didn't have to revise my thinking because my prediction was correct. Now I think the larger the wheel, the farther it goes. My group's test results were consistent, but I think why other group's results were inconsistent was because there might have been more than one changed variable. Now I want to investigate what would happen if you used different materials for the wheels.

FIGURE 6–7 *Anna's complex conclusion*

the wheel, the farther it goes." (Some of the students who were concerned about the design of the go-carts might question whether she can make this generalization because they would think that the larger the wheel, the less stable it might be.)

She uses scientific thinking as she notes that her group's test results were consistent, but that other groups might have had inconsistent results because they did not conduct a controlled investigation. Finally, she ends her conclusion with a good question for which she could plan a new investigation.

Overall, this is a strong conclusion. You would give her feedback about how she included all the components, and then specifically name some strengths. Then you could say, "Another scientist might wonder what evidence you have to support your inference about the revolutions of the small and large wheels." She then could conduct some tests and add a note to her notebook entry.

Notebook Entry: Jasmine

Prediction

Jasmine wrote the prediction and reasoning in Figure 6–8. She is quite articulate when she speaks but has trouble expressing herself in English when she is writing. Talking to someone just before she writes a sentence is an effective strategy for her because her oral language is fresh in her mind.

Jasmine predicts that the small wheel will make the go-cart travel farther than the large wheel. She reasons that the large wheel is heavier, which she thinks will make the go-cart travel a shorter distance. Although she has a misconception that weight affects the distance the go-cart will move, her reasoning is logical. If she believes that less weight makes the go-cart travel a shorter distance, then a small wheel would make the go-cart travel farther than a larger wheel. She adds that the small wheel also is closer to the ground so it can move more than the big wheel. This part of her reasoning might reflect something she has figured out in her retesting and revising of her own go-cart. The smaller wheels made with the materials these students have often are more stable than the larger wheels. So again, her reasoning makes sense.

In talking with her about her prediction and reasoning, you would discuss the strengths of her argument based on the thinking she has included. She needs to know that she is thinking like a scientist. If you have time, you might ask her to draw a diagram or use a go-cart to explain her ideas. After she sees the results of her investigation, she will revise her thinking.

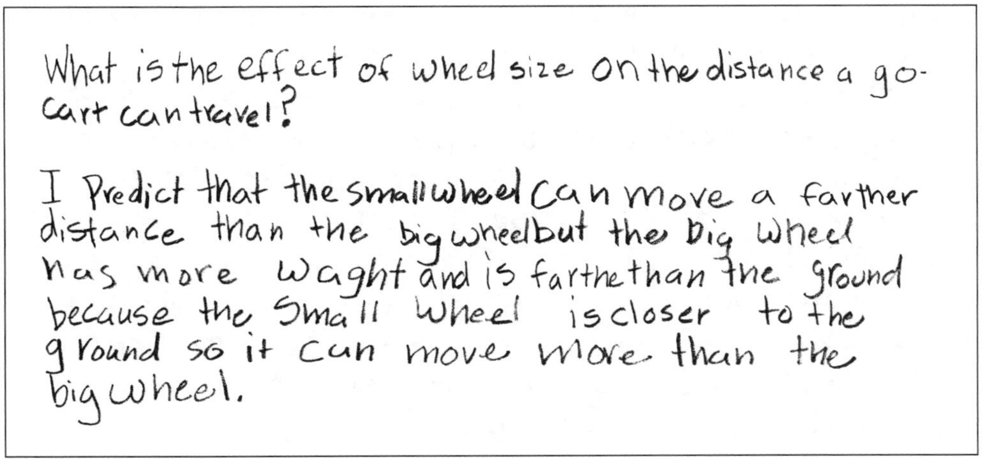

> What is the effect of wheel size on the distance a go-cart can travel?
>
> I Predict that the small wheel can move a farther distance than the big wheel but the big wheel has more waght and is farthe than the ground because the small wheel is closer to the ground so it can move more than the big wheel.

FIGURE 6–8 *Jasmine's prediction*

Complex Conclusion

In Jasmine's conclusion to the investigation (Figure 6–9), she answers the question, then supports the claim with accurate data for both the small and large wheels, including an *In fact* statement that is accurate and a generalization that makes sense.

As she writes about the next parts of the conclusion, she has some trouble with the language, but she clearly knows that the data do not support her prediction. You would point out the specific strengths in the first half of the conclusion. Then you could ask, "Another scientist might wonder what you mean when you say, 'the small wheel will go faster than the large wheel, but the larger wheel has more waght [weight] than the small one.' What could you tell her about what you mean by *speed* and *weight*?" This will help Jasmine think more deeply about what she means and you can determine whether she has a misconception and/or a problem with the language. (Students often talk about speed in this investigation because the small wheels spin faster on the axles than the large wheels do. Thinking that weight makes objects move faster also is a common misconception.)

On the whole, especially for a student who is learning how to write in English, this is a strong conclusion that communicates quite clearly how she is thinking. To help her construct an understanding about the effect of circumference, she needs to do more than listen to people talking about it. She needs to work with concrete materials, a measuring tape and the wheels, and actually see the effect.

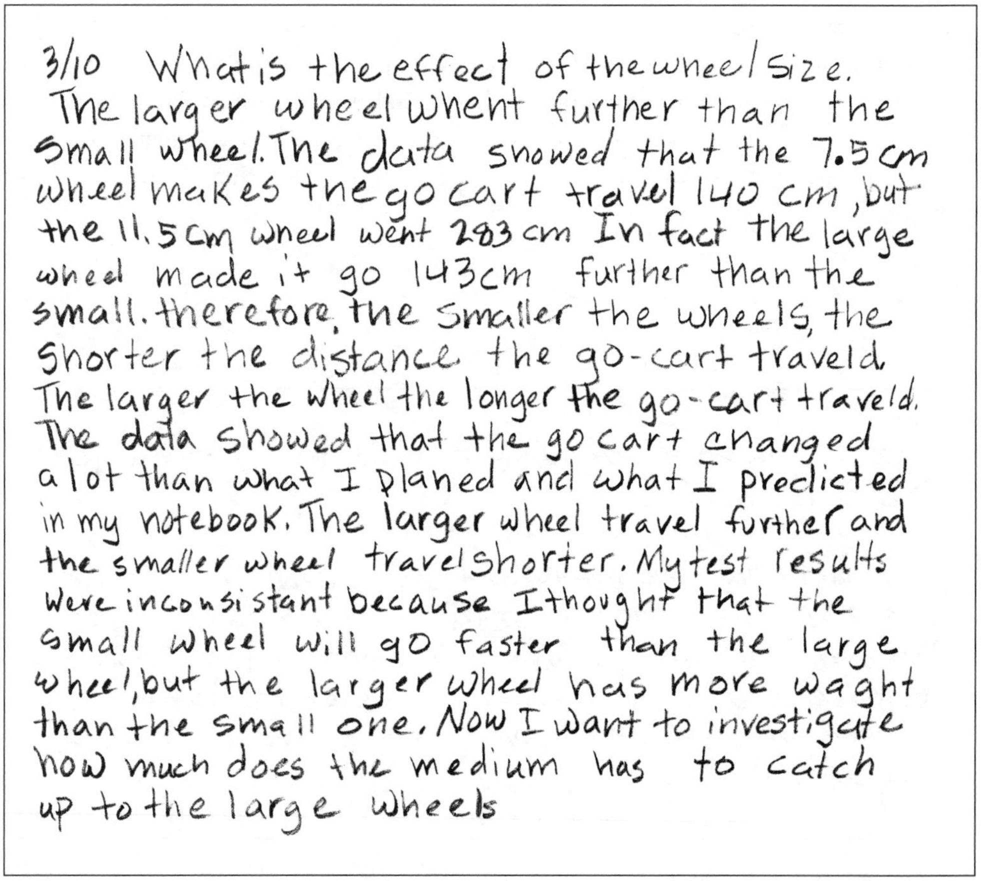

> 3/10 What is the effect of the wheel size. The larger wheel whent further than the small wheel. The data snowed that the 7.5 cm wheel makes the go cart travel 140 cm, but the 11.5 cm wheel went 283 cm In fact the large wheel made it go 143cm further than the small. therefore, the smaller the wheels, the shorter the distance the go-cart traveld. The larger the wheel the longer the go-cart traveld. The data showed that the go cart changed a lot than what I planed and what I predicted in my notebook. The larger wheel travel further and the smaller wheel travel shorter. My test results were inconsistant because I thought that the small wheel will go faster than the large wheel, but the larger wheel has more waght than the small one. Now I want to investigate how much does the medium has to catch up to the large wheels

FIGURE 6–9 *Jasmine's complex conclusion*

Other Highlights of the Video Episode

Dealing with a Misconception

After this videotaped episode, when looking over the students' conclusions, the teacher realized that the inference they had made (for every revolution of the large wheels the small wheels would have to go around twice to equal the same distance) was incorrect. At this point, she did not have time to do a lesson in which all her students could measure the circumference of the wheels and determine the correct inference. So she posed a question to the class that another scientist might ask about evidence for the inference, then requested volunteers to investigate the question. A group of six girls conducted an investigation and determined that there is no evidence for the inference. They then shared the results of their investigation with the class. This is an effective way of dealing with misconceptions if you already have invested a lot of class time in an investigation and cannot add another investigation.

Teaching Notes

The teacher has made her own scaffolding—her teaching notes. When she planned the lesson, she wrote a series of questions she wanted to remember on note cards. She has taught this unit many times, but regardless of how many times a teacher teaches a unit, teaching notes are still critical to the success of the lesson.

Related Material

Chapters

- Chapter 9: "Group Critiquing and Teacher-Student Conferences"
  - Assessment 2 and Teacher-Student Conference Video Episodes are about this go-carts investigation and complex conclusion

- Chapter 11: "Sample Minilessons"
  - Includes a minilesson for writing conclusions

Website

- Checklists for Exemplary Notebook Entries
  - Includes the checklists in this chapter as well as checklists for other types of notebook entries (for example, scientific observations, comparisons)

- Student Notebook Entries, Pre-kindergarten Through Fifth Grade: Scientific Conclusions
  - Read samples from your own grade level and a grade level above and below to get a sense of the how to meet students' needs.

- Stories from Schools
  - "Essential Keys to Equitable Achievement for Underserved Students"

- Background Information About the Video Episodes: Go-Carts

CHAPTER 7

Using Modeling and Scaffolding with English Language Learners

Before You Watch

Teachers often ask how they can teach inquiry-based science and, in particular, science writing, to their students who are learning English. The first part of the answer is that in inquiry-based science, students initially work with concrete materials, constructing their understanding of particular science concepts from those physical experiences. This part of the learning does not depend on their ability to read, speak, and write English.

Second, in this approach to teaching science writing and scientific thinking, the teacher continually models and provides a variety of visual, oral, and written scaffolding to support students as they learn science concepts, scientific thinking and skills, and scientific language. This scaffolding is helpful in different ways for most students, including those who are learning English, have special needs, or have strong academic skills.

In the Animals Video Episode, only one of the twenty students in the class speaks English as his native language. Most of the strategies that the teacher uses are part of this science-writing approach. She also uses some other strategies for teaching English language learners (ELLs). All the strategies are appropriate, to varying degrees, with elementary students of all ages who are learning English.

While You Watch

As you watch the video, consider these questions.

1. What kinds of scaffolding does this teacher use in the science and the writing sessions?

- Visual (for example, word banks and word cards, scientific illustrations)

- Oral (for example, modeling specific phrases and sentence starters)

- Written (for example, providing writing frames)

2. How does the teacher embed the language instruction naturally within the science and science-writing instruction?

After You Watch

The modeling and scaffolding in this science-writing approach help students learn to work, think, talk, and write like scientists. The scaffolding supports students as they move from not knowing certain common or scientific words (for example, *rough* and *smooth surfaces*), to knowing the words when they are reminded (by visual and oral cues), to knowing the words and not needing any support in using them.

Language learning happens as a natural, integral part of the lesson. For example, the teacher begins the science session by engaging the students in reflecting on their prior experiences with land snails. At the same time, she also naturally embeds language instruction in the science lesson. Talking about *where* students remember seeing snails (for example, on sidewalks and sand) leads to the categorizing of the *surfaces* into *rough* and *smooth*. The three terms are critical in the lesson's focus question. As the students continue through the process of planning their fair test, they continue to build their understanding of these terms as well as the term *fair test*.

Strategies for Your Classroom

For all students, whether they know English or are learning English, scientific language and thinking are different from what they usually hear and read. So you continually need to teach and model how to use new vocabulary and language, and give students many opportunities to use the language orally before they use it in their writing. Four teachers in our program (Jim Buckwalter, Ana Crossman, Kirsten Nesholm, and Stephanie Chen) who have had a great deal of experience teaching inquiry-based science and science writing to ELLs have recommended using the strategies in the next sections. The strategies are effective with all students, especially those who are learning English.

Strategies for Learning Vocabulary

- Have students put word cards in the word bank during discussions. This helps students know where to find words they need to use.

- Add sketches or pictures from the computer to word cards as well as concrete materials (see information about word banks in Chapter 1). In some cases, writing a short definition is helpful as is color-coding words that go together. For example, in a unit on sound, you could write the following words in the same color because they all relate to pitch: *pitch*, *high*, *medium*, *low*. Then you could use another color for words related to vibration: *vibration*, *fast*, *medium*, *slow*.

■ Provide small word cards like the ones in the word bank at the students' table groups. Having the words right there when they are writing makes the language more accessible.

■ Have ELLs draw what they see or draw it as you draw it, labeling the parts of the drawing. This is critical to their language and conceptual development. See Chapter 3 for more information.

■ Use concrete materials (for example, in the video episode, the teacher used a tray with wax paper, sandpaper, and a snail) to help students visualize something they are going to do, or to remind them of something they have done.

Strategies for Learning Language Structure

ELLs need more access to models of how language looks than English-speaking students do, so keep scaffolding up on the walls for extended periods of time in a designated science area so everyone knows where to look.

■ Sentence starters are especially important for ELLs, both in discussions and in their independent writing. They need continual repetition and practice of new language.

■ Keep referring back to class tables and charts, saying things like, "Stop and tell your partner the function of . . ." or "Everyone point to . . ."

■ Model how to use gestures (as the teacher did in the video episode) that help students hear each word in a sentence you are speaking or reading together. The kinesthetic response helps engage the students and reinforce the learning.

■ Have the class practice saying a sentence with you, then write it together, then read it together.

■ When conferencing with a student, help him form a sentence, first by helping him say his sentence and then by supporting him as he writes it. Sometimes just saying the sentence before writing it will get the student started. If the student is in the emergent writing stage, you can write the words he says on a sticky note, then he can copy the words into his notebook. For additional strategies for emergent writers, see Chapter 12.

Strategies for Grouping Students

■ During the science session when students are working with concrete materials, you might want to pair students with others who speak their language. At the beginning of language acquisition, the real learning initially happens in the student's native language.

■ During the reflective discussion and the writing session, you might want to pair ELLs with students who know English, so the ELLs can hear the language they need to use in their writing.

Strategies for Discussions

Holding students accountable while also providing support and encouragement is important because some students with limited English skills are reluctant to speak in front of a large group of their classmates. They need to know that you have the same high expectations for them that you do for all your other students.

■ When beginning a lesson and connecting students with their prior knowledge, have each pair of students turn and talk with each other. If possible, pair ELLs with students who are more verbal and have more developed English skills. Scan the discussion area or room as students are talking and go to individual ELLs and ask them questions (for example, "Where have you seen . . . ?") that help them activate their prior knowledge about the question. Often students realize they do know a lot about the subject, which increases their confidence as well as their interest in the discussion. To facilitate student conversations, strategically place yourself so you can provide support to those who most need it.

■ When you begin a whole-class discussion, have pairs of students turn and talk with each other about a question before discussing it as a whole class. For each pair, designate the student who will ask the question and the one who will answer it. You will need to repeat the question, pointing to the words in the question as you say it together. Keep these questions simple. This pair discussion gives all students a chance to think and talk before sharing their ideas with the whole class. Tell one pair ahead of time that you will call on them first during the discussion. This will give them a little time to get ready, which will build their confidence about sharing their ideas.

■ Discuss the key words in the focus question. Give examples of the meaning of the terms and ask students for examples. If there are words that sound the same but have different meanings, point out the distinctions.

■ Model using simple frames for discussions, such as "I think this happened because . . ." and "My evidence is . . ." This keeps all students focused on their discussion and teaches ELLs new language structures. As ELLs become more confident, expect them—and your other students—to speak in complete sentences, beginning with the sentence starters when needed.

■ Listen in on a discussion between students who do not yet have enough confidence to share their ideas. Then, during the class discussion, refer to what you heard during their discussion. This will help build their confidence in their speaking and scientific thinking. By listening in on different groups, you can get a sense of which students have meaningful ideas that are accurate enough to share. Call on them first, before other students with more developed English skills speak up and say everything that the less verbal students would have said.

■ If an ELL cannot answer a question, have her go to the white board or whatever visual scaffolding you have posted and ask her to point to the answer. Or suggest two possible responses and have her choose one. If you think she just needs more time, tell her to continue discussing the question with her partner and say that you will call on them later in the discussion.

- Post simple sentence starters for discussion, including sentences that teach students how to be respectful of each other. For example, a frame might be, "I agree with his idea about . . . I have another idea about . . ." When reflective discussions are such a critical part of the science and writing sessions, students need to learn how to be respectful of each other so that every student feels comfortable about contributing to the discussion.

Strategies for Using Bilingual Aides

For students who do not yet have much academic language, having a bilingual aide in the classroom can make them feel more comfortable, and thus more able to learn. If bilingual aides are available to you, you can support them in several ways.

- Meet with the aide before the science or writing session and share the learning objectives for the lesson.

- Provide a list of questions to ask the students. This is critical because inquiry-based science instruction requires teachers to ask the kinds of questions that make students think. Aides and other adults who assist in your classroom need to know the appropriate questions to ask in specific lessons, and they need to understand that they do not give answers to students. The aides are there to clarify questions and to use the students' native language to help them express their ideas.

- *As you are teaching a lesson or leading a class discussion*, have the aide sit with a group of ELLs who need the most support. As you and other students are talking, the aide can translate and ask questions to check for understanding, and support them if they want to contribute to the discussion.

Feedback and Assessment Strategies

The notebook entries of ELLs are going to be different from other students' entries because of the additional scaffolding they need and the amount of writing that they do. You also need to assess the entry and give feedback in ways that fit the student's stage of language development. But even with limited English, these students have ideas to communicate. You will need to speak with them in order to find out what else they know. Regardless of the language development or age of your students, however, you still critique and talk with them about their notebook entries in terms of the Three Key Elements of this science-writing approach: science concepts, scientific thinking, and/or scientific skills.

- In giving students feedback, simplify the wording of the feedback.

- Have the student read the feedback with you or to you, which will give him additional practice with the language while also helping him understand your comments.

- Also look back at a student's earlier entries to find evidence of improved understanding and thinking. Point out this growth to the student before you share feedback about a single entry. Building a student's self-esteem and confidence is an important part of any teaching, but it is even more critical with students who are learning a new language.

- Copy entries or keep a student's complete science notebook in his portfolio. Because science writing begins with concrete experiences, ELLs often produce more and better writing in their science notebooks than in their other writing.

Sample Notebook Entries from the Video Episode

The three students who wrote the entries in this section are in different stages of learning English and live with parents who do not speak English. They also are only halfway through kindergarten, their first year of schooling. Yet all these students are making a claim and supporting it with evidence, a skill that many older students who already know English have not mastered.

Notebook Entry: Jialang

In Jialang's entry (Figure 7–1), he copies the first sentence accurately and completes it with the correct type of surface, sandpaper. He then copies some of the words for the second sentence and adds the correct data. So the entry states that he thinks snails crawl more on the sandpaper. He supports this claim by including *34* [tally marks] as his evidence, which also is accurate. So Jialang clearly is doing more than just copying words.

In talking with Jialang, you would have him read the entry to you or with you. Then you would point out that he has answered the question the class has been investigating and then he has given the evidence, which shows that he has strong scientific skills and he is thinking like a scientist.

After discussing the strengths of the entry with Jialang, your next steps would depend on your knowledge of the student. If you think that asking him to do something more will be too much for him at this point, then you would talk with him just about the strengths of his entry. If you think he could do a little more thinking, and perhaps writing, then you would address the weaknesses. To help Jialang move to the next level in his writing, you could say, "Another scientist would need to know what you found out about the wax paper. How many times did the snail go to that surface?" Then Jialang might add the numeral *29* and the words *wax paper*.

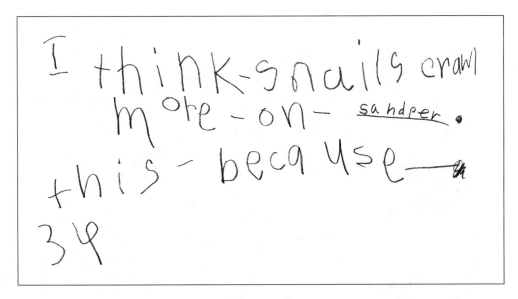

FIGURE 7–1 *Jialang's entry*

Throughout elementary school, even when students have well-developed writing skills, they typically do not include the data for both tested surfaces; they include only the data for the one that answers the question. In this case, snails crawled more on the sandpaper, so that is what most students naturally will write about unless they are taught to provide both sets of data. Teaching this skill to the youngest students, including those who are learning English, helps them build a strong foundation of scientific thinking and writing.

Notebook Entry: Kristine

Kristine begins her entry (Figure 7–2) with the first three words from the writing frame. Then she copies words, all of which are pertinent to the investigation. She then writes "34 timd [times]" in the blank part of the frame, which indicates that she seems to know that thirty-four is the important number.

In giving Kristine feedback about the strengths, you would read the entry with her, pointing out the strengths just noted, including how important it is that she reported the "34 timd [times]," just as scientists report the important results of their tests.

After noting the strengths, you would ask Kristine to read the words for the complete first sentence with you: "I think snails crawl more on sandpaper." Then you would write those words on a sticky note so she could copy the sentence into her notebook. Having her read the words on the note with you is important support. Like many students who are learning English, Kristine is very good at copying the words but does not yet recognize and read the words fluently and with understanding.

Notebook Entry: Jamie

In her entry (Figure 7–3), Jamie completes the writing frame completely and accurately. She speaks another language at home, but her English skills already are quite developed. The more open frame for the second sentence ("I think this because") enables her to include more independent thinking and writing because of her language skills. She includes the data

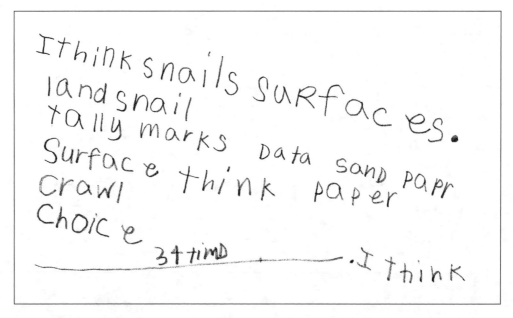

FIGURE 7–2 *Kristine's entry*

Writing in Science in Action

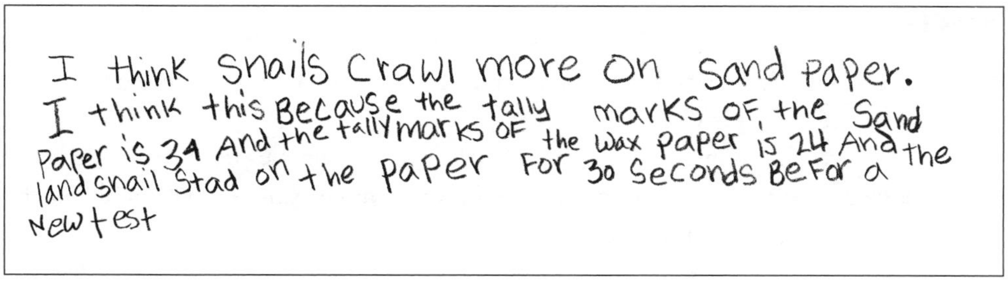

> I think snails crawl more on sand paper.
> I think this because the tally marks of the sand
> paper is 34 And the tally marks of the wax paper is 24 And the
> land snail stad on the paper for 30 seconds befor a the
> new test

FIGURE 7–3 *Jamie's entry*

for *both* surfaces, which is not structured into the frame and which is unusual for elementary students of all ages to think of doing. The writing frame that the teacher provides gives students scaffolding for their response while also allowing them to express their scientific thinking more independently if they have more developed skills. This is the ideal kind of frame.

Jamie also adds to her entry something about the students' fair test, which is not in the frame: "And the land snail stad [stayed] on the paper for 30 seconds befor a new test." This might be her way of saying, "We conducted our test fairly, which is another reason I think our evidence is accurate and that more snails actually did go on the sandpaper."

When talking with Jamie about her entry, first have her either read it to you or with you, then give her feedback about the strengths in her entry. She reports the wrong data for the wax paper (twenty-four instead of twenty-nine), which she might realize when she rereads what she has written. If she does not, you could say, "Another scientist might wonder about the data you have reported. What do you notice about your numbers here?" Jamie probably will recognize the error.

Other Highlights from the Video Episode

When the teacher does a shared-writing minilesson in this video episode, the following is the writing structure she provides for her students: "I think snails crawl on _____." After they finish their shared writing, the teacher removes that writing and replaces it with this writing frame: "I think snails crawl more on _____."

Normally, you would use the same frame for independent writing that you do in the shared writing. But the second version actually is a better frame because it makes the students think about, and include, their data: Which of the surfaces did their snail crawl on *more* times? The writing frame thus teaches the students a critical practice in scientific thinking and writing: to provide evidence to support statements or claims. Even kindergartners who are learning English can learn this scientific practice.

Related Material

Chapters

- Chapter 5: "Scientific Investigations and Supporting Claims with Evidence"
- Chapter 8: "Meaningful Assessment and Effective Feedback"
- Chapter 12: "Emergent Writing"

Website

■ Student Notebook Entries, Pre-kindergarten Through Fifth Grade: *Because* and *I Think This Because*; Scientific Conclusions
  • Read examples from your own grade level as well as samples from the grade levels above so you can see how the writing becomes more complex but builds on the foundations laid in kindergarten.

■ Stories from Schools
  • "Reflections and Suggestions from a Science Coach"
  • "Young Students' Science Writing: Raising the Bar"

■ Background Information About the Video Episodes: Animals

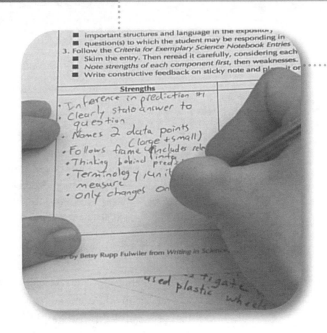

CHAPTER 8

Meaningful Assessment and Effective Feedback

This chapter provides some guidelines and strategies for assessing your students' notebook entries formatively so that you can determine what your students know and are able to do, and what you need to do in your instruction to take them all to the next level. The process also involves sharing specific, positive feedback with students that is effective because it motivates and guides them in further developing their content understanding, and scientific thinking and skills.

From the very beginning of developing this approach to science writing, several principles have guided how teachers assess science notebook entries and provide feedback to their students:

1. Teachers do not score or grade students' entries in their notebooks.

2. When they provide written or oral feedback to students, they always begin by describing specific strengths in terms of scientific criteria (the Three Key Elements) rather than making superficial evaluative statements such as "Good work!" or by focusing on weaknesses.

3. If they find weaknesses in an entry they are assessing, teachers address them in their feedback to students through questions another scientist might ask ("A scientist might wonder . . . How do you think you could make this part easier for him to understand?") rather than making evaluative or judgmental statements ("But you didn't . . .").

4. Teachers conduct informal assessments on a regular basis by quickly reading student notebook entries while students are writing. Teachers provide oral, positive feedback and ask scientists' questions during these times.

5. Teachers look carefully at students' notebooks, assessing them in terms of the Three Key Elements and providing written feedback to students, three or four times in the course of a science unit. They then use what they learn from their assessments to inform further instruction both for individual students and for the class as a whole.

This assessment process is *formative* in that it is done throughout the unit and thus continually informs the teacher's instruction. In contrast, *summative* assessment, which usually comes at the end of a unit, cannot affect instruction or further learning for those students in that unit of study.

Extensive research supports these principles of assessment.

> Research studies have shown that, if pupils are given only marks or grades, they do not benefit from the feedback. . . . Feedback has been shown to improve learning when it gives each pupil specific guidance on strengths and weaknesses, preferably without any overall marks. Thus the way in which test results are reported to pupils so that they can identify their own strengths and weaknesses is critical. Pupils must be given the means and opportunities to work with evidence of their difficulties. For formative purposes, a test at the end of a unit or teaching module is pointless; it is too late to work with the results. We conclude that the feedback on tests, seatwork, and homework should give each pupil guidance on how to improve, and each pupil must be given help and an opportunity to work on the improvement. (Black and Wiliam 1998, 8)

This approach to science writing has produced very positive outcomes for students who typically do not meet state standards, such as those who are learning English or who have special needs (Stokes, Hirabayashi, and Ramage 2003, ii). Such students benefit not only from the scaffolding and modeling that are a major feature of this instruction but also from formative assessment and unscored, positive, constructive feedback, both of which, research has shown, can increase self-esteem and motivation.

> Perhaps the most significant finding from the research is that the practice of formative assessment benefits all students, but the increase in levels of achievement is particularly marked for lower achieving students. Thus the effect is to decrease the gap between the more and less well achieving students. This contrasts with the evidence of the impact of [high-stakes] tests, which favour the higher achieving students and create a downward spiral for the lower achieving students, whose constant failure leads to loss of self-esteem and effort. (Harlen 2004, 9)

Unfortunately, many teachers do not use these practices. In a study of secondary teachers' science assessment practices with science notebooks, researchers explained what they called a "troublesome finding":

> [T]he majority of teachers' feedback practice is not aligned with the recommendations on effective feedback by researchers. Instead of providing descriptive and prescriptive information, teachers often offered to their students evaluative information either as quantity of work (e.g., "more examples") or the general level of understanding (e.g., "wow," "unclear!," a smiling face, or a question mark) as 20.34% and 40.4%, respectively. Therefore, it is not a surprise that due to the lack of information on what can be done next, few students were able to take advantage of teacher comments to modify their work. (Li et al. 2010, 15)

The strategies in this chapter will help you provide two types of effective feedback:

■ *descriptive feedback*, in which you explain the strengths and ask questions about weaknesses in an entry; and

■ *prescriptive feedback*, in which you provide suggestions and support, either individually or through whole-class instruction, for how students can improve their thinking and skills.

Although in this program we do not grade or score notebook entries, teachers often are held accountable for providing science grades in progress reports. Suggestions for determining those grades are included at the end of the chapter.

Strategies for Your Classroom

The next sections will give you some guidelines for formally and informally assessing science notebook entries and providing effective feedback. When you *formally* assess notebook entries or other science writing, you need to look carefully at students' work following an assessment process (see below), so you do this assessment during your time away from students. When you *informally* assess students' entries, you move around the classroom, checking in with students as they write in their notebooks, getting a sense of what they are writing and giving them positive, effective feedback as described in this chapter.

Strategies for Formal Assessment

■ Look briefly at each entry in the notebook prior to the entry you are assessing to give you a general idea of the quality of the student's entries.

■ Focus your assessment of the notebook entry on the Three Key Elements, asking yourself, What does the entry tell another scientist about the student's:

1. Understanding of the *science concepts* in the unit?

2. Ability to *think scientifically*?

3. Ability to use *scientific skills*?

■ In Checklists for Exemplary Notebook Entries (provided at www.heinemann.com/wisia, and in earlier chapters), select the checklist for the type of entry you are assessing and use it as you do the following:

• Skim the entry. Then reread it carefully, considering each of the characteristics. Do not assess other criteria, such as grammar, spelling, voice, sentence fluency, or neatness (unless the entry is too illegible to read). Notebook entries are rough drafts.

• *Note strengths of each component first*, then weaknesses. Identify any issues that you think will require further instruction for the student or class.

• On a sticky note, write constructive feedback to address strengths. To address a weakness, write a question that a scientist might have about the entry. Place the note on the entry. You will refer to the note during a conference with the student, or the student will read the note and revise or add to her entry in answering the scientist's question. You will read the revised entry later on.

■ One reality of the assessment and feedback process is that if you try to assess all of each student's entries, you will have to resort to the most superficial of feedback responses (for example, writing "Good job!" or "Great!" or adding smiling faces or stickers). You do need to check in with students during science investigations and independent writing times to be sure that each student is writing an entry, and to monitor progress and provide support. But you cannot fully assess and provide feedback for every entry. Instead, you should plan to do that for only three or four entries in the course of a unit, depending on the grade level.

- In many units, you will see that certain concepts and skills are developed through several successive lessons. For example, in a unit about sound, students might do three or four lessons in which they explore the effect of the length of an object on its pitch. You would assess the notebook entry and provide feedback after the last lesson. Later, students might do several investigations to explore the effect of string tension on pitch and vibration. At the end of that series of investigations, you again would assess your students' entries and provide meaningful feedback.

- In some units, students plan and conduct a controlled investigation in which they must collect data over a period of time. You can assess their growth in conceptual understanding and scientific thinking, and their ability to express their understanding and thinking, by critiquing their prediction and then their conclusion a number of weeks later.

- At the beginning of some science units, students write an entry that you can assess and save as a pre-assessment of what they know at the beginning of the unit. At the end of the unit, students make another entry that you assess and use as a post-assessment or summative assessment of what they have learned during the unit. (If the unit does not have these assessments, you can develop them yourself.) This will give you an opportunity to get an overall picture of what each student has learned. Teachers often use these when writing progress reports, as described later in this chapter.

Strategies for Providing Effective Feedback

- After you have assessed an entry, provide feedback that describes three things about the entry, in this order:

  1. The *strengths* of the entry in terms of the Three Key Elements.

  2. The *weaknesses* framed as queries that a scientist might have about parts of the entry that are missing, inaccurate, or unclear.

  3. *Something the student can do differently* the next time he writes this type of entry. For example, you might say, "Next time, you can check off each property in your data table after you write about it." This prescriptive feedback often is given as verbal feedback and frequently is part of the further instruction that you provide for the whole class.

- In your feedback, do not use the word *but*. For example, you might say or write, "This is a strong conclusion because you accurately answer the question and you support your answer with accurate evidence. *But* you don't include evidence from the other part of the manipulated variable." Using the word *but* undermines the effect of your first positive statements and does little to motivate the student to improve future entries. In contrast, you could say or write it this way: "This is a strong conclusion because you accurately answer the question and you support your answer with accurate evidence. Another scientist might wonder what your data are for the other part of the manipulated variable. What would you tell her?" This kind of feedback is much more positive and engaging.

- As an extension of this idea, keep your use of *I* and *me* to a minimum. Teachers typically say things such as, "I noticed" or "Tell me" or "I really liked the way . . ." The more you create this typical teacher-student interaction, the more you undermine the motivating effect of having scientists as the audience and scientific practices as the guidelines for the students' work.

- The list in Figure 8–1 provides a variety of questions that you can ask students when you notice that something in an entry is unclear, missing, inaccurate, unnecessary, or inappropriate (for example, a personal feeling or opinion). Using this method to address weaknesses in a notebook entry instructs students without making them feel as if they have not measured up to some standard—an all-too-common and unnecessary experience for many. This positive approach not only increases students' confidence and motivation, but also improves their ability to communicate with an audience outside the classroom.

Strategies for Informal Assessment and Feedback

You can learn a great deal about individual students and the class as a whole just by informally checking in with students during every science investigation and independent writing time.

- Ask questions to probe students' understanding and thinking, and observe and give instruction as needed about scientific skills (for example, using a measuring tool such as a thermometer or measuring tape, or conducting a controlled investigation).

- Some teachers have a pad of sticky notes on a clipboard, and when they observe something they want to remember when they are working with a student, they quickly write a note. In their planning book or grade book, they have a sheet of paper for each student. At the end of the day, they place each dated note on the appropriate student page. These anecdotal records are useful in planning instruction, writing narratives for progress reports or report cards, and planning conferences with specialists and parents or guardians.

- Many teachers (especially primary teachers) have students keep their notebooks open after they finish writing their entry for the day. The teachers then close each notebook after they read or at least scan the entry to get an idea of how the student is doing. Keeping the notebooks open ensures that the teachers remember to glance at each child's notebook to be sure everyone is writing. This system keeps the students accountable and saves teachers from discovering missing entries when they sit down to assess them. Scanning the students' entries like this also is helpful because it gives teachers an idea of what they need to do next with their instruction as well as what kind of individual support each student needs.

Strategies for Teacher–Student Conferences

- Many teachers who use this science-writing approach have one-on-one conferences during independent working times. No one has more than two of these formal

Questions to Ask Students
About Notebook Entries

Another scientist/researcher/physicist/biologist/botanist/geologist/ meteorologist/ engineer might wonder/need to know/question . . .

In a laboratory/out in the field, a scientist might wonder/need to know/question . . .

- ☐ *What did you actually observe? (i.e., What did you actually see rather than infer?)*

- ☐ *What are the important details that other scientists would need to know? Did you include all of them?*

- ☐ *Have you recorded/reported the observations/data/test results/evidence accurately and honestly?*

- ☐ *Does what you have written agree with the observations/data you recorded in your notes/data table/graph?*

- ☐ *What did you observe that makes you think that?*

- ☐ *What evidence do you have to support your idea/thinking?*

- ☐ *Do your test results support your prediction? If not, how has your thinking changed because of your test results?*

- ☐ *How is what you have reported similar to/different from . . . ?*

- ☐ *How could you explain your thinking/results in a different way?*

- ☐ *What do you think could have happened during the investigation to cause those inconsistent/inconclusive data? (i.e., Which variable or variables might not have been kept the same/controlled? Which part of the test might not have been fair/controlled?)*

- ☐ *What question would you like to investigate next?*

Scientists reread their entries to be sure everything they have written is clear, accurate, and honest.

- ☐ *When you reread your entry, what (if anything) do you need to add/change to make this entry more clear and/or accurate?*

FIGURE 8–1 *Questions to Ask Students About Notebook Entries* conferences with each student during a science unit. In the intermediate grades, teachers might meet with each student once, and then meet more often with students who need more support.

■ Teachers of younger students have fewer, if any, of these longer conferences during independent working times because the students need more supervision but they do meet informally more often with individual students during the writing session because it takes less time to read an entry and discuss it with a child. On average, kindergarten and first-grade teachers are able to meet informally with each child during the science sessions or independent writing times once each week (if they teach science four or five times a week) or at least once every two weeks (if they teach science two or three times a week).

Strategies for Summative Assessment and Progress Reports

As noted earlier, in this science-writing approach, teachers do not put any scores or grades on their students' notebook entries. However, in most districts, as in Seattle Public Schools, teachers are required to report scores or grades at the end of reporting periods. The following strategies can help you produce grades from summative assessment (typically given at the end of a unit) while still using formative assessment (done throughout the unit) and positive, unscored feedback with your students.

■ Ideally, if a science unit has a pre-assessment and a post-assessment, you can assess and grade them, record the scores, and factor them into the overall scores or grades for progress reports or report cards. But have students do these assessments on separate sheets of paper so that they are not part of the science notebook, which is not graded or scored. Keep these assessments in a separate file or portfolio, or in some other assessment system.

■ Many teachers do not share the scores on these assessments with their students (because of what research shows about sharing scores), but do share positive, constructive feedback with them. Teachers also might assess specific notebook entries during the unit to evaluate students' understanding of certain concepts being developed through a number of lessons (as noted in the previous sections). If teachers are going to score these assessments, they have students perform them also outside the notebook.

■ When it is time to complete a progress report for each student, consider a student's scores from mid-unit and end-of-unit assessments you have done of students' work and any anecdotal notes you have recorded on sticky notes. Refer to the student's science notebook to get a better sense of how the student is doing in terms of the Three Key Elements. Also, consider your observations during science investigations and independent writing times. This, as one master teacher puts it, "is in my brain" rather than written down, but is factored into the overall assessment.

■ For your summative assessment of their work, young students can write only a limited amount, but this gives their teachers some sense of what they can do and understand. To get a better picture of some students' understanding, teachers will need to talk with those students.

■ When preparing for a conference with a student's parent or guardian, look through the student's science notebook and place sticky notes on entries that show growth in understanding and skills as well as areas in which the student needs to work on developing his skills or understanding of concepts. You also can have students place a sticky note on an entry that they want you to share in a conference. Have them tell you, or write, why they think the entry is strong. Teachers report that sharing these notebook entries that you and the student have selected often is a particularly meaningful part of the conferences, not only because the parents and guardians are so impressed with what their children are able to write in their notebooks about their scientific thinking and understanding, but also because the level of sophistication is greater than the parents or guardians have seen before or expected to see.

Sample Notebook Entries

Notebook Entry: Kimberly

Even a high-achieving child needs formative assessment and specific feedback so she can move along a developmental continuum. Figure 8–2 shows the way that many teachers might give feedback on an assessment. About halfway through a unit on land and water, fifth graders in Seattle Public Schools write a response to the question that Kimberly has written at the beginning of her entry. Teachers assess these entries to determine what their students understand so far in the unit about the effect of water flow on erosion and deposition. Teachers use the results to plan further instruction and give students feedback that will help them move to higher levels in their conceptual understanding, scientific thinking, and scientific skills.

As you look at the score (4/4) and feedback the teacher has given Kimberly, think about whether they will help Kimberly improve her scientific thinking and conceptual understanding. How would you improve the feedback?

Kimberly was very excited that she had received the highest score possible, but she could not say specifically *why* she thought the entry deserved the score. All that she noticed when she reread the entry on her own was that she had not identified the antecedents for "it." She is a strong student who is accustomed to getting exemplary scores and wants to be a conservation zoologist when she grows up.

Although the teacher has underlined key phrases that do indicate conceptual understanding, she does not write any comments that would communicate that to her student. "Good start!" is an accurate comment in that Kimberly does answer the question in a general way, but comments like this are not specific enough for Kimberly to understand what characteristics of the beginning of the entry indicate this "good start." The feedback would be more effective if it were something like the following: "This is a strong entry because you begin by answering the question in a general way. Then you provide evidence for what happened to the land with both slow- and fast-moving water. A scientist might ask what evidence you have of erosion and what you mean when you use the word *it*." This alternative feedback provides meaningful comments that identify the strengths of the entry and then poses a scientist's questions that would have Kimberly address explicitly the effects of water speed on erosion and the antecedents for each *it*.

While the score on her entry does not diminish Kimberly's self-esteem (as scores typically do with students who have less developed skills), the teacher's feedback does not help Kimberly further develop her proficiency in scientific thinking and writing. This is no

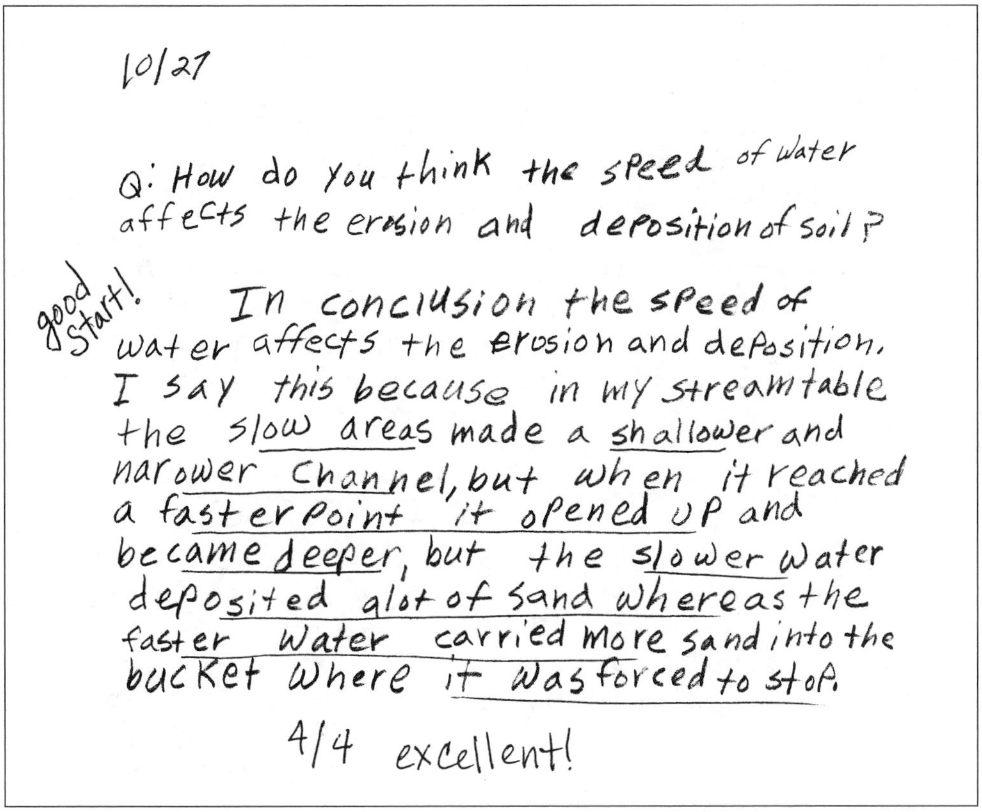

10/27

Q: How do you think the speed of water
affects the erosion and deposition of soil?

good Start!   In conclusion the speed of
water affects the erosion and deposition.
I say this because in my streamtable
the slow areas made a shallower and
narower channel, but when it reached
a faster point it opened up and
became deeper, but the slower water
deposited alot of sand whereas the
faster water carried more sand into the
bucket where it was forced to stop.
4/4 excellent!

FIGURE 8–2 *Kimberly's entry*

less an omission with students who have strong academic skills than it is with students who
have less developed skills.

Notebook Entry: Aneke

Aneke's entry in Figure 8–3 includes an example of a fourth-grade teacher's written feedback. The class is studying ecosystems, and in this entry, students are supposed to write
about what they think would happen to their ecosystem if the plants died, and then answer
the same question about the effect of not having snails and cloudfish in the ecosystem. In
the original entry (before Aneke revises it), she accurately states *what* would happen, but
she does not explain her reasoning for *why* she thinks this would happen except to say that
the organisms are interdependent.

In her comments, Aneke's teacher (who provides feedback like this to each student four
or five times during every unit) points out the strength of Aneke's initial answers and then
notes that Aneke needs to "explain *how* these plants and animals are interdependent!" Both
comments communicate important points, although the teacher recognized when she later
reread her note that by using *but*, she diminished the impact of her first, positive statement.

After Aneke reads her teacher's comment, she and the teacher talk about how to use
asterisks and arrows so she can add more to her entry. In the revised response, Aneke shows
that she understands the science concepts and how to be more specific in communicating
her thinking about cause-and-effect relationships. This is important for all her classmates
to know and could be part of a class discussion and a writing minilesson as the class con-
tinues to explore relationships in their ecosystems.

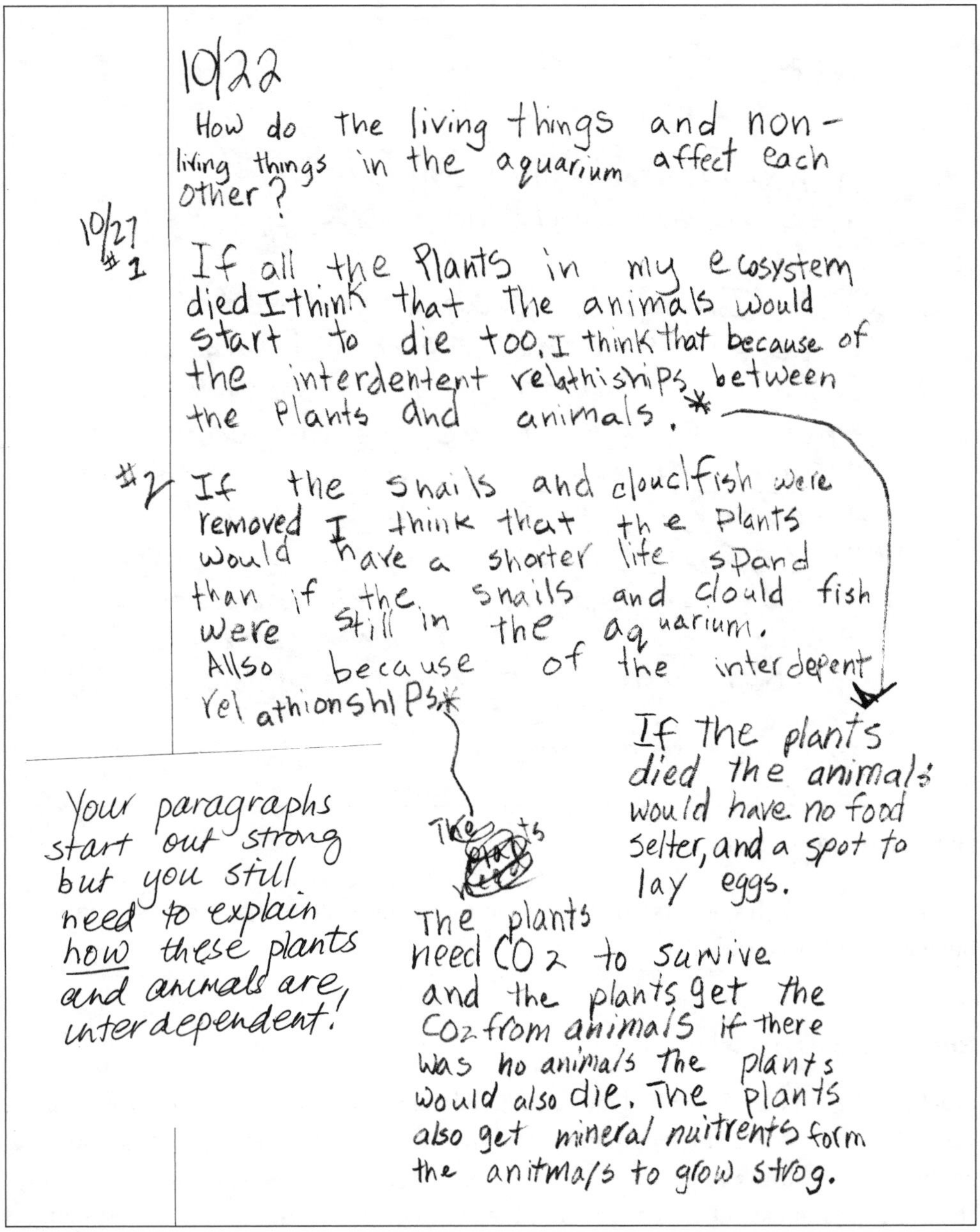

10/22
How do the living things and non-living things in the aquarium affect each other?

10/27
#1 If all the Plants in my ecosystem died I think that the animals would start to die too, I think that because of the interdentent relathiships between the plants and animals.*

#2 If the snails and cloudfish were removed I think that the plants would have a shorter life spand than if the snails and clould fish were still in the aquarium. Allso because of the interdepent relathionships*

If the plants died, the animals would have no food selter, and a spot to lay eggs.

The plants need CO_2 to survive and the plants get the CO_2 from animals if there was no animals the plants would also die. The plants also get mineral nuitrents form the anitmals to grow strog.

Your paragraphs start out strong but you still need to explain how these plants and animals are interdependent!

FIGURE 8–3 *Aneke's entry*

Aneke's example illustrates how a student can revise and improve an entry in response to her teacher's feedback. However, all our teachers say it is hard to consistently follow up with a student to see if she revises the entry at all, let alone effectively revises it. You can keep track of these revisions by having students leave their notebooks open until you have looked at them, as mentioned earlier. Or, some teachers make notes on a clipboard to remind themselves to follow up with individual students.

Notebook Entry: Thien

Thien, who wrote the entry in Figure 8–4, is in a classroom of high-functioning students with autism. The class has been investigating what effect wheel size has on the distance a

The larger wheel goes the farthests. The data shows that the 7.5 cm wheels make the go-cart travel 144 cm. The 11.5 cm wheel went 149 cm. In fact, the large wheel went 5 cm futher. Therefore, the smaller the wheels, the shorter the distant the go-cart travel. My prediction was right because the large wheel went futher than the small wheel but medium wheel went the furthest. Now I think the large wheel went the farthest because the shape was bigger. My test results were inconsistent because the medium wheel went the furthest. It went 206 cm. I think this happened because I put to many rubber bands. Now I want to investigatate what would happened if I rounded out more.

FIGURE 8–4 *Thien's entry*

go-cart can travel. After the investigation and reflective discussion, the students use a handout (such as the one in Figure 6–2 in Chapter 6) that guides them, step by step, through the writing of a complex conclusion that has seven parts. (In "Benefits of Modeling and Scaffolding for Students with Special Needs" in Chapter 2, Thien's teacher, Shelly Hurley, describes how she used this handout with her students.)

On the whole, this is a good conclusion that indicates that Thien has developed strong scientific skills in terms of conducting a controlled investigation and understanding controlled variables. He understands the outcome of the investigation and has used logical reasoning in trying to make sense of why the large wheel makes the go-cart travel a longer distance than the small wheel does. As with most students at this point in their conceptual development, he needs more concrete experiences and discussions in order to understand that the circumference of the wheels is affecting the distance the go-carts travel. In terms of his writing, the modeling and scaffolding that his teacher has provided have supported him in successfully writing a complex scientific conclusion.

In talking with Thien about his conclusion, you would point out these strengths. Then you could show him the measuring tool he used in the investigation and ask him if he thinks five centimeters is that great a difference. Modeling new thinking by using concrete materials is important with all students and essential with students who have special needs. Having the tool right there helps students connect with their concrete experiences—in this case, making sense of measuring the distances in metric units.

As a general practice in this science-writing approach, teachers address weaknesses and ask questions about an entry in terms of queries that a scientist might make. But the idea of a person outside the classroom asking questions can be too abstract for students with autism, who usually relate better to questions that are close to their immediate, concrete experiences. So asking Thien what *he* thinks about the five-centimeter distance is a more effective strategy in this case.

Partway through his conclusion, Thien states that his prediction was correct, which it was because he predicted the large wheel "goes the farthest." But his data do not support his prediction or his answer to the investigative question because in his trials, the medium wheel made the go-cart go the longer distances. So his "My prediction was right" sentence is not accurate. However, as his teacher said, "In his world, the large wheel did go farther than the small wheel. It doesn't matter to him that the medium wheel went farther than either of them because we were only talking about this small wheel and this large wheel, and his statement is true for those wheels." So asking questions about the medium wheel would not be productive in this case. It would be better to spend time using concrete materials, the wheels, as you talk together about his changing ideas and his skills as a scientist.

Related Material

Chapters

- Chapter 1: "Overview"
- Chapter 9: "Group Critiquing and Teacher-Student Conferences"

Website

- Checklists for Exemplary Notebook Entries

Group Critiquing and Teacher-Student Conferences

 ASSESSMENT VIDEO EPISODES

The video episodes in this chapter feature groups of teachers who meet about once a month throughout the school year. The purpose of the meetings is for teachers who highly value science and science writing to assess some of their students' notebook entries together and to discuss further instruction. Each of these science-writing reflection groups is made up of participants who are teaching the same inquiry-based science units at the same grade level. (The teachers are paid a nominal sum and receive professional development credits for their participation.)

VIDEO EPISODE: ASSESSMENT 1

Before You Watch

In the Assessment 1 Video Episode, teachers are critiquing basic conclusions from the same *Soils* unit lesson that was featured in an earlier video episode (see Chapter 2). One of the main *science concepts* in this unit is that soil components—sand, clay, and humus—have distinctive properties. By using *scientific skills* in making observations and conducting specific tests, students can determine the properties of the soil components. Knowing these properties, and then conducting tests and using *scientific thinking*, students can identify each soil component when it is in a mixture of soil components.

Before you watch the video episode, read Gavin's data table and conclusion (Figures 9–3 and 9–4 at the end of this chapter). This is the first sample the teachers are critiquing in the video episode. Write some notes about what you notice about his entry just as if you were assessing your own student's work. Then skim the other entries from this episode, by Tajinai and Dorothy (Figures 9–5 through 9–8 at the end of this chapter), as well as the tools for the group meetings (Figures 9–1 and 9–2 in the "After You Watch" section that follows).

Note that in the course of developing the materials for this book and the website, we have revised some of the forms shown in the video episodes. The main difference is that we now refer to the Three Key Elements of this science-writing approach (science concepts, scientific thinking, and scientific skills) instead of the Big Four components, which included expository writing. As discussed in Chapter 1, the traits of expository writing that we are targeting (idea or content, organization, and word choice) are too integrally connected with communicating about science concepts and scientific thinking to assess them as a discrete element. So when the facilitators in the video episodes refer to The Big Four, think about the Three Key Elements.

While You Watch

As you watch this video episode, consider the following questions:

1. How is the way the teachers assessed the first entry (Gavin's) similar to and different from the way you assessed his entry?

2. How is the teacher-student conference similar to and different from the way you talk with your students about their notebook entries?

3. In what ways do you think the guidelines or protocols are affecting the teachers' assessment of these entries?

After You Watch

In this videotaped meeting, the teachers spend more time on the first entry than they normally do. But the way they discuss the entry is typical of how the group assessment process works in this science-writing approach. The process is scaffolded by three group-meeting assessment tools: group-meeting guidelines, a general form for assessing entries and planning instruction, and the checklist for the appropriate type of notebook entry.

Group-Meeting Guidelines

The meeting guidelines shown in Figure 9–1 are essential when teachers work together to assess science notebook entries and talk about further instruction. One of the group members acts as a facilitator, following the guidelines or protocol. This scaffolding helps everyone focus effectively and productively on the assessment. Of particular importance is the emphasis on:

■ *strengths* in the students' work,

■ the *Three Key Elements*, and

■ having the *students' work stand on its own* without their teacher's explaining anything about the student or the entry. The group critiques each entry without preconceived

Group–Meeting Guidelines for
Assessing Notebook Entries

The facilitator's role is to ensure that the guidelines are followed.

1. **Consider the specific concepts, scientific thinking, and scientific skills that pertain to the selected lesson and entry.**

2. **From the Checklists for Exemplary Notebook Entries (on the website and in earlier chapters), choose and briefly go over the appropriate checklist for the type of entry you are assessing.**

3. **Silently, and fairly quickly, read through the first student sample without looking for anything in particular.**
   - *The teacher who provides the sample should* not *explain anything about the student or the entry.*

4. **Read the entry again, focusing on only the strengths in terms of the characteristics from the checklist.**

5. **Discuss the *strengths* of the sample.**
   - *Do not mention any weaknesses.*
   - *Do not discuss any other criteria (e.g., spelling, grammar, neatness).*
   - *List the strengths on the Assessing Notebook Entries and Planning Instruction form (Figure 9–2). All teachers can do this, or one teacher can volunteer to record these notes for the teacher whose student's entry is being assessed.*

6. **Discuss the *weaknesses* of the sample in terms of the characteristics from the checklist.**
   - *List the weaknesses on the assessment sheet.*

7. **Discuss and plan further instruction and feedback that could build on the strengths and improve the weaknesses.**
   - *Make notes on the form regarding further instruction. (All teachers might want to take notes as this discussion can impact their own future instruction as well.)*

8. **Give a completed form to the teacher whose student's entry was assessed.**

FIGURE 9–1   *Group-Meeting Guidelines for Assessing Notebook Entries*

Assessing Notebook Entries and Planning Instruction

1. **Look briefly at each entry in the notebook prior to the entry you are assessing to give you a general idea of the quality of the student's entries.**
2. **Focus your assessment of the selected entry on the Three Key Elements, asking yourself, What does the entry tell another scientist about the student's:**
   - ☐ *Understanding of science concepts in the unit?*
   - ☐ *Ability to think scientifically?*
   - ☐ *Ability to use scientific skills?*
3. **Follow the appropriate checklist from the Exemplary Notebook Entries (provided on the website and in earlier chapters) for the type of entry you are assessing as you do the following:**
   - ☐ *Skim the entry. Then reread it carefully, considering each of the characteristics. (Do not consider other criteria such as grammar, spelling, voice, sentence fluency, or neatness.)*
   - ☐ *Note strengths of each component first, then weaknesses. Determine further instruction for the student or class.*
   - ☐ *On a sticky note, write constructive feedback to address weaknesses. To address a weakness, write a question that a scientist might have about the entry. Place the note on the entry.*

Strengths	Weaknesses	Further Instruction

This is a revised version of a chart featured in *Writing in Science*.

FIGURE 9–2 *Assessing Notebook Entries and Planning Instruction* notions about the student's abilities. As a result, often they notice aspects of an entry, particularly strengths, that the student's teacher has not noticed.

Form for Assessing Notebook Entries and Planning Instruction

Whether you are assessing notebook entries alone or in a group, the guidelines in the form shown in Figure 9–2 can help you focus your assessment of any type of notebook entry. (You also will use a specific checklist for assessing each type of entry.) Even teachers who are experienced in this science-writing approach follow the guidelines and checklists because they help them stay focused on the critical things to consider in an entry.

Checklist

The third form used in assessing notebook entries is the checklist showing the exemplary characteristics of the appropriate type of entry. In this video episode, the teachers are assessing a conclusion using the checklist shown in Figure 6–3 in Chapter 6 and the paragraph about the Three Key Elements that precedes the checklist.

Sample Notebook Entries from the Assessment 1 Video Episode

Notebook Entry: Gavin

The teachers begin by critiquing Gavin's data table and conclusion (Figures 9–3 and 9–4). His conclusion for the investigation is:

> I thik [think] the locol soil has clay and humus I pirtic [predict] that bucus [because] I tred [tried] to roll it into a ball I cold [could] but abut [about] 10 segnts [seconds] later it bork [broke] so that how I now [know] it is clay and humus My settling test the dint [they didn't] look like clay at oll [all]. But at the beging [beginning] it looked like clay

Gavin is communicating both scientific thinking and understanding of science concepts in his conclusion. In talking with him after assessing his entry, you would focus on specific strengths in the entry (as the teachers mentioned in the video episode). Then you could say, "Another scientist might wonder what you observed about the soil in the water that made you think it had the properties of clay at first, but not later on." He then could share his observations and scientific thinking with you. If he has the time and energy for writing more in his entry, he could add information. Otherwise, he could dictate his thinking to you and you could put a sticky note with his comments on his entry.

This student receives special education services and has an Individual Education Plan (I.E.P.) in writing. What contributions did the focus on *science content* and *scientific thinking* and *skills* make to the assessment of this student's work? What might the teachers have focused on without this framework?

Notebook Entry: Tajinai

When Tajinai finished writing her conclusion (shown in Figures 9–6a through 9–6c at the end of the chapter) during the independent writing time, she left her notebook open so that her teacher could check it as he moved from desk to desk. When he read Tajinai's entry, he noticed that before her concluding statement, she had not completed her writing about the smear test. So he asked her some questions to elicit the rest of the evidence from her, and then showed her how to use an asterisk so she could complete her entry below her concluding statement. (He mentions this to her during their conference in the video episode.)

This is a good example of informal formative assessment and differentiated instruction, because the teacher has seen that she has left out some additional information and Tajinai has demonstrated that she can write at this level. Other students in the class have not yet progressed this far on the writing-development continuum. So the teacher expects some of them to focus on writing about the results of only one test but encourages Tajinai to increase the complexity of information she includes in her entry. He supports all the students in ways that challenge them but do not make them feel frustrated or overwhelmed.

Notebook Entry: Dorothy

The teachers briefly assess Dorothy's entry at the end of the meeting. As is the case with many students who have strong thinking and writing skills, her conclusion is detailed and accurate. In talking with Dorothy, you would point out the strengths in her data table and her conclusion (Figures 9–7a through 9–8). Then you would ask a question that helps her realize that she has included details in her conclusion that she did not record in her data table. To address this, you could say, "Another scientist might ask you to support the statements you have made in your conclusion with test results from your data table. Can you match up each of your statements with data from the table?" It will become clear to her that even though her conclusion has accurate evidence, it is not the evidence she has recorded. You then would talk about including more details in her notes as she makes her observations.

Dorothy also might benefit from using the strategy of checking off each detail of the evidence as she includes it in her conclusion in order to focus her on her recorded data. Students like this, who have strong academic skills, benefit from learning skills for organizing all their data and scientific thinking.

VIDEO EPISODE: ASSESSMENT 2

Before You Watch

In the Assessment 2 Video Episode, the science-writing reflection group is assessing entries from the go-carts investigation featured in the Go-Carts Video Episode (see Chapter 6). Students have been working with small model go-carts and have conducted an investigation of this question: "What is the effect of wheel size on the distance a go-cart can travel?" Students have been testing go-carts with three different sizes of wheels and have measured and recorded the distance the go-carts travel.

In their conclusion, students need to answer the question (for example, "Larger wheels make the go-cart travel farther than smaller wheels do."). Then for evidence, they need to report the distance traveled for the largest and the smallest wheels. This is much easier thinking and writing than what students need to do in the first two parts of the basic conclusion for the soils investigation, which requires interpreting and reporting qualitative (unmeasured) data from multiple tests.

However, the science concepts and scientific thinking in this investigation are much more complex than those in the soils investigation. After finishing the basic conclusion in number 4 of the checklist for Characteristics of an Exemplary Basic or Complex Conclusion (Figure 6–3), the students must then communicate about their metacognitive development—the ways their thinking has changed since they made their prediction and conducted the investigation. To do this requires them to revise (if necessary) and communicate their hypothesis—the reason *why* they think the larger wheel made the go-cart go farther. Note that the checklist for a complex conclusion now has seven points instead of the eight shown in the video episode (two were combined to simplify the form). The handout the students use as scaffolding for their writing is included and discussed in Chapter 6.

Assessing these conclusions takes time, but they are summative, coming at the end of a series of investigations, and reveal a great deal about students' understanding of science concepts and their ability to think scientifically and use scientific skills.

Before watching the episode, read Austin's entry (Figures 9–9 and 9–10 at the end of the chapter) and assess it by using the assessment tools shown earlier in the chapter. If possible, go through the process with a small group of teachers so you can get a sense of how to critique entries in this way with your colleagues.

To assess this entry, you need some background about the science content the students are learning in this investigation:

- Larger wheels make the go-cart travel farther than smaller wheels do. This happens because larger wheels have a larger circumference than smaller wheels do, so every time a wheel makes one complete revolution on its axle, the larger wheel makes the go-cart go farther than the smaller wheel can with one revolution.

- The smaller wheels *spin* faster than larger wheels do, so students may think that go-carts travel *faster* with smaller wheels. But students are testing distance, not speed. Teachers often have to ask students to clarify their statements about speed and distance.

While You Watch

Think about the following questions as you watch the episode:

1. How is the teachers' discussion in this episode similar to and different from the first group's discussion?

2. How might this discussion affect Austin's teacher's conference with Austin as well as each teacher's whole-class instruction?

After You Watch

This group has a much longer discussion of the entry than they normally have, partly because of the videotaping. But the complexity of the science concepts and thinking also warrants a more in-depth discussion. This group meeting thus underscores the importance of:

- understanding the science content in a lesson;

- thinking deeply about students' misconceptions and what might be causing them; and

- developing ways to help students construct deeper understanding through concrete experiences and discussion.

When the teachers are discussing the entry, they focus on the students' *thinking* and *concepts* because the problems that their students are having at this point in the unit are related to their reasoning and their depth of conceptual understanding. Note that one of the teachers mentions that if this one student is having problems with his thinking and understanding, other students probably are confused as well, which means that the whole class would benefit from more concrete experiences and discussions. The facilitator also recommends that the teacher bring a set of concrete materials (the cardboard wheels) to the discussion because the concepts that the students are trying to explain are abstract. Using concrete materials can help them explain their reasoning. (Students also can draw pictures of what they are thinking, although using the concrete materials often is an easier place for students to begin to develop their reasoning and explanations.)

When you think of your own units, what are some common misconceptions that students have? How do you help them construct deeper understanding of the science concepts as well as reflect about how their thinking has changed?

If you would like to see the teacher's discussion with Austin, watch the Teacher-Student Conference Video Episode.

Teacher-Student Conferences

A common question teachers ask about the videotaped teacher-student conferences (both in the Assessment 1 Video Episode and the separate Teacher-Student Conference Video Episode) is how teachers have time to sit down with a student and focus in such a detailed, formal way on her entry while the other students are working independently. Typically, the teacher shown in the Assessment 1 episode has individual formal conferences of about three to five minutes only once or twice with each student during a science unit. But he informally talks with each of his students during investigations and independent working times throughout a science unit, as shown in the Soils Video Episode. Because of the videotaping of the Assessment 1 episode, he conducted one conference in an empty classroom for a longer period of time so that the video episode could highlight the format and content of these conferences.

The second conference with Austin (in Assessment 2: Teacher-Student Conference) is even longer, but demonstrates the most important features of a successful conference:

1. First, point out specific strengths in science content understanding, scientific thinking, and/or scientific skills. You do not need to address every example of every strength, but you do need to provide at least one example of each strength so the student understands what you mean. For example, you might say, "This is strong scientific thinking." You then need to provide evidence and reasoning for your comments: "This is strong scientific thinking *because* you include evidence for the distance that both the small and large wheels made the go-cart travel to support your answer to the question."

2. Next, ask a question or questions that a scientist would have about parts of the entry. In some cases, students then will revise their entry. Make sure, though, that they do not cross out predictions and reasoning. Like adult scientists, students need to keep a record of their evolving thinking.

3. Finally, reiterate the overall strengths of the entry, then make a suggestion (prescriptive feedback) about a practice or particular strategy that will help the student write stronger entries. For example, in this conference, the teacher advises Austin to use concrete materials to help him think through what he wants to communicate before he begins to write.

In a formal conference of a more realistic length (about three to five minutes), you would follow the same format but include less feedback. One reason this conference is especially long is because we wanted to show the "further instruction" that needs to occur after some investigations. In this case, many students in the class still are constructing their understanding of why the go-carts travel farther with larger wheels, a struggle that does not become obvious until the teacher reads the students' complex conclusions. Ideally, what Austin's teacher does with the concrete materials (the cardboard wheels with the black marks) as he guides Austin in constructing his deeper understanding is what the teacher would do with his whole class.

Related Material

Chapters

- Chapter 2: "Modeling and Scaffolding"
- Chapter 6: "Predictions, Graphs, and Complex Conclusions"
- Chapter 8: "Meaningful Assessment and Effective Feedback"

Website

- Checklists for Exemplary Notebook Entries
  - Includes the checklist for conclusions as well as for other kinds of notebook entries (for example, scientific observations and comparisons)

- Reproducibles
  - Includes the forms used in the group meetings in these two video episodes

Sample Notebook Entries
for Science-Writing Group Meetings

This section includes the notebook entries that the teachers critiqued during the two group meetings.

Assessment 1 Video Episode: Sample Notebook Entries

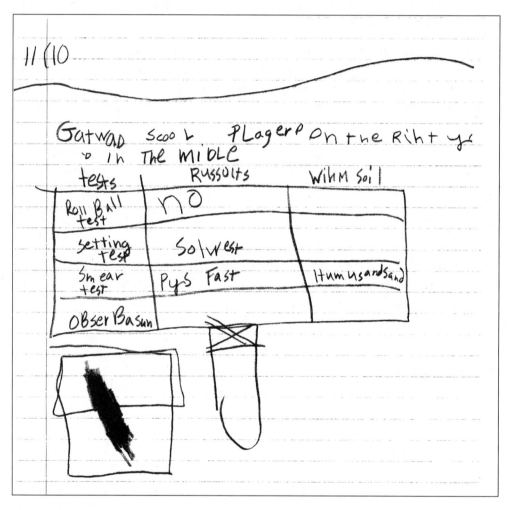

FIGURE 9–3 *Gavin's data table*

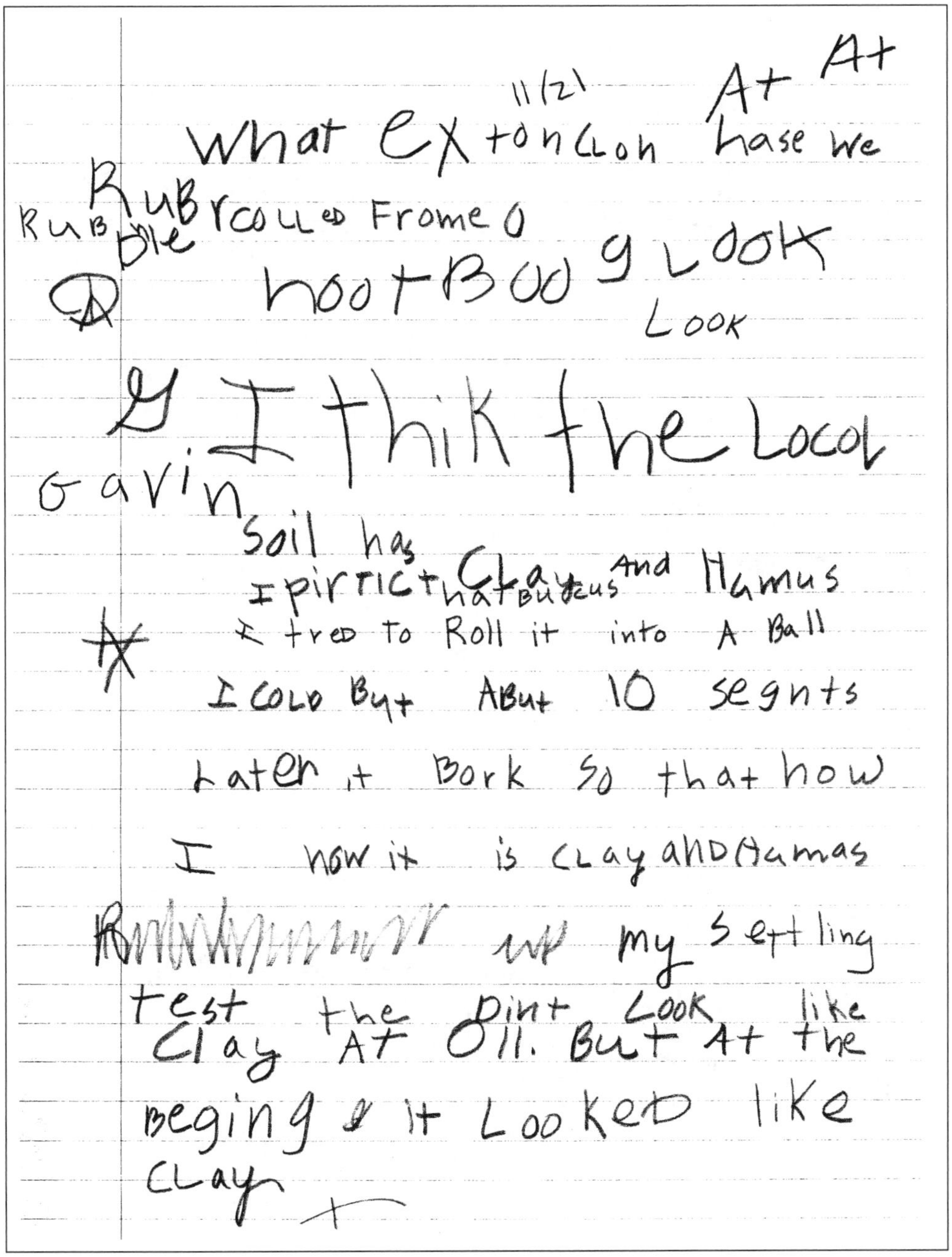

what ex ton(2)tonc on At At hase we
RuB Ru Broou Frome o
      hoot Boo g Look
            Look

g I thik the Locol
Gavin
      soil has
      I pirric that Clay And Humus
      I treo To Roll it into A Ball
      I colo But About 10 segnts
      Later it Bork So that how
      I now it is Clay anDHumas
      with my settling
      test the Dint Look like
      Clay At Oll. But At the
      beging it Looked like
      Clay

FIGURE 9–4   *Gavin's conclusion*

What is in our local soil?

tests	Observations		which soil?
observation	roots plants Black white speckts rocks wood chips rough/soft smells like tree		humus? sand? clay?
Roll a ball tests √	no Ball smoth/rough/roky dark Blak		humus
Smear tests	rough little lighter easy to smear some Particle Stickt		local soil
Settling tests	Day 1 ring around light water roots Dark Soil settled fast Particles- floating	Day 3 roots layers of sand ring around Particles- floating roots Dark Soil clear water	humus sand

FIGURE 9–5 *Tajinai's data table*

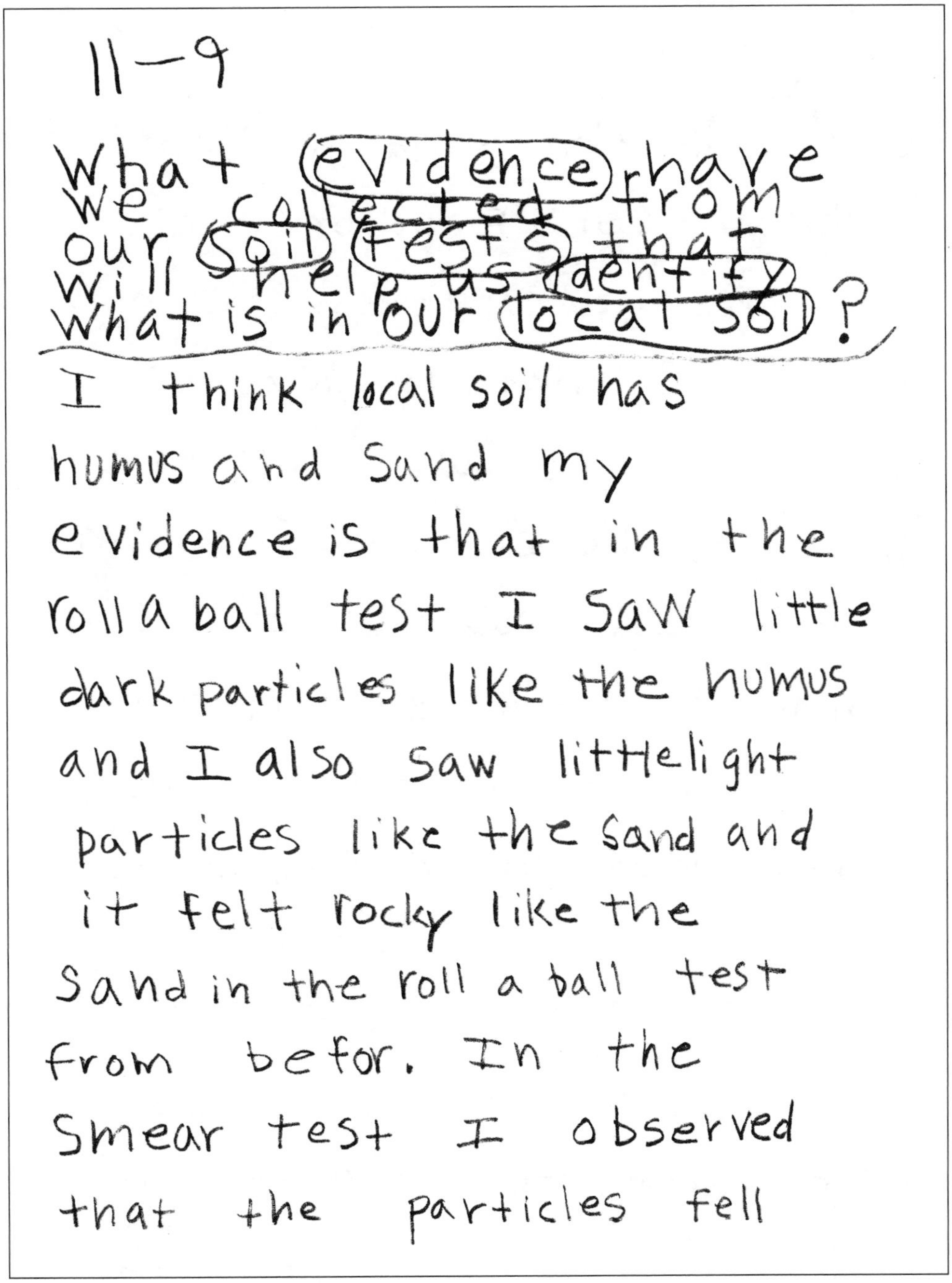

11-9

What evidence have
we collected from
our soil tests that
will help us identify
what is in our local soil?

I think local soil has
humus and sand my
evidence is that in the
roll a ball test I saw little
dark particles like the humus
and I also saw little light
particles like the sand and
it felt rocky like the
sand in the roll a ball test
from befor. In the
smear test I observed
that the particles fell

FIGURE 9–6a *Tajinai's conclusion*

off like the Sand in the
Smear test from before
in the Smear test I
Observed that it was
easy to smear and the
particles were kind of darkish
like the humus but it was
kind of lightish like the
Sand in the Smear test
from befor. my evidence
is that in the settling
test I Observed that
the particles got darker
and also the water got
murky and the paticles

FIGURE 9–6b *Tajinai's conclusion continued*

got stuk to the tude.*
So that is why I think
there is humus and sand
in our local soil.

* like the humus and I
also saw sand in the tude
because there were little
light paticles at the bottom
and also it settled
quickly like the sand
in the settling test
from befor.

FIGURE 9–6c *Tajinai's conclusion continued*

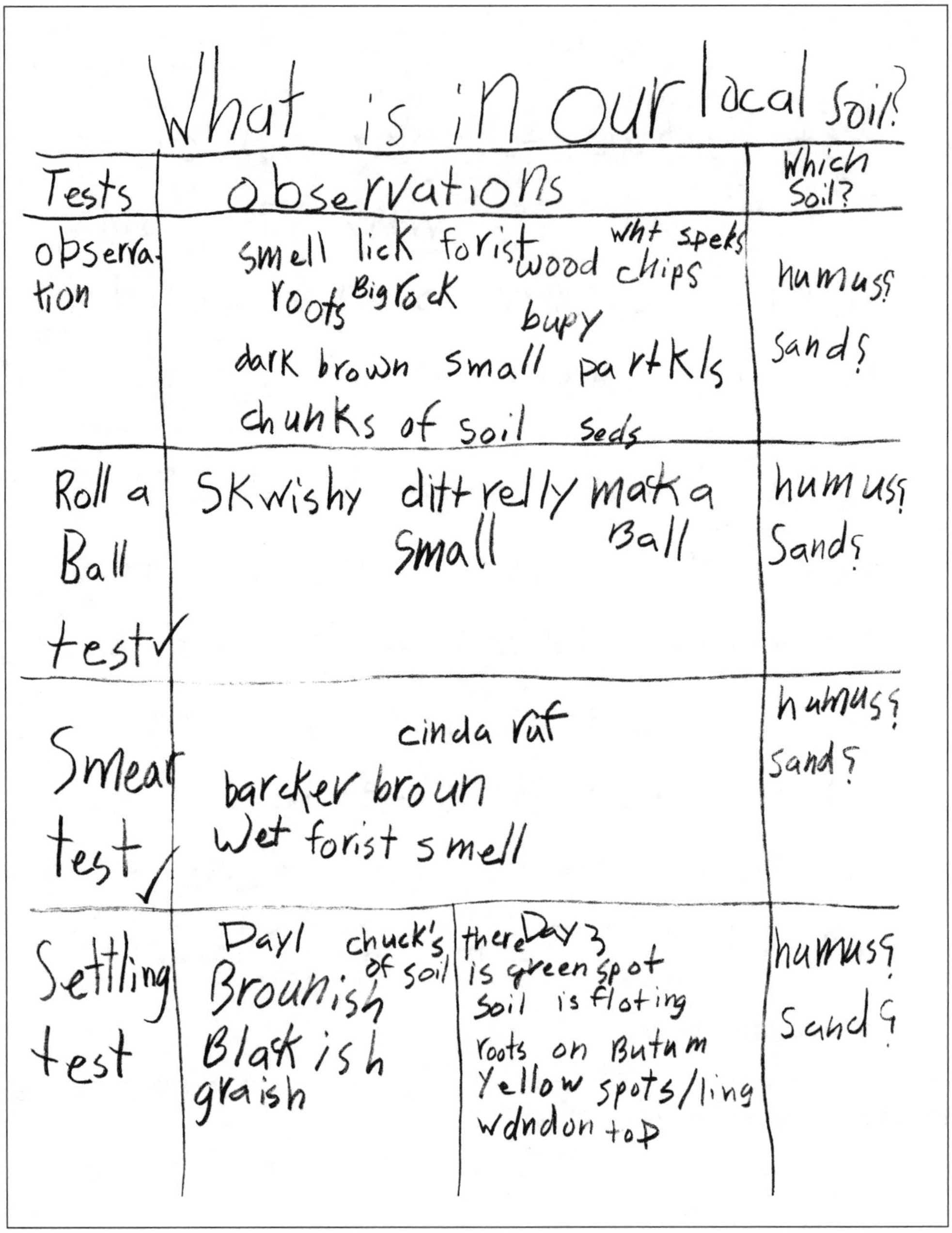

Tests	Observations	Which Soil?
observa-tion	smell lick forist wood chips wht speks Roots Bigrock bupy dark brown small partkls chunks of soil seds	humus? sand?
Roll a Ball test ✓	SKwishy ditt relly mak a small Ball	humus? Sand?
Smear test ✓	cinda ruf barcker broun Wet forist smell	humus? sand?
Settling test	Dayl chuck's of soil Brounish Blakish graish	there Day 3 is green spot soil is floting roots on Butum Yellow spots/ling wdndon top	humus? sand?

What is in our local soil?

FIGURE 9–7a *Dorothy's data table*

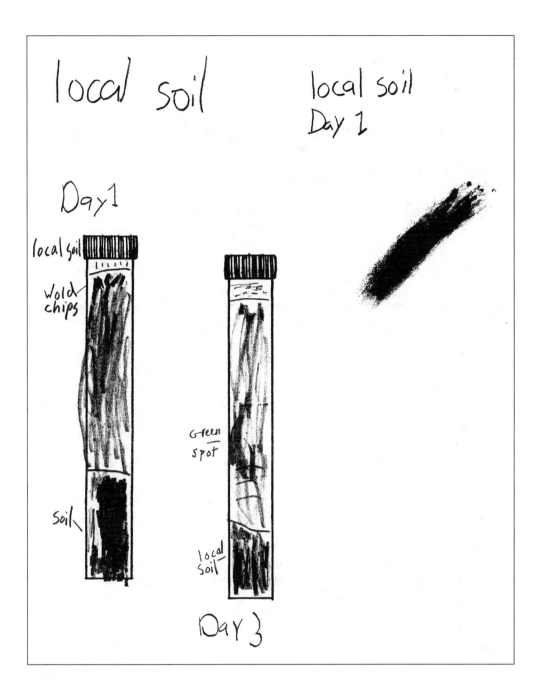

local soil

local soil
Day 1

Day 1

local soil

Wold
chips

soil

Green
spot

local
soil

Day 3

FIGURE 9–7b   *Dorothy's data table continued*

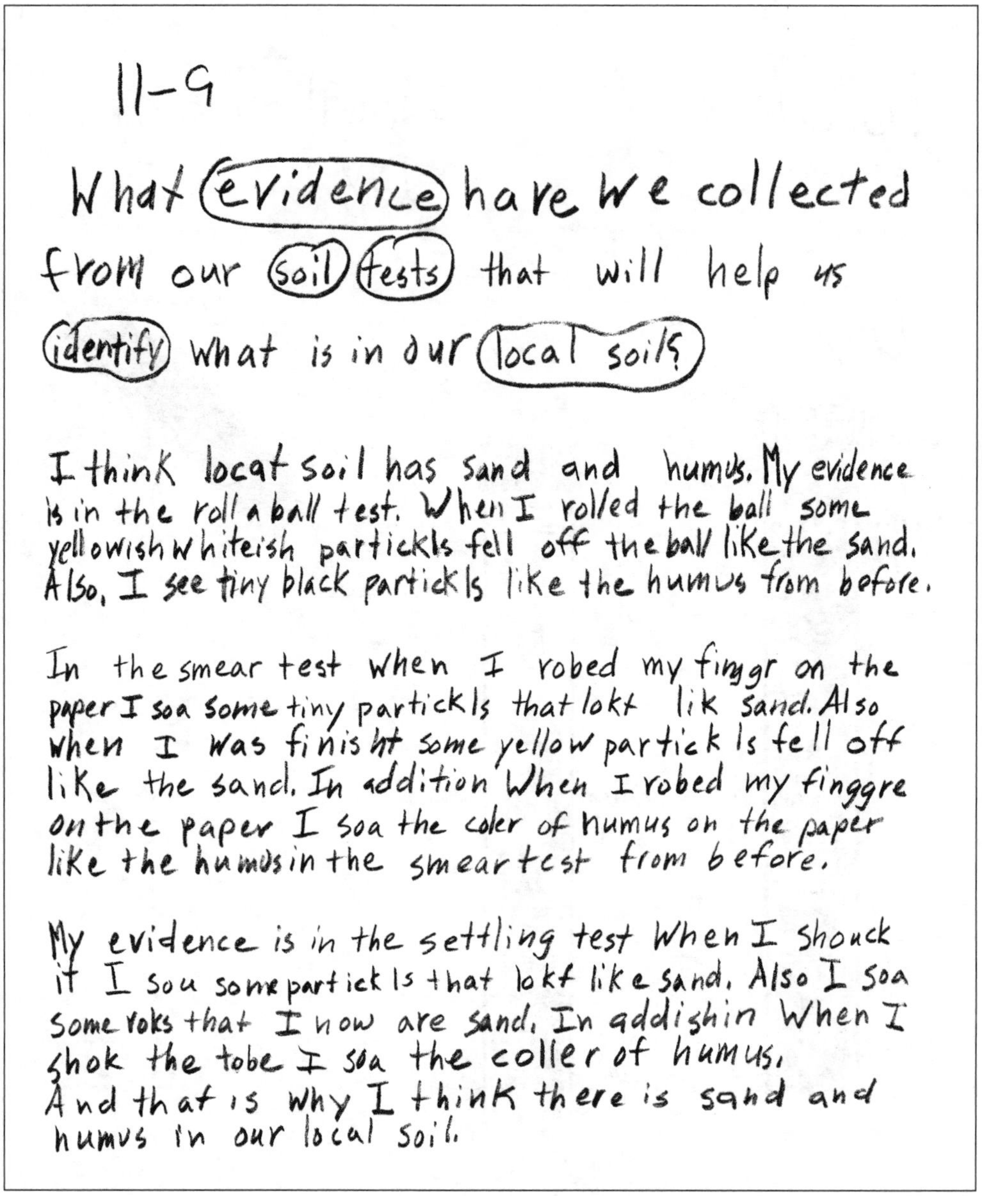

11-9

What (evidence) have we collected from our (soil) (tests) that will help us (identify) what is in our (local soils)

I think locat soil has sand and humus. My evidence is in the roll a ball test. When I rolled the ball some yellowishwhiteish partickls fell off the ball like the sand. Also, I see tiny black partickls like the humus from before.

In the smear test when I robed my fingr on the paper I soa some tiny partickls that lokt lik sand. Also when I was finisht some yellow partick ls fell off like the sand. In addition When I robed my finggre on the paper I soa the coler of humus on the paper like the humus in the smear test from before.

My evidence is in the settling test When I shouck it I sou some partickls that lokf like sand. Also I soa some roks that I now are sand. In addishin When I shok the tobe I soa the coller of humus. And that is why I think there is sand and humus in our local soil.

FIGURE 9–8 *Dorothy's conclusion*

Assessment 2 Video Episode and Teacher-Student Conference Video Episode: Sample Notebook Entries

1/12

FQ: How does the size of wheel affect the distance the go-cart travels?

I predict the that the smaller the wheel the shorter the cart goes because a large wheel will have a longer circle spin. Most of the time something goes it spins at least once, and if the wheel is smaller one spin isn't as long.

FIGURE 9–9 *Austin's prediction*

Investigative question: What is the effect of the size of the wheels on the distance a go-cart can travel?

The effect of the size of the wheel is. Each size wheel goes a different speed. Because the 7.5 cm wheels makes the go-cart travel around 200 cm. The 11.5 cm wheels travels around 299 cm. Therefore, the smaller the wheels, the shorter the distance the go-cart travels.

At first, I thought the small and large wheels will go around the same distance. Because if you hold both wheels up together and turn them once they both end at the same point. Then I got both wheels rolled them the smaller wheel stoped first while the large wheel kept going.

Now I think they both go different speeds Because if you wind up your go-cart all wheels go at least 1 full circle.

My group's test results were inconsistent. I think this happened because with our small wheel we did test 1 with a different go-cart. All the others had the same cart.

Now I want to investigate what would happen if we used plastic wheels.

FIGURE 9–10 *Austin's conclusion*

CHAPTER 10

Planning Instruction

Focus Questions and Meaningful Notebook Entries

As you implement this science-writing approach in your classroom, you will need to begin developing focus questions for your own science units and planning the kinds of entries your students will be making in their science notebooks. This takes time, so be patient with yourself as you go through the process. Even if you begin by writing just a few focus questions for a unit rather than one for every lesson, your efforts will positively affect your instruction and your students' learning.

If you can, it is very helpful to work with another teacher who is teaching the same science unit. In our work with teachers who are new to this science-writing approach, we have found that teachers feel supported and motivated when they are able to work with someone else. But when that is not possible, we also have found that teachers can learn a great deal and be very successful when they do this planning on their own. This chapter is designed to help you think about the basic issues in developing focus questions and notebook entries whether working alone or with other teachers.

Developing Effective Focus Questions

In an inquiry-based science lesson, a focus question helps students engage their minds and focus their attention on a specific question just before, during, and after their investigation. In writing effective focus questions, you first need to consider what science concept or concepts students will be learning as they conduct investigations during the science lesson. You also need to consider how the lesson fits in the flow of the unit. Inquiry-based science units are designed so that through a progression of lessons, students incrementally construct their understanding of key science concepts and develop their abilities to work and think like scientists. A focus question zeroes in on an important scientific concept, skill, and/or thinking, which helps students focus their thinking and ultimately contributes to deeper understanding of a concept as they progress through the unit.

The following list shows some possible focus questions, grouped according to the types of science lessons that you will find in inquiry-based science units.

For Lessons About Prior Knowledge, Initial Observations, and Comparisons

- What do you think you already know about . . . ?

- What can you observe about . . . ?

- What do your senses tell you about . . . ?

- What do you observe happening when . . . ?

- How can we measure . . . ?

- What are some properties/characteristics of . . . ?

- How are . . . and . . . similar and different?

- What differences do you observe?

For Lessons That Are More Focused or Are Part of Ongoing Investigations

- What differences do you observe?

- How has . . . changed over time?

- How has . . . changed since . . . ?

- What properties or characteristics do you think affect . . . ?

- What roles do the . . . play in the system?

- What do you think would happen to the system if . . . ?

For Controlled Investigations

- What should you consider in planning a controlled investigation about . . . ?

- What do you predict will happen and why?

- What do you think would happen if . . . ? Why do you think that would happen?

- What is the effect of . . . [the manipulated variable] on . . . [the responding variable]? Example: What is the effect of *wheel size* on the *distance a go-cart can travel*? This kind of focus question is called an *investigative question* and includes the manipulated (changed) variable and the responding (measured or observed) variable.

- What does the graph tell us about our test results and the answer to our investigative question?

For Lessons About Applications and Connections to the Real World

- What can you do to . . . [make something in particular happen]? Example: What can you do to make a sinker float?

- How is our model similar to and different from . . . ?

- How can what we have learned help us figure out how to . . . ?

Relating Focus Questions to Concrete Experiences

To develop deep conceptual understanding in science, students need first to relate to and answer a question based on their concrete experiences. To begin developing effective focus questions, consider two fundamental questions:

1. Can students answer the question after *concrete* experiences, such as after actively observing objects or organisms, or conducting tests on them, or after making a series of observations and/or tests and making an inference?

2. Does the question relate *directly* to the students' concrete experiences? (In other words, it is not a general or abstract question.)

Questions That Can Be Answered Through Concrete Experiences

One of the common pitfalls in writing effective focus questions is using certain types of *Why* or *How* questions. For example, in a unit about electricity, we might ask, "Why [or How] do longer wires make bulbs dimmer in a complete circuit than shorter wires do?" The problem with this question is that it demands that students have an understanding of the underlying physical science concept of resistance, which is an abstract concept: as the length of wire increases, there is more resistance in the circuit, and that is why the bulb shines increasingly less brightly. Students cannot actually see resistance; they just can observe its effect. In other words, students can observe that complete circuits with longer wires have dimmer bulbs than identical circuits that have shorter wires. But they cannot know from direct observation *why* or *how* that happens.

A much more effective question for elementary students to investigate and answer is: "What is the effect of different lengths of wire on the brightness of a bulb in a complete circuit?" This is a more effective question because students actually can observe the changing brightness of the bulb as the length of wire increases. They then can answer the question using their observations as their evidence. After more investigations in which they change the thickness of the wire and the material of which the wire is made, students can begin to infer and construct an understanding of the concept of resistance. But asking them to make that abstract leap with few if any concrete experiences in making circuits means that students probably will not develop a deep understanding of the concept of resistance.

Questions That Relate to Students' Experiences

Consider this focus question from the science lesson in the Ecosystems Video Episode (Chapter 4): "How are the real terrestrial ecosystem outdoors (the park) and our model terrestrial ecosystems indoors similar and different?" This question asks the students to reflect on *their own concrete scientific experiences* outdoors and with their *own* model ecosystems in order to construct their understanding and their response. Because students are focused on a question about the similarities and differences between the park *they have experienced* and the models *they have built and observed over time*, they will be much more successful in developing and communicating their understanding of the concept that underlies the question than if they were asked to answer a generic or abstract query. Eventually, after more concrete experiences, they will be able to make generalized statements about physical models, but they need the concrete experience first.

In contrast, a typical reading comprehension question intended to elicit understanding of a similar concept might be one of the following:

1. Why do scientists make physical models?

2. How are a model and a real ecosystem similar and different?

3. What is the definition of a physical model?

The first and second questions are abstract. Students would have to think about their concrete experiences (if they have had them) and then generalize from those experiences to answer the questions in the way that the questions demand. That is a very difficult thinking and writing task for elementary students. The third question would probably entail a restatement of a definition that the students have encountered in their reading rather than in scientific experiences.

Planning Meaningful Notebook Entries

After you have written an effective focus question for an inquiry-based science lesson, you need to plan what kind of notebook entry will help students think even more deeply about their thinking and their understanding of science concepts. As explained in Chapter 1, you do not want students to be writing about what they *did*. Procedural writing does not meet the criteria for this science-writing approach because writing about what they did does not help students deepen their understanding of science concepts or their development of scientific thinking.

Again, the critical question to consider when you are thinking about effective notebook entries is this: How will writing this notebook entry help develop students' understanding of science concepts and/or scientific thinking as well as scientific skills? The scientific skills are important prerequisites to the development of the other two Key Elements. For example, if students do not have the scientific skill of accurately measuring and recording data, they will not be able to develop their scientific thinking and understanding of the pertinent concepts. Thus, the scientific skills are important as a means to that end. Those skills are directly involved in making scientific illustrations and diagrams, observation notes, data tables, and graphs.

What ultimately is most important—but often overlooked in teaching elementary science writing—is scientific thinking because students must use that thinking in constructing their evolving understanding of science concepts. You want to be sure that when students are writing scientific observations, comparisons, interpretations of data, and conclusions, their entries require them to explain their thinking and/or conceptual understanding.

Let's look at three plans for focus questions and notebook entries based on the *Plant Growth and Development* unit published by Science and Technology for Children (STC). In each case, we will evaluate the plans based on the goals for each Key Element below.

1. Important *science concept*:

   • A plant has a life cycle that is made up of distinct stages over a period of time.

2. *Scientific skills* necessary for constructing understanding of that concept:

   • Collecting quantitative (measured) data of height and calculating growth

- Making scientific observations and recording them in note form in a data table

- Making detailed, accurate scientific illustrations with accurate labels

3. *Scientific thinking* involved in constructing understanding of that science concept:

- Comparing the different observations, data in the data table, and data on a line plot to determine how the plant is growing and developing over time

Now, consider the following focus questions and the writing that the teachers model for their students to do. Which of the questions is effective and which of the entries will result in meaningful writing in terms of the unit's important science concept?

First Plan

Focus Question: How are the seed leaves and the true leaves similar and different?

Written Entry: Make a box and T-chart to organize the similarities and differences between the two types of leaves. Then write a comparison of the leaves following the Compare and Contrast writing frame.

The question is not important enough for students to spend time writing about because the fact that there are two types of leaves is only a small part of what happens during the plant's life cycle. In the time it takes students to make a box and T-chart and then write a comparison, they would benefit much more from making detailed notes and a scientific illustration and then writing about all their observations of the plant that day. Those observations are critical in helping students develop the idea that the plant is changing as it goes through its life cycle.

This question is an excellent one to *ask* students, however, because it makes them focus on the distinct differences between the two kinds of leaves. It also is important for students to include these differences in their scientific illustrations and notes in their data table.

Second Plan

Focus Question: How do observable characteristics and scientific illustrations help us see changes in an organism?

Written Entry: Make a box and T-chart to organize the similarities and differences between observable characteristics and scientific illustrations. Then write a comparison of the characteristics and illustrations, following the Compare and Contrast writing frame.

Students should understand, in terms of scientific skills, the importance of making detailed scientific observations and scientific illustrations (and you should be sure to model those skills), but they do not need to spend their writing energy and time comparing and contrasting the two skills. It is most important for students to write their notes, make their scientific illustration, and write about their scientific observations. By doing so, they not only are learning how to write scientifically, but they also are spending time thinking as they write about what they observed. This whole process then deepens their understanding of the main science concept of growth and development over time.

The box and T-chart and Compare and Contrast writing frame (see Figure 11–3 in Chapter 11) are an extremely useful and effective means of helping students make and write strong comparisons. As a result, many teachers, as they are beginning to implement this science-writing approach, overuse the strategy and the writing frame. When you are planning a notebook entry, you need to ask yourself in what way repeatedly making box and T-charts and writing comparisons is going to help students develop their scientific thinking and their understanding of science concepts.

Third Plan

> *Focus Question*: What can we observe about a plant's growth and development over time?
>
> *Written Entry*: In your data table, write notes and measured data from your observations of your plant today. Then write a scientific observation of what you observed today, using your data table and the scaffolding on either side of the class data table. (The scaffolding includes a list of characteristics, such as the plant's height and number of leaves, as well as words and phrases, such as *I observed*, *Also*, and *Furthermore*.)

This focus question is effective because it gets to the heart of one of this unit's main concepts, and overarching in that it applies to ongoing investigations. The notebook entry also is effective because the process of recording their observations, then writing about those observations, helps students develop a deeper understanding of what they are observing as they also are learning how to write about this understanding and thinking.

Avoid Spoon-Feeding

In planning your instruction and notebook entries, you need to think about how to provide students with enough scaffolding to write their entry independently, but not so much scaffolding that students are just copying cloze sentences and filling them in with a few words and phrases. This spoon-feeding does not build students' writing skills or their confidence in their writing abilities nor does it deepen their thinking or understanding of science concepts.

Look at Samples A, B, C, and D in Figure 10–1. The teacher of the students who wrote samples A and B had modeled, using the following scaffolding, how to write about the growth of the class plant. After the minilesson, he asked them to write about the class plant (rather than their own plant) and provided the scaffolding below (italicized in the figure) for students to use during their independent writing:

> On Day 19, I observed that the plant was _____ high. It has grown _____ since _____ days ago. I think that means it has been growing _____.

The teacher of the students who wrote samples C and D modeled how to use words from the focus question to begin writing about the plant's growth. As she modeled how to write about the plant's growth, she referred students to the class data table and modeled one way

Effective Scaffolding or Spoon-Feeding?

Sample A

On Day 19, I observed that the plant was 18 cm *high. It has grown* 2 cm *since 5 days ago. I think that means it has been growing* slowly.

Sample B

On Day 19, I observd the plant was 18 cm *high. It has grown* 2 cm *since 5 days ago. I think it has been growing* kinda slow.

Sample C

I observed that my plant has been growing slowly the last 5 days. On Day 14, it was 14 cm tall, and on Day 19, it was 16 cm tall. That's only 2 cm of growing in 5 days.

Sample D

From Day 14 to 19, I observd plant grow reely slow. On Day 19, it was 15 cm. That only 1 cm taller.

FIGURE 10–1 *Effective Scaffolding or Spoon-Feeding? samples*

to talk and write about the growth (for example, "On Day 14, I observed . . ."). Then she showed them how to use the data table to structure their writing. She did not say that the students had to write about the growth data in a particular order but instructed them to include all the information that was on that part of the data table. In doing so, she also modeled a strategy in which students check off the data from the table after they have included it in their written entry. She also modeled how to use certain words and phrases (from a list at the front of the room) as they wrote different parts of the entry together. Then the students used their own data table as they wrote about their own plant.

The spoon-fed nature of samples A and B results from scaffolding that is too detailed. The scaffolding creates cloze sentences that require students to fill them in with single numerals or single words. Also, students wrote about the class plant instead of using their own data and writing about their own plant, which would have required them to think and write more independently. The second teacher, by contrast, provided some needed structure but did not spoon-feed most of the words in the entry.

A Last Thought: Talking Before Writing

Regardless of how effective your focus questions and notebook entry plans are, students will have difficulty making strong notebook entries if you do not have a rich and interactive shared reflection discussion after students have conducted their investigations during the science session and a shared review discussion at the beginning of the writing session. Students, especially those who are learning English or have special needs, need to hear and speak the language before they can use it effectively in writing. It is important for you to model scientific thinking and language during discussions, and also provide opportunities for students to talk with each other in pairs, in small groups, and in whole-class conversations. You can see some excellent examples of these practices in the Plants (Chapter 3) and Animals (Chapter 7) Video Episodes.

CHAPTER 11

Sample Minilessons

Having students simultaneously learning how to write scientifically and constructing understanding of new science concepts can be challenging both for you and them. When students need to learn a new form of scientific writing, they can learn the skill more easily if they first observe, think, and write about something that is familiar to them or is simple to understand. In the following sections, you will find sample minilessons for making a scientific observation as well as some common forms of science notebook entries: a scientific illustration, written scientific observation, comparison, data table, and basic conclusion.

You also can use these minilessons as models for the writing lessons you develop for your science units. When you are planning a lesson, be sure to write the entry yourself. This is worth the time because you will see what might be confusing or challenging for your students and can change the lesson accordingly before the students try it.

Making a Scientific Observation

Preparation

1. Have a sharpened wooden pencil for each student or pair of students. The pencils should be identical, if possible.

2. Make a large copy of the Observations organizer (see Figure 11–1) on chart paper so that you can easily refer to it during discussions.

3. Make copies of the organizer so each student can have her own copy to use as she makes her observations.

Observations

Think of the four senses (not taste).

Size, shape, color, lines, patterns, texture, weight, smell/odor, sound, behavior . . .

I observed _____.

I noticed _____.

Connect it with what you know or have investigated.

It reminds me of _____ because _____.

Observe and record cause and effect.

When _____, it _____.

Note any changes.

At first, _____. But now _____.

Be curious, and ask questions you might investigate.

I am curious about _____.

It surprised me that _____.

I wonder what would happen if _____.

What is the effect of on _____?

This organizer is generic. You probably will want to revise it for your science lessons so it better facilitates the kinds of observations you want students to make in each case.

(This is a slightly revised version of the Observations organizer featured in Writing in Science.*)*

FIGURE 11–1 *Observations organizer*

Conducting the Minilesson

1. *Let students explore freely as they observe their pencil.* Ask them to talk with their partner about what they are noticing.

2. *Introduce the Observations organizer (Figure 11–1).* Tell students that the organizer will help them look for specific details, give them some language to use in their observations, and help them think scientifically about the properties of the pencil.

3. *Model using scientific language in discussions with partners.* As you go through the Observations organizer, model how students could speak with each other. For example, model how they could say, "I observed that the pencil is . . ." and "I think . . . I think this because . . ." This oral sharing works best when you have students work in pairs that are also part of groups of four, so they can have small-group discussions when necessary as well. By sharing their observations with each other, they enhance their individual observations and develop language skills that they can use in their writing.

4. *Make a distinction between scientific observations and inferences.* For this lesson, students can call the object a *pencil* from the beginning, but tell them that they should not use any terms for the parts during this lesson. Instead, they should use descriptive, general vocabulary and talk only about what they observe. For example, instead of saying, "The pencil has an eraser," a student might say, "I observed a red, rubberlike material that is connected to one end of the pencil."

    This might seem contrived because most students probably know that that part of the pencil is an eraser. But this lesson will help students learn to describe what they actually observe rather than labeling it or making inferences about it. Typically, for example, a student would say or write, "The goldfish is sleeping" or "The goldfish is dead." These are inferences. The following statement is an observation: "The goldfish is floating on its side at the top of the water and has not moved for the last hour." Students can make the inferences as long as they state the observation as well and indicate their thinking—"I observed that the goldfish is . . . I think this means that the goldfish is dead."

5. *Help students see the difference between creative analogies and scientific analogies.* For example, a student might say or write, "It reminds me of a rocket ship because it is pointed in the front and the back looks like flames could come out of it." This is a creative analogy. In contrast, a student could say or write, "It reminds me of a mechanical pencil because it has a similar shape and one end can make dark marks on paper and the other end can rub away the marks." This is a scientific observation that is comparing similar properties of two objects.

6. *Model how to use* because. Share with students the importance of using the word *because* in their statements. When students include this word, they share their reasoning, which is a critical skill in science and science writing.

Drawing a Scientific Illustration

After students have spent some time observing the pencil, model how to make a scientific illustration. The process of drawing what they observe will help them notice even more details. Students either can make their own illustration as you model how to draw the different parts, or they can make their illustration independently after you have finished the modeling.

Conducting the Minilesson

1. *Begin with the outside contour.* Model how to begin the illustration by thinking out loud: "What is the outside contour or shape of the main part of this pencil?" In this way, you are modeling to start the illustration by thinking about the overall shape. After they tell you what they have observed, draw a rectangular shape for the main part of the body.

2. *Ask about details.* Next, ask them what details they observe that you should add to the illustration (for example, the horizontal ridges, the letters, the color). By doing this type of modeling, you are not just drawing the pencil and having students copy the drawing. You are helping them learn the thinking process and some of the drawing techniques while using their observations as the *content* of the drawing. This is similar to a shared-writing minilesson in which you model the *structure* of the particular kind of scientific writing while the students contribute the *content* of the writing.

3. *Draw in 3-D.* Show them how to add lines and shading to give a 3-D effect, which will help them learn how to notice and add details.

4. *Focus on one part of the object.* Direct the students' attention to one end of the pencil, asking them what they observe there. Breaking the illustration into parts like this helps students focus and see more details, and it helps break the drawing into different segments, which helps students who are not confident in their drawing abilities. (Another helpful strategy, using quadrant perspectives, is explained in Chapter 3.) Then ask students what they observe at the other end of the pencil, and add the details as they share them.

5. *Add a title.* Tell them that another scientist looking at the illustration might not know for sure what it is. Elicit from the students that you need to add a title (*Pencil*) above the illustration so other scientists will know what you have drawn.

6. *Label the parts.* Then model how to add a label for each part, telling students that now that they have closely observed the object, you all can discuss the term for each part (for example, *eraser*, *graphite*). Show them how to draw a straight line that clearly goes from the label to the correct part, and talk about how important it is for other scientists to know exactly which parts go with which labels. Also, tell them that they should not use arrows unless they are showing the direction or movement of something.

7. *Have students draw independently.* Have students make a scientific illustration of their own pencil.

Writing a Scientific Observation

After students have carefully observed an object or organism and, when necessary, made a scientific illustration, they sometimes will need to write a scientific observation. (In other cases, jotting down observation notes will be sufficient.)

Conducting the Minilesson

1. Do a shared-writing minilesson (similar to what you did in modeling how to draw the illustration of the pencil) to model how to write a scientific observation of a pencil:

   - Provide the words to begin each sentence (see the finished example that follows). The students provide the content of the rest of each sentence.

   - Model how to use the Observations list to organize the written observation.

   The following is an example of a shared writing that a teacher did with intermediate students. (Younger students would write a shorter observation.) The words the teacher modeled are italicized:

   > *I observed* that the pencil is 18 cm long and 0.5 cm wide for most of its length. *I noticed* that the body is shaped like a solid, narrow cylinder. *Also*, one end has a metal piece with a pink, rubber-like material attached to it. The other end becomes narrower and ends in a point. The wider part of the point is tan with some wood-like grain markings. The tip is pointed and black.
   >
   > *The pencil reminds me of* the mechanical pencil I use *because* they have similar shapes and they both make black marks on paper. *When I* put the black tip on paper and moved the tip across the paper, the tip made a black line on the paper. *When I* rubbed the pink part over the mark, the mark almost went away. *I noticed* that a gray smudge is still on the paper.
   >
   > *I am curious about* how the pencil was made. *I wonder what would happen if* everyone in the world used pencils made of wood. Would we run out of trees?

2. At the end of this minilesson, remove the shared writing and replace it with a writing frame with the italicized words.

3. To help students get started with their own entry, have them turn to their science partner and say the sentence they want to write. Reading words out loud from the organizer can help as well.

4. Students then follow the Observations organizer and use the provided words when they need them as they write their own scientific observation.

5. If you have a group of students who need more support with writing than the majority of the class does, you either can have them sit together and work with them as a group or pair them with students who have more developed language skills, then stop by their desks to give them individual support. (See Chapters 7 and 12 for other strategies for helping students who need extra support in writing.)

Making and Writing a Comparison

In this minilesson, students compare and contrast a wooden pencil and a colored marker.

Preparation

1. Each student or pair of students will need a sharpened wooden pencil and a colored marker. All the pencils should be identical, as should all the markers.

2. To make the box and T-chart organizer (see Figure 11–2), you can use a large piece of chart paper, white board, document camera, or overhead projector.

Box and T-chart Strategy for Making Comparisons

Similar or Same

> Tools for writing
> Hold in your hand
> . . .

Different

Pencil	Colored Marker
Yellow	White with purple
18 cm long	13.5 cm long
0.5 cm wide	1.5 cm wide
Graphite	Colored ink
Erasable	Not erasable
. . .	. . .

FIGURE 11–2 *Box and T-chart Strategy for Making Comparisons*

3. Make a large copy of the Compare and Contrast writing frame (see Figure 11–3) on chart paper so that you can easily refer to it during the shared-writing minilesson.

4. Make copies of the writing frame so each student can have his own copy in his notebook.

This minilesson is most effective if students draw an illustration and write an observation about each of the two objects before you begin the comparison. Plan to have students draw and write about the pencil on a left-hand page and the marker on the facing right-hand page. They will make a box and T-chart on a separate sheet of paper so they can look at both pages as they fill out the organizer. When they finish, have them glue or tape the finished box and T-chart on the next (left-hand) page. They then can write the comparison on the facing right-hand page so they can see the organizer as they write. This approach works well for any such comparison, whether using objects, events, or organisms.

Conducting the Minilesson

1. Tell students that they are going to learn a strategy for comparing and contrasting two objects or organisms, in this case, a wooden pencil and a colored marker.

2. Draw a box and write *Similar* or *Same* above it. Ask students to share the ways in which the pencil and the marker are similar or the same. Write each property in the box.

3. Next, write *Different* and make a T-chart with *Pencil* above the left-hand column and *Colored Marker* above the right-hand column. Ask the students how the pencil and marker are different. List the differences horizontally by category as students mention

Compare and Contrast

Start with how things are the same or similar.

The _____ and the _____ are similar because they both _____. In addition, they _____.

Add more as needed.

. . .

Explain how they are different. You can compare the same property or characteristic in the same sentence. Use *and*, *but*, or *whereas* to set up the contrast.

The _____ and the _____ are different because the _____, but the _____. Also, the _____, whereas _____.

Add more as needed.

. . .

Remember to ask yourself, Will it be clear to another scientist what I mean when I use pronouns such as *they* and *it*? If not, how can I edit the sentence to make it clearer?

(This is a slightly revised version of a writing frame featured in Writing in Science.*)*

FIGURE 11–3 *Compare and Contrast writing frame*

them. For example, the color of the pencil should be listed in the same line horizontally as the color of the marker; the length of the pencil should be listed in the same line horizontally as the length of the marker. Emphasize this point so that students understand how important it is to organize these differences in this way. A T-chart is the most basic form of a data table, which is an essential organizer in science.

Also model the use of contrast words (for example, *but, whereas*) as you add differences to the T-chart. For example, write and say, "The pencil is yellow," then say "but" as you write the word just above the T-chart on top of the vertical line. Then complete the contrast as you write and say, "but the marker is white with purple." Calling the line down the middle of the contrasting properties "the but line" gets students' attention and helps them learn the structure and the language of contrasts. Write other contrast words above the line as well.

4. Referring to the box and T-chart as a prewriting organizer or scaffolding, model how to write a comparison using the Compare and Contrast writing frame in Figure 11–3. Involve the class in writing each part of the comparison, following the box and T-chart to help write organized and detailed paragraphs.

For example, you could say, "One way we could start our comparison is to use this frame: 'The pencil and the colored marker are the same because . . .' Now, what can we use from the information in the box to complete that sentence?" In this way, you are modeling a *structure* for the comparison and the students are providing the *content*.

5. Continue using the frame in this way. At the end, model how to add more to the frame if students have more to include. Your resulting shared-writing comparison might look like this (italicized words are from the writing frame and a chart of useful words and phrases listed next to the shared writing):

> The pencil *and the* colored marker *are similar because they both* are tools. *In addition*, we use our hands to write and draw with them.
>
> The pencil *and the* marker *are different because* the pencil is yellow, *but* the marker is white and purple. *Also*, the pencil is 4.5 cm longer than the marker, *whereas* the marker is 1 cm thicker than the pencil. The pencil has graphite and makes black marks, *but* the marker has colored ink and makes purple marks. *Finally*, we can erase the graphite marks but not the ink.

6. Use this writing frame only as initial scaffolding. After students have had some experience, model how to follow the box and T-chart organizer and make the writing more fluent. For example, you can teach students to combine differences: "The pencil is yellow, and it is 18 cm long and 0.5 cm wide. In contrast, the marker is white with purple, and it is only 13.5 cm long, but it is 1.5 cm wide." Some students naturally do this more complex writing, but typically they will not include as many details or organize the information so clearly. The box and T-chart organizer helps support these students.

Making a Data Table for a Controlled Investigation

To help students learn how to make a data table for a controlled investigation, it is helpful to work beforehand with a table for an investigation that they are not planning and conducting. Figure 11–4 is a handout students can use in deconstructing a data table to see how

Making a Data Table for a Controlled Investigation

Investigative question

What is the effect of wheel size on the distance a go-cart can travel?

Wheel Size vs. Distance Traveled

Wheel Size (cm)	Distance Traveled (cm)			
	Trial 1	**Trial 2**	**Trial 3**	**Mean**
7.5				
9				
11.5				

1. ***Title***
   - *Include the name of both the manipulated (changed) variable and the responding (measured) variable separated by* vs. *(versus).*

2. ***Manipulated (Changed) Variable***
   - *Make a column, then write the variable's name as the title.*
   - *Include the abbreviation for the unit of measurement.*
   - *Make a row for each type of the manipulated variable.*

3. ***Responding (Measured) Variable and the Trials (Tests)***
   - *You should conduct at least three trials, then calculate and record the mean (average) of those three trials. So you need four narrower columns under the responding (measured) variable title.*
   - *The responding variable title should include the abbreviation for the unit of measurement.*

FIGURE 11–4   *Handout for Making a Data Table for a Controlled Investigation* the components of a controlled investigation determine the parts and structure of a data table. When planning their own controlled investigations, students can use this handout to create their own data tables.

Preparation

1. Copy the handout for each student.

2. Make a copy of the data table in the handout on chart paper or the white board, or so you can project it onto a screen.

Conducting the Minilesson

1. Read the investigative question together and discuss the parts of the question. Circle the manipulated (changed) variable, "wheel size," and draw a rectangle around the responding (measured) variable, "the distance a go-cart can travel." (If you use other terms for these variables, change the handout so students can work with the terms they need to learn.)

2. Ask students what they notice about the title of the data table. The title should include both the manipulated and the responding variable separated by "vs." Again, if you prefer a different title or use of vocabulary, edit the handout to correspond with what you want students to learn.

3. Point out that the manipulated variable is in the first column and the results of the trials or tests are divided evenly among four columns under the responding variable.

Interpreting Data and Writing a Basic Conclusion

The following minilesson will help students learn how to write a basic conclusion using a data table. (The sample below uses the data table shown in Figure 11–4.)

Preparation

1. Make copies for each student of the writing handout in Figure 11–5. Do not give students the handout until after they have discussed the investigative question (see the section that follows).

2. If you cannot project an image of the handout onto a large screen, then make a large copy of the investigative question and the data table so all the students can see them while you are doing the minilesson.

Conducting the Minilesson

Discuss the Investigative Question

1. Describe the following scenario: Students have decided to investigate whether changing the size of the wheels on their model go-carts (all of which are made of the same materials and are constructed in the same way) affects how far the go-carts can travel.

Investigative question

What is the effect of wheel size on the distance a go-cart can travel?

Wheel Size vs. Distance Traveled

Wheel Size (cm)	Distance Traveled (cm)			
	Trial 1	Trial 2	Trial 3	Mean
7.5	127	159	134	140
9	198	209	223	210
11.5	267	299	283	283

Three Components of a Basic Conclusion

1. **Answer the investigative question.**

   Use words from the question in your answer.

2. **Include evidence from the data table to support your answer.**

   The data show that *[Remember to include* only *and* but*]*

   ☐ the 7.5 cm wheels make the go-cart travel _____ cm.

   ☐ *11.5 cm wheels—distance in cm*

   ☐ In fact, _____ *[use numbers you computed to the right of the data table]*

3. **Write a concluding statement.**

   Therefore, the *[smaller/larger]* the wheels, the *[shorter/longer]* the distance the go-cart travels.

FIGURE 11–5 *Handout for writing a basic conclusion*

2. Show students the investigative question.

3. Ask them to talk with a partner and identify the manipulated (changed) variable and the responding (measured) variable in the question.

4. As you are discussing and identifying the variables together, draw a circle around the manipulated variable (wheel size) and a rectangle around the responding variable (distance the go-cart can travel). This visual organizer helps students remember that there are two variables in the question. Referring frequently to the variables highlighted in this way helps students think about the test results and write about them in terms of both variables. Later, they will use the data table as more complex visual scaffolding for the components that they need to write about in their conclusion.

Discuss the Data Table

1. Give students the handout for writing a basic conclusion (Figure 11–5).

2. Ask students to identify the variables in the title of the data table.

3. Discuss what they think the data in the table are telling them about the answer to the investigative question.

4. Teach them how to *summarize the data* in their discussions and how to use comparative language. One way to help them identify the data they need to summarize is to circle the smallest wheel size, *7.5 cm*, as well as the mean distance it made the go-cart travel, *140 cm*. Connect those two numbers with an arching line (see Figure 11–6). Do the same thing with the largest wheel and the corresponding mean distance.

   Ask students to do the same on their own copies of the data table. This helps them focus on the most important data to cite as evidence. This strategy also helps them remember to write about both wheel sizes and both mean distances. Otherwise, many students will write about only the data that support their conclusion ("The largest wheel made the go-cart travel a mean distance of 283 cm.").

5. Teach them how to use *only* and *but* when comparing data, and write the words on the data table in the appropriate places (as shown in the figure): "The smallest wheel made the go-cart travel a mean distance of *only* 140 cm, *but* the largest wheel made the go-cart travel 283 cm."

6. Next, show them how to compute the difference between the two means to the right of the Mean column on their data table. For example, they can subtract the smallest mean distance from the largest mean distance.

7. Discuss the relationship between the two means. Using a phrase such as *In fact*, show them how they can add more information about the data: "*In fact*, the largest wheel made the go-cart travel about twice as far as the smallest wheel did." Add the phrase *In fact*, to the data table next to the calculations.

Model How to Write a Basic Conclusion

As you go through each part of the conclusion, refer students to their handout. Model how to check off each step on the handout as you write about it. (The italicized words that follow are in the students' handout.)

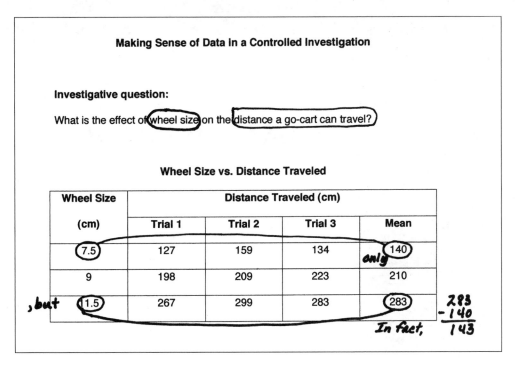

FIGURE 11–6 *Data table as scaffolding*

1. *Answer the investigative question.* Talk about answering the question by comparing both the manipulated and responding variable. For example, "Larger wheels make the go-cart travel farther than the smaller wheels do."

2. *Provide evidence to support your answer or claim.* Ask students to use their data table to structure their writing: "*The data show* that with 7.5 cm wheels, the go-cart travels a mean distance of *only* 140 cm, *but* with 11.5 cm wheels, the go-cart travels a mean distance of 283 cm." (The handout abbreviates the second part of the sentence so students have to think about how to write it.) Ideally, students should say and write, "The 7.5 cm wheels make the go-cart travel *a mean distance of* only 140 cm . . ." But this language and writing are more complicated. Sometimes it is appropriate for elementary students to use a kind of shorthand language until they are ready for more complex phrasing.

3. *Write a concluding statement.* This statement is more of a generalization than the opening sentence in the conclusion. For instance, one sentence could be, "Therefore, I think that the larger the wheels, the longer the distance the go-cart travels." Or "Therefore, I think that as the wheel size increases, the go-cart travels farther."

Note that the first three components of the basic conclusion consist of answering the question (making a claim), then supporting that answer with evidence, and finally, adding a generalized statement that requires a higher level of understanding and language skills. When needed, the fourth component of a basic conclusion refers back to the student's prediction and explains whether or not the data support the prediction. If students had been doing this investigation, rather than just reading the data, they would have made a prediction before they conducted the trials and could add this fourth component.

After you finish modeling the process, remove the shared writing. Have students follow their handout as they write their own conclusion.

CHAPTER 12

Emergent Writing

One of the remarkable outcomes of over a decade of work in this science-writing project is the high level of writing and thinking that is evident in the notebook entries of kindergartners and other emergent writers, including pre-kindergartners. The students are able to draw and write about their scientific thinking and conceptual understanding at higher levels than many adults would expect of them. We think the following factors have contributed to this outcome.

1. The teachers use *inquiry-based methods and science units*, so the students are engaged in their learning and excited to think and communicate about it.

2. The teachers *model* how to work, think, talk, draw, and write like scientists, and *provide scaffolding* to support this learning.

3. The teachers ask them to write about their *thinking* and *what they have learned* through working with concrete materials and discussing their investigations.

4. The teachers value the *content*, *scientific thinking*, and *scientific skills* shown in a science notebook. They overlook conventions (spelling, grammar, punctuation) and handwriting because notebook entries are rough drafts. (If students "publish" their entries as scientific articles, then they revise their writing for conventions and neatness.)

5. The teachers *see science as driving literacy instruction*, rather than vice versa. They embed literacy instruction in the lessons in ways that help students understand concepts and learn to think and write scientifically. Learning to write different forms of expository text, especially in the meaningful context of "doing science," also develops students' informational reading skills.

6. The teachers *expect students to be able to communicate as young scientists*, and provide the time, science experiences, modeling, and scaffolding to support students in being successful. They treat the students as scientists working in the larger community of scientists.

In teaching science writing, teachers face greater challenges with kindergartners and emergent writers than with students who have more developed handwriting and writing skills. But there are strategies that help even students who do not yet have well-developed fine-motor skills and/or do not yet know their letters. The experiences and successes that kindergarten teachers in our science-writing project have had over the years make clear that, regardless of what skills students have when they begin kindergarten, writing in science notebooks is developmentally appropriate.

An Example: Encouraging a Reluctant Writer

When the physical process of writing is challenging, it is understandable that students are reluctant to write. Yet such students also often love science and quickly develop good observational and scientific thinking skills.

Jack wrote the entry in Figure 12–1. He is a kindergartner for whom holding a pencil (which he does with two hands) and writing and drawing with it are extremely hard work.

FIGURE 12–1 *Jack's entry*

But his teacher also knows he has important observations to communicate. She meets him where he is with his writing and helps him move to the next level, just beyond where he feels comfortable.

The class has been studying the *Fabric* unit, published by Full Option Science System (FOSS). Jack has dated the entry and glued in the focus question. (His teacher makes copies of the focus question, which students glue in their notebook. Some teachers print focus questions on address labels to make the process even easier.) After the science lesson (sometime later in the day or the next day), the teacher models how to make a scientific entry during a shared-writing minilesson. For this lesson, the focus is on making a scientific illustration and writing a caption using the words *I think*.

During the independent writing time, the teacher checks in with Jack. He tells her, "I can't write it." So she asks him to write the word *I*. He says, "I know that," and writes the letter. Then the teacher writes the words *I think* on a sticky note, which she puts on the page. He copies the words and works on his drawings. When she returns, she asks him what he thinks fabric is. He says his drawing shows a blanket, which she writes right next to his illustration in quotation marks to show that it is his word and his thinking.

In Figure 12–2, Jack makes another entry. He writes the date and glues in the focus question, then, as everyone discusses the question together, he circles the important words that the class has found. During the independent writing time after the teacher has modeled how to draw another kind of fabric and write about a property they have observed, Jack begins his drawing and copies the word *fabric* from a word card.

When the teacher checks in with him, she asks what he has observed about the fabric he has drawn. He says, "It has little squares." In this case, the teacher feels Jack needs modeling of how to include this important detail in his drawing. She writes his words in quotation marks, but draws a little square instead of writing the word *squares*. Jack practices drawing a few squares on the side of the page. Then he copies multiple squares on his drawing to show that property he has observed. His drawing is detailed and accurately communicates his scientific observation.

Later, students are to write one property they have observed about fabric. In Figure 12–3, Jack tells the teacher he has observed that some fabric is smooth. She writes the words for him on a sticky note, and then he copies his own words, which are an accurate generalization, for his notebook entry.

When the teacher works with Jack, she emphasizes his scientific thinking, his observational skills as a scientist, and his ability to communicate as a scientist. Reluctant writers usually become much less reluctant when they realize how much science they know and can do. And the more they write, the more their physical skills develop as well.

Specific Strategies for Supporting Emergent Writers

Adapting science-writing experiences for students who are learning to recognize and form letters and/or who are in the earlier stages of developing fine motor skills, as Jack is, requires teachers to meet the students where they are in their development and expect them to write at the edge of the place where challenge becomes frustration. Teachers use a variety of strategies to do this.

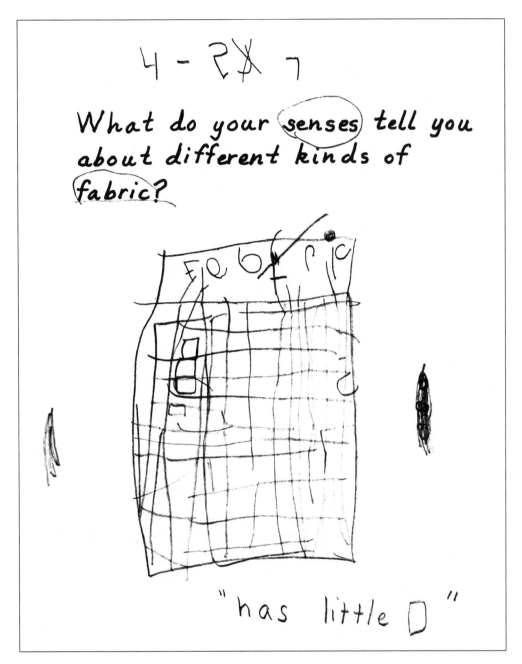

FIGURE 12–2 *Jack's entry*

■ One useful strategy is writing words in highlighter for students to trace. In the sample in Figure 12–4, the teacher has written the date and a writing frame in yellow highlighter (not visible in the figure) on a student's page. She asks the student, Micah, about the missing part in the frame, and he says that organza and burlap are both fabric. Micah understands the concept and the words, which he traces while the teacher works with other students. This process helps Micah communicate his thinking while also working on developing his fine-motor skills. It also allows the teacher to help different students during the independent writing time.

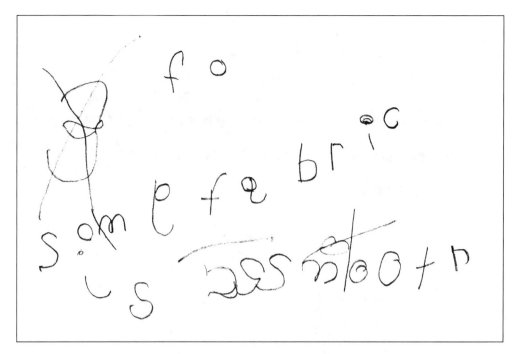

FIGURE 12–3 *Jack's entry*

- Another, related strategy involves the teacher's writing the student's own words on a sticky note for the student to copy (as with Jack in the example above). In Figure 12–5, Micah dictates to the teacher, "Burlap is scratchy." The teacher writes this observation on a sticky note, which she puts on the bottom of his notebook page. Micah then copies his own words into his notebook while she moves on to help other students.

- Avoid using typed cloze (fill-in-the-blank) writing frames for students' notebook entries. Although these frames might result in a nicer "product," they do not help students learn how to write on their own. The students who wrote the entries that are featured in this chapter are moving along the writing developmental continuum because their teachers provide scaffolding and strategies that teach them how to write independently. And the students know their entries are valued and valuable because of the students' scientific understanding, thinking, and skills, not because of the appearance of the entries or the number of words on each page.

Strategies for Using Word Banks

A science word bank is a critical component of this science-writing approach. The first time you teach a unit, making word cards and other materials will feel very time-consuming. But the next time you teach the unit, you will have prepared all these materials.

- In addition to having a regular-sized word card in the word bank, many kindergarten teachers make multiple small copies of each word card, which they place in the word bank next to, or behind, the main word card. Students then can come up and borrow words they need from the bank. Many kinesthetic learners especially benefit from this strategy.

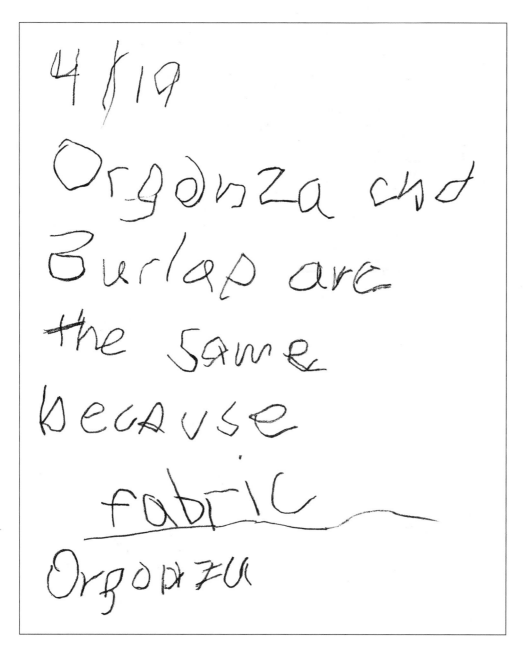

FIGURE 12–4 *Micah's entry*

- For other students, leaving their desk during independent writing time is distracting. So another strategy is to have a clear plastic stand (available at office or restaurant supply stores) for each group and insert a list of typed words that you know will be in a given lesson. Micah's teacher used this approach. Micah referred to the typed list to find *terrycloth* and *absorb* to use in his conclusion, shown in Figure 12–6: "Terrycloth absorb [water.]" This is a kindergarten version of a very simple scientific conclusion, which Micah has written on his own.

- Another strategy for making words accessible to students is to make small word cards for each word in the lesson. Make one set of cards for each group. When it is time for

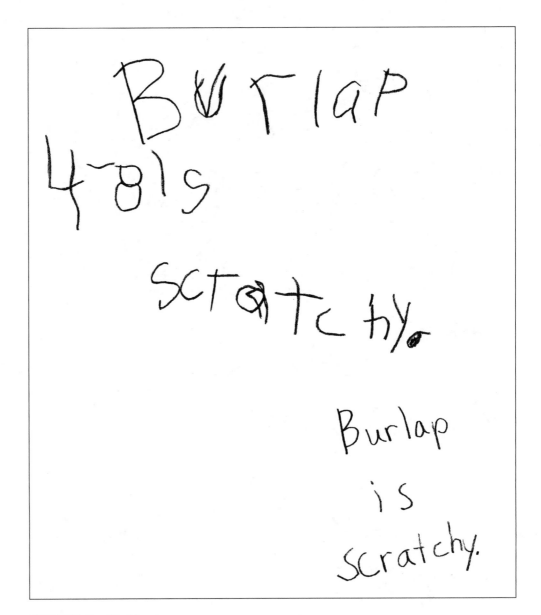

FIGURE 12–5 *Micah's entry*

independent writing, hand out an envelope or basket to each table group for students who prefer to use the small word cards. For some students, being able to handle the card and have it close to where they are writing is helpful.

■ Students also should learn that many of the words they need to use in their writing are in the classroom environment. So as you are modeling, during the shared reflection in the science session and during the shared-writing minilesson in the writing session, ask them where you should look for a certain word you need to use in the writing. In this way, you model how to use such tools as the science word bank, class data tables and charts, the focus question for the science investigation, word family lists, and charts of frequently used words or word walls.

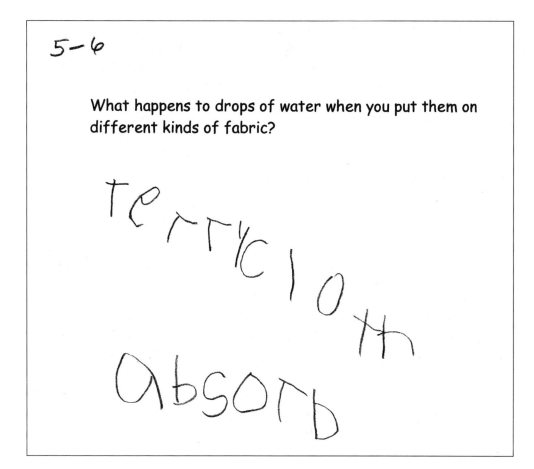

FIGURE 12–6 *Micah's entry*

Spelling Strategies

As mentioned before, in this science-writing approach, we consider notebook entries to be rough drafts, so we do not address spelling when we talk with students about their entries. However, emergent writers need to learn spelling strategies so that they can communicate their ideas independently in writing. So we teach them spelling strategies during the writing sessions, but then talk about their entries in terms of the Three Key Elements.

Emergent writers should learn to use the environment (as mentioned earlier) to help them in spelling words they do not know how to spell. If they cannot find a word they need in the environment, model other ways to help them write words, not necessarily so that the words are spelled correctly, but so that "other scientists" (the audience for their notebook entries) can understand them. The following questions cover some of the common strategies learned in writing and reading programs:

- Where have you seen the word?

- Does it look like a word you already know?

- Is it like a word in a word family you already know?

- What sounds do you hear?

As you are writing with students as a group or individually, continually model these strategies, including identifying the sound-letter associations in a word as you sound it out and write the letters for the sounds you hear. Students will write increasingly independently if we do not emphasize, in these rough-draft entries, that words must be spelled correctly; what is important is that someone else can understand the content of what they are communicating about their thinking.

Strategies for Making Scientific Illustrations

An important skill in making many science notebook entries, regardless of the age or writing skills of the student, is drawing scientific illustrations or diagrams. Often, emergent writers may be able to communicate details in a drawing that they cannot yet put into written words. During the reflective discussions after students have conducted an investigation, you need to model—in small, incremental steps—how to draw what they have observed. For example, in modeling the drawing of how cedar changes when it is stained, you would draw a "before and after" illustration that shows that the cedar becomes darker and the grain more pronounced after staining. This focuses students on the concept (the surface of cedar changes when it is stained because of the wood's properties and those of the stain) rather than the procedure used.

In Figure 12–7, Jazmine has made a scientific illustration. Her teacher had modeled how to make illustrations after investigations of different fabrics they had been observing. He showed them how to write a title so that another scientist would know what they had drawn, and he modeled how to add details of what they had observed in each kind of fabric.

In Jazmine's entry, she writes the date and glues in the focus question at the very beginning of the science lesson. During the class discussion, her teacher models how to draw another piece of fabric as the class discusses their observations.

During the independent writing time, Jazmine writes a title for the illustration using a word card, then she makes her illustration. The details she includes are distinctive properties of burlap: the square shape of the piece of fabric, the horizontal and vertical threads with large holes in between them, and the frayed edges. In the fall of kindergarten, she is probably not ready to communicate these properties in writing, but because her teacher continually has modeled how to observe and then draw details as accurately as possible, she is able to make a scientific illustration that communicates as much as words do.

Strategies for Moving Emergent Writers to Increasing Independence

One of the leaders in our project, Paula Schachtel, has taught both kindergartners and first graders how to write like scientists. Although the way she teaches a science session is similar throughout the school year, she changes the way she teaches science writing to young students as they move from not knowing their letters in the fall to writing multiple complete sentences in their notebooks about their scientific thinking and understanding in the spring of kindergarten.

As an example, we can use the Wood and Water lesson from the *Wood* unit (published by FOSS). During this lesson, students first develop an understanding of the terms *soaks in*, *absorbs*, *repels*, and *beads up* by observing what happens to drops of water placed on paper

How are fabrics alike and how are they different?

10-12

GUR LAP

FIGURE 12–7 *Jazmine's entry*

towels and wax paper. The teacher models how to draw the different results. Students then test five different types of wood by placing drops of water on them. During the class discussion, the teacher and students make a class data table that summarizes the students' test results, and then students produce drawings based on their observations.

Regardless of the time of year, you would teach this science lesson in the same way. But you would teach the writing lesson differently depending on whether you taught it in the fall, the winter, or the spring because you would be providing less modeling and scaffolding as the students develop more independent skills.

The following sections describe how Paula suggests teaching the science writing for the Wood and Water lesson at different times of the school year. If in the fall you know you have students who have more developed writing skills, then you would provide them with less scaffolding but just as much modeling so that they learn how to think and write like scientists.

Fall Notebook Entry

SHARED-WRITING MINILESSON
(You are at the document camera, overhead, or white board; students are at their desk with their notebook.)

- Select one kind of wood (for example, cedar). Hold it up and ask students how to draw it. As students share their ideas, make a drawing while the students make a similar drawing in their notebook.

- Think out loud as you draw and write. For example, you might say, "I need to add a title to my drawing so that other scientists will know what kind of wood this is. What should I write?" Students will tell you to add the title *Cedar*.

- Draw what happened to water on the cedar and add the label *water*. Students will continue adding to their drawing as you discuss with them and model adding details to the entry.

INDEPENDENT WRITING
- Students select a word card from the word bank to copy in their notebook to describe what happened to the water—*beads up, repels; soaks in, absorbs*. Make multiple copies of word cards so students who need to may take cards to their desk to copy.

Winter Notebook Entry

SHARED-WRITING MINILESSON
(Students are on the carpet because they will not be drawing or writing in their notebook while you model, on chart paper, how to write a sample notebook entry based on what the students share.)

- Select one wood (for example, cedar). As students share their ideas, model how to draw cedar and water, add a title and labels, and write a simple caption. (For example, "The cedar absorbs water.").

INDEPENDENT WRITING
- Students choose one of the other kinds of wood to draw and write about in their own notebook. Students write and draw independently using the word bank and other strategies, and referring to the sample entry that the class created together.

Spring Notebook Entry

SHARED-WRITING MINILESSON
(Students are at their desks; you are at the document camera, overhead, or white board.)

- Remind students of resources and strategies they can use in their independent writing (for example, class results, the word bank, sketches from the shared reflection discussion during the science session, and phonemic or phonetic spelling).

- Tell them that they will choose one wood that absorbs or repels water and take it to their desk.

- Have them put their hand on the left-hand page of their notebook. This is where they will make a title for their first wood, a scientific illustration, and a sentence about what happened in their tests (for example, "The particleboard repels water.").

- Have them put their hand on the facing right-hand page of their notebook. This is where they will do the same thing for a different piece of wood that had different test results (for example, "The water went in the plywood."). They will bring that piece of wood to their desk after they draw and write about the first piece.

INDEPENDENT WRITING

- For this lesson, you do not need to provide a writing frame. Students can write a sentence for each illustration on their own by this time of the year.

- Students make their notebook entries while you give support as needed.

A Last Thought: Time

The most common challenge in this kind of teaching is finding the time to do it. As the students' skills increase, so does the amount of time they need to do higher-level writing. Teachers who choose to spend additional time on science and science-writing instruction have students who make greater gains in both science and expository writing, and yet, many teachers are not comfortable "taking all that time away from literacy instruction in order to do science."

Science is an area in which emergent writers can learn how to write expository text that includes scientific observations, comparisons, cause and effect, and simple conclusions. These are not types of writing that young students typically learn in other parts of their school day. Nor is scientific thinking—a valuable higher-level thinking skill—something that they learn in other subjects, especially in the primary grades. Furthermore, students are learning these skills in a meaningful context in which their learning begins with hands-on, concrete experiences that are exciting for them. That is why so many students, especially those who have challenges in learning how to write, often are likely to have their first exciting successes in writing when they are making an entry in their science notebook. Teachers who have seen these successes never question the value of the time their students spend doing science and writing about it.

Related Material

Chapter

- Chapter 7: "Using Modeling and Scaffolding with English Language Learners"

Website

- Student Notebook Entries, Pre-kindergarten Through Fifth Grade
  - Read samples from your own grade level as well as from other grades to see how the samples have similar components but increase in complexity as students get older and have more experience with science and science writing.

- Stories from Schools
  - "Young Students' Science Writing: Raising the Bar"
  - "Reflections and Suggestions from a Science Coach"

CHAPTER 13

Frequently Asked Questions and Next Steps

As you implement this approach to science writing, you will encounter various challenges, as well as successes, with your students. In years of feedback from hundreds of teachers, certain questions arise over and over again. This chapter addresses the most common and fundamental questions and provides suggestions for the next steps you can take in implementing this approach in your classroom.

Question

What do I do when students miss a science and/or a writing session?

Possible Cause

A student misses a science investigation because he was absent from school or was out of the classroom for some reason.

Potential Solutions

- If the investigation is relatively easy and if the student is old enough either to do it with a partner or alone, have him do the investigation during recess or some other appropriate time.

- If the student cannot make up the investigation, he can learn something about it by having a partner explain what their group did and talk about the results the partner has recorded. The student can copy the results into his notebook. If there are class results on a data table, he can record those instead and then refer to those data and/or observations during the writing session. His partner also can explain other class charts or lists that the class made while the student was absent.

- If the student has missed only one day, he might be able to learn something during the class discussion before students do the next investigation, especially if one investigation builds on another. During that engagement discussion, you can have students summarize the reflective class discussion that the student missed at the end of the previous investigation. This also can help the other students remember and show what they discussed. Using the concrete materials from the investigation as well benefits both the student who missed the investigation and the rest of the class.

Possible Cause

A student was in class during an investigation but missed the writing session.

Potential Solutions

- If the student is in kindergarten or first grade, have her skip the writing part. If she is older, have her talk about it with her partner, then write the entry during an independent work time or silent reading period.

Question

What can I do to make my students less dependent on writing frames?

Possible Cause

Students need to see more modeling of how to write independently.

Potential Solutions

- Model how to use words from a question to begin an answer instead of providing the words in a frame. For example, students might be writing an entry to respond to this question: "What is the effect of the amount of light on a plant's growth and development?" You could say, "One way we could begin our entry about this question is to write, 'The amount of light does affect a plant's growth and development.'"

- When you finish a shared writing of a sentence or an entry, ask, "What's another way we could write this?" Ask students to share another sentence with a partner or the class. During this shared writing, students also can write their own sentences on their own white board or on a separate blank sheet of paper so that each student can practice writing different ways of expressing the same observations or ideas.

- Model how to find words and phrases in the classroom (for example, in the word bank, on class charts and data tables, in the focus question). Gradually introduce words and phrases from the list of useful words and phrases found in Figure 1–2 in Chapter 1. Create a similar chart; add words as you use them in discussions and writing lessons.

- Remove the shared writing that you did as a class so that students do not copy it. Replace it with the scaffolding or structure that you have modeled. After the beginning of the school year, offer a more skeletal version of the scaffolding: list the components of the entry, which the class will have discussed during the shared reflection in the science session. (For an example of this type of scaffolding, see the "Strategies for Writing: Supporting Claims with Evidence" section in Chapter 5.)

■ When students use words or phrases that are not in the scaffolding but that are equally effective, call attention to their independence as a strength when you give them feedback. The more successful students feel, the more confidence they have to move away from the writing frames.

Possible Cause

The writing frames might have more scaffolding than students need. At some point virtually all teachers (including the author and those who are master teachers in this science-writing program) provide writing frames that are too heavily scaffolded. They do this with the best of intentions, most often when they have a lot of students who are learning English, have special needs, and/or are at the very early stages of writing development. Sometimes teachers provide such frames because they want students to include everything in a complex entry, and providing detailed scaffolding seems to be a good way of ensuring that students will include each part.

The following is an example of such scaffolding. Fourth-grade students conducted tests to determine which foods contain certain nutrients and then compared their results to what the labels on the foods said. Students were to answer the following question in their science notebook: "How does the information we have from our tests compare with the information found on food labels?" Most students then followed scaffolding based on the Compare and Contrast writing frame (see Figure 11–3 in Chapter 11). The teacher gave the following frame to a few students who struggle with writing:

Conclusion:

There are some similarities between the information we learned about flour from our tests and the information I learned about flour by reading the food label. First, both the tests and the food label show _____. Also, both show that _____.

There are also some differences between the information from the tests and the information on the food label. The food label _____, but our tests _____. Another difference is that the food label _____, whereas our tests _____.

I have some ideas about why the information from our tests does not match the information on the label. First, _____. In addition, _____.

Students for whom writing is a challenge will get physically and mentally tired by copying all this scaffolding in their notebook and will be doing very little thinking.

A related issue is the use of typed, fill-in-the-blank worksheets. Figure 13–1 is an example of a typed frame that a teacher made for some students who have special needs in writing. (Other students copy from the white board as they write their entry.) Students had observed soil components when they placed the soil in water and then several days later. The teacher wanted to develop her students' scientific thinking, and expected them to report what they observed about each soil and about the water in each case. This means that in each paragraph they needed to report two observations—"Last time" and "but

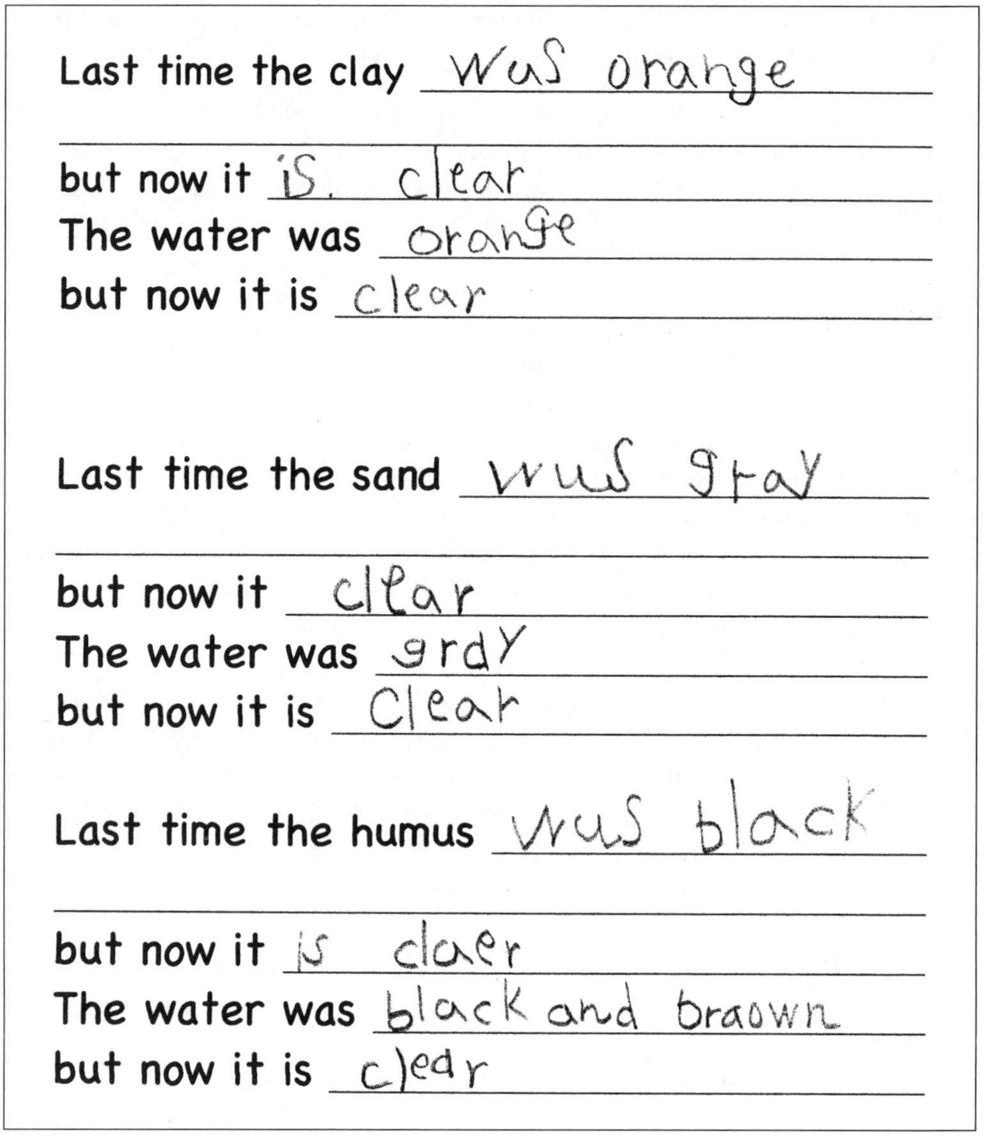

Last time the clay __Was orange__

_____

but now it __is. clear__
The water was __orange__
but now it is __clear__

Last time the sand __wus gray__

_____

but now it __clear__
The water was __grdy__
but now it is __clear__

Last time the humus __wus black__

_____

but now it __is claer__
The water was __black and braown__
but now it is __clear__

FIGURE 13-1 *Kalevi's entry*

now"—about a soil component and two observations about water. This is complex thinking and writing, and the scaffolding is designed to help students remember what to include
in their entry.

Giving a worksheet like this to students who have not yet developed strong writing skills
might seem like the kind of support they need in order to write what other students are writing. Yet they will learn more, and gain more confidence in their writing abilities, if they write
more independently rather than filling out a worksheet. The student, Kalevi, has written
nineteen words on his own, which is about the same number of words in each of the three
paragraphs in the scaffolding. He clearly understands a lot about the properties of these soil
components, and would benefit from choosing one soil component and writing one paragraph on his own, copying words from the writing frame that the teacher used in the shared-
writing minilesson, and then adding his own words, which he has shown he is capable of
doing.

Potential Solutions

■ The following frame could be used in the previous example about the food labels. Based on a structure students already know from the Compare and Contrast writing frame, the frame provides additional support for students without providing too much of the wording and structure.

> The information from our tests and on food labels is similar because they both _____. In addition, they _____.
>
> > *Add more with* Also, *and* Furthermore, [Include the commas to remind students to use them in these cases.]
>
> The information from our tests and on food labels is different because the tests _____, but the food labels _____.
>
> > *Add other differences. Use* whereas *and* In contrast, [Include the comma.]
>
> I think the information could be different because _____.

This structure might seem to be too open, but if the students have engaged in a meaningful discussion during the shared reflection and you have modeled using this scaffolding in the shared-writing minilesson, even students who have not yet developed the same level of writing abilities as their peers likely will be able to write at least one paragraph in this way.

■ If a student cannot do this much writing, then have her write less rather than providing more scaffolding. In this case, she could choose to write one of the three paragraphs that she finds most interesting. Also, make sure to check in first with struggling writers during the independent writing stage of the writing session. These students also benefit from telling a partner what they are going to write before they start writing.

■ Some students will find it helpful to have a typed copy of the frame at their desk to copy (rather than having to look up at the board or screen).

■ For additional support for emergent writers, see Chapter 12.

Question

What do I do when my students seem to understand the science concepts during the class discussion, but their notebook entries do not reflect that same level of apparent understanding?

Possible Cause

In the discussion, students might seem to understand the concept, but they actually do not understand it well enough to write about it.

Potential Solutions

■ Students might not yet have had enough experiences with the materials to be able to construct an understanding of the new science concept. During the active investigation stage of the science session, allow more time for students to work with concrete materials, especially in those lessons and controlled investigations that require more complex thinking and/or involve more complex concepts.

■ Students can get confused when teachers move them too quickly from having experiences with concrete materials to talking about concepts in the abstract. When students are learning complex concepts through multiple investigations, provide scaffolding that supports them in each stage of their learning. The following examples, from the teacher in the Go-Carts Video Episode (Chapter 6), provide some ways to do this.

  • In the investigations leading up to the videotaped session, students began by constructing go-carts and figuring out ways to make them move (through winding rubber bands around the axles). During their initial discussions, they made a class diagram of the go-cart and labeled its parts.

  • Later on, as students had more experiences with the go-carts and began to construct an understanding of energy, the teacher began to draw the flow map shown in Figure 13–2. This helped support students as they constructed their understanding that the stored energy in the rubber band is transformed into kinetic energy, which is transferred to the axle and wheel, which makes the go-cart move. The teacher continued to refer to this visual scaffolding during class discussions.

  • By starting with the concrete experience, introducing terms in a diagram of that concrete object, then making a representation of the abstract concepts in a fairly abstract graphic organizer, the teacher helped students build their understanding, gradually moving from the concrete to the visual to the abstract in a way that supported students at each stage of this learning process.

Possible Cause

Students can talk about the science concept with complete understanding but not write about it because they have not yet heard and spoken the language enough and/or participated in a modeled minilesson.

Potential Solutions

■ During the shared reflection, model using scientific language and scientific thinking (for example, using *because* and providing reasoning).

■ When you introduce words, phrases, and sentences, say, "Say this with me." Then throughout the discussion, regularly ask all the students to say the words out loud as you hold up or point to a word card or sentence strip.

■ Regularly during discussions, ask students to turn to another student and talk about a question you have asked. This will give every student a chance to use the language orally, not just the students who speak during discussions.

■ Remind, and expect, students always to speak in complete sentences and to use scientific language (for example, "I observed," "I think this because," "So I think this means," "Therefore, I think").

■ During the discussion, show students where they can find words they need (for example, in the word bank, class data table and charts, and the focus question).

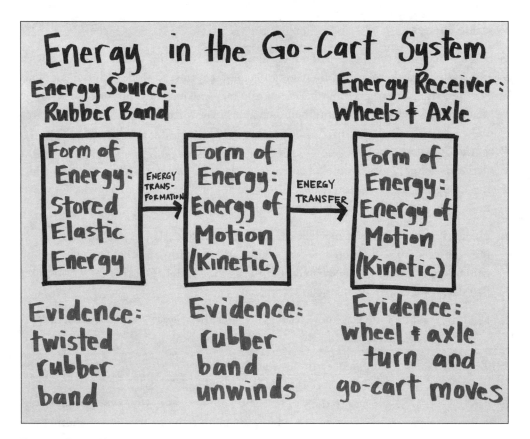

FIGURE 13–2 *Flow map*

- Be sure to have a shared review to start the writing session, which will remind students what they were discussing during the shared reflection discussion during the science session. Have a set of concrete materials at this discussion, too.

- During the shared-writing minilesson, use the same language in your modeling that you had students use during the discussions. (When you plan your science and writing sessions, remember to make note of language you need to use during the discussions to prepare students for the kind of writing they will be doing in their notebooks later on.) Then your modeled writing will be easier for students to understand and to use as scaffolding for their own entry.

- Before students write the first sentence of their own entry, ask them to turn to their partner and say the sentence they are going to write.

- Provide copies of the scaffolding for students who have trouble seeing or focusing on the board or screen at the front of the classroom. Plastic stands (from restaurant or office supply stores) also can display the scaffolding where several students can easily read it at their table.

Question

How can I support and motivate students who struggle when they try to write their entries, even when I provide scaffolding?

Possible Causes

"Doing science" in active inquiries fascinates most students. They can get frustrated with writing in their notebooks when they do not get enough time to work with the materials and/or the writing interrupts that time. They also may lose focus and attention when they become tired, or lack confidence in their own abilities as writers.

Potential Solutions

- Be sure to allow plenty of time for active investigation during the science session. During an investigation, have students do only the following in their notebooks: jot down notes, record data, and/or make illustrations or diagrams.

- Students need a significant break between the science and writing sessions. Otherwise, they get too tired or distracted to concentrate on the writing. Rather than having the writing session during or immediately after the science session, schedule the writing later that day or sometime during the following day.

- Hold the writing session no more than a day after the science session or students will have trouble reconnecting with their experience and thinking.

- To build students' confidence, always start by pointing out specific strengths in the entry based on science practices (for example, saying, "This is a strong observation because you . . ."). Never use the word *but*, because it negates whatever you say about strengths. If you see any weaknesses, address them from the perspective of another scientist: "Another scientist might wonder . . ."

Questions

How do teachers make time to teach science and science writing in this way? How do I get my principal's support in doing this when literacy and mathematics are the focus of instruction in my school?

Potential Solution

These questions are closely related and are two of the most common questions we are asked. The questions are of particular concern to teachers in schools where many students enter with undeveloped academic skills and/or are learning English.

The challenging solution is that teachers have to make time. Stories from Schools (see www.heinemann.com/wisia) includes a Blue Ribbon School principal's testimonial about why she advocates inquiry science and science writing as critical foundations for increasing achievement in schools with high numbers of students who are not meeting academic standards and/or are learning English.

No teacher in our program will say that his job is easy, but all will say that teaching science and science writing is extraordinarily worthwhile because of the positive impacts on students' learning in science, critical thinking, and expository writing. Research on this science-writing approach, as noted in the introduction, supports this. The results are particularly dramatic with students who typically have not been doing well academically. The hands-on learning, which increases students' motivation, and the support of modeling and scaffolding mean they do much better in science and science writing than in other academic areas. They often have their initial breakthroughs in academic achievement in science, and gain self-esteem because they see themselves as successful students.

Another benefit is that in learning to write the text structures of different forms of expository text (for example, a comparison or conclusion), they are developing their ability to read and make meaning of those text structures. In addition, they often must apply math skills in their science investigations (for example, in the Go-Carts Video Episode when students need to collect data in metric measurements, calculate means, and analyze data in a scatter plot). These are ideal opportunities to apply math skills, starting in kindergarten, in the context of authentic experiences.

When teachers teach science and science writing, they are, in fact, not taking time away from literacy and math. They are providing opportunities to develop those skills at even higher levels and in meaningful contexts.

Next Steps

This science-writing approach is as complex as it is rewarding. Teachers generally find that it takes about three years to feel confident teaching an inquiry-based science unit and science writing. But as they begin to implement different strategies, they also see dramatic improvement in their students' thinking and writing skills. If you are just beginning to learn this approach, the following "next steps" will quite quickly result in positive outcomes. Begin by implementing just one or two of these components of the approach, then, gradually, add more as you and your students become more confident and successful.

■ Have students routinely use *because* and *I think this because* in their talking and writing.

■ Use a focus question for every science session.

■ Make and use a science word bank and a word bank or chart of useful words and phrases in scientific writing (see Figure 1–2 in Chapter 1).

■ Use graphic organizers to help students develop their thinking and understanding (for example, a box and T-chart for making a comparison).

■ Model and provide sentence starters and simple writing frames for different forms of notebook entries.

After teaching at least one science unit using this approach, add other, more complex components of the approach:

■ Provide less scaffolded writing frames.

■ Provide more intentional modeling as well as opportunities for students to talk with each other using the modeled language.

■ Provide constructive, positive, formative feedback about notebook entries, starting with strengths, and addressing weaknesses by posing questions that scientists would ask.

■ Develop formal and informal ways of regularly providing feedback to students.

Collaborating with Colleagues

In both the original science-writing project in Seattle Public Schools and in the field-test sites during our National Science Foundation grant work in the last five years, teachers met by grade level almost monthly to support each other in planning instruction and assessing notebook entries. These Science-Writing Reflection Groups are a type of professional learning community (PLC) that is especially helpful for teachers interested in developing their practices in science and science-writing instruction. Typically, these are areas in which teachers have little access to professional development opportunities and other forms of support.

In the assessment video episodes, you can see teachers collaborating for these purposes. The website for this book and for *Writing in Science* includes meeting guidelines that will lead you and your colleagues through two years of collaboration—to plan and discuss instruction, write focus questions and plan appropriate notebook entries, and assess student work. The guidelines are designed to support you as you use the materials in this book and the DVD. Additional guidelines will help you use *Writing in Science* and this book together. To increase your students' achievement in science and science writing, you certainly can effectively use these materials on your own. And if you have the opportunity to work with others in your school or with teachers from throughout your district, you might find the experience even more rewarding.

Final Thoughts

As the video episodes, Stories from Schools (see www.heinemann.com/wisia), and other parts of this book illustrate, students from all backgrounds and academic abilities can be successful in science and in writing about science. For those who struggle in school and/or who lack interest or motivation, actively engaging in doing and writing about science can be the one part of their school day where they feel successful, show breakthroughs in their academic development, and discover the excitement of learning. As you begin or continue to implement this approach, our hope is that you will experience the rewards and joys that we have felt as we have watched our students embark on the exciting journey toward becoming scientifically literate citizens—and, in some cases, adult scientists.

References

Black, Paul, and Dylan Wiliam. 1998. "Inside the Black Box: Raising Standards Through Classroom Assessment." *Kappan Home.* www.pdkintl.org/kappan/kbla/9810.htm.

Common Core State Standards Initiative. 2010. *Common Core State Standards for English Language Arts & Literacy in History/Social Studies, Science, and Technical Subjects.* Posted on www.commoncorestandards.org. Washington, D.C.: National Governors Association Center for Best Practices (NGA Center) and the Council of Chief State School Officers (CCSSO).

Donovan, M. Suzanne, and John D. Bransford, eds. 2005. *How Students Learn: Science in the Classroom.* Washington, D.C.: The National Academies Press.

Fulwiler, Betsy Rupp. 2007. *Writing in Science: How to Scaffold Instruction to Support Learning.* Portsmouth, NH: Heinemann.

Harlen, Wynne. 2004. "The Role of Assessment in the Implementation of Science in the Primary School." Posted at www.science.uva.nl/scienceisprimary/.Plenary#2.

Herman, Joan L. 2005. "Seattle School District—Effects of Expository Writing and Science Notebooks Program: Using Existing Data to Explore Program Effects on Students' Science Learning." Report for the Stuart Foundation. Los Angeles: National Center for Research on Evaluation, Standards, and Student Testing (CRESST), University of California.

Li, Min, Ian Clark, Ayita Ruiz-Primo, Shinping Tsai, Jim Minstrell, and Ruth Anderson. 2010. Secondary science teachers' written feedback practice in science notebooks. Paper presented at the annual meeting of the American Educational Research Association.

National Research Council. 2010. *A Framework for Science Education: Preliminary Draft.* Washington, D.C.: The National Academies Press.

National Research Council. 1996. *National Science Education Standards.* Washington, D.C.: National Academy Press.

Stokes, Laura, Judy Hirabayashi, and Katherine Ramage. 2003. "Writing for Science and Science for Writing: The Seattle Elementary Expository Writing and Science Notebooks Program as a Model for Classrooms and Districts." Posted at www.inverness-research.org/reports-projects.html#su. Inverness, CA: Inverness Research.

Writing in Science
How to Scaffold Instruction to Support Learning

Betsy Rupp Fulwiler

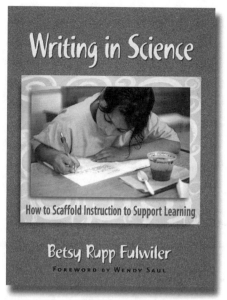

978-0-325-01070-0 / 2007 / 224pp / $25.00

Research-based and field tested in the Seattle Public Schools, Betsy Rupp Fulwiler's classic resource has helped tens of thousands of teachers move their students to higher levels of achievement in both science and expository writing. *Writing in Science* is packed with everything you need to get started:

- the how, why, and when to use science notebooks (and what the research says)
- over 50 annotated science notebook entries
- how to use science word banks and graphic organizers
- how to assess science notebook entries
- planning writing instruction for a science unit
- blackline masters for graphic organizers and writing frames
- focus and investigative questions for inquiry-based science units, Grades K-5.

Heinemann
DEDICATED TO TEACHERS

CALL **800.225.5800** FAX **877.231.6980** VISIT **Heinemann.com**